THE DILEMMA OF AUTHORITARIAN LOCAL GOVERNANCE IN EGYPT

THE DILEMMA OF AUTHORITARIAN LOCAL GOVERNANCE IN EGYPT

Hani Awad

EDINBURGH
University Press

Edinburgh University Press is one of the leading university presses in the UK. We publish academic books and journals in our selected subject areas across the humanities and social sciences, combining cutting-edge scholarship with high editorial and production values to produce academic works of lasting importance. For more information visit our website: edinburghuniversitypress.com

Edinburgh University Press Ltd
The Tun – Holyrood Road
12 (2f) Jackson's Entry
Edinburgh EH8 8PJ

First published in hardback by Edinburgh University Press 2022

Typeset in 11/14pt Adobe Garamond by
Cheshire Typesetting Ltd, Cuddington, Cheshire, and
printed and bound by CPI Group (UK) Ltd,
Croydon, CR0 4YY

A CIP record for this book is available from the British Library

ISBN 978 1 3995 0253 5 (hardback)
ISBN 978 1 3995 0254 2 (paperback)
ISBN 978 1 3995 0255 9 (webready PDF)
ISBN 978 1 3995 0256 6 (epub)

CONTENTS

ILLUSTRATIONS

Figures

Appendices

ACKNOWLEDGEMENTS

This book would not have been possible without the help of so many wonderful people, from those who invested in me, to those who supported me.

I owe a deep debt of gratitude to the Arab Center for Research and Policy Studies (ACRPS), which not only funded my doctoral journey at Oxford University, but also extended its full support to develop my doctoral thesis into a book. In particular, I extend a huge thank you to Haider Said and Mohammad al-Masri for encouraging me to pursue this project and giving me the time and space to revise the original thesis.

I would also like to thank my colleagues in the ACRPS and the Doha Institute for Graduate Studies, whose intellectual insights helped in the development of this work; in particular, Marwa Farag who read the early drafts of some chapters, and made an insightful and thought-provoking contribution to our many discussions. Thank you also to Dana El Kurd and Ismail Nashif who read and commented on an early draft of Chapter 1, and especially to Abdel Fattah Madi, Khalil al-Anani, Ibrahim Fraihat and Jamal Barout for their support at different stages of the work.

At Oxford, I owe a debt of gratitude to Walter Armbrust for his key role as my supervisor. Walter knows that I cannot thank him enough. Special thanks also go to Dominique Atallah for her help and guidance from my very first day at Oxford, and which continued throughout my time there. It would also be remiss if I did not thank the people who engaged with my project at different stages during my studies at Oxford, Jocelyn Alexander, Indrajit Roy, Leïla Vignal, Adeel Malik and Reem Abou-el Fadl.

The EUP team – Emma Rees, Louise Hutton and Eddie Clark – I thank for their patience throughout the review process. I acknowledge that the feedback of both anonymous reviewers was insightful and constructive, helping to improve the manuscript and strengthen the quality of the final product.

To Hussain Saleh and Sherif Mohyideen, whose help in facilitating my research was indispensable during the early stages of this project, I owe tremendous thanks. Thank you also to everyone who provided me with technical support, especially Mo'ataz Mikkawi, Khaled Abbas, Nerouz Satik, Yasir Ashour, Ismail al-Iskandrani, Ahmed al-Shami, Sara al-Masri, Rania Abdel Azim, Saif Al-islam Eid and Yara Nassar. The text as a whole benefited from Jane Clark's critical reading, comments and careful editing, but most importantly her constant support and encouragement.

I am thankful to all who encouraged me to write this book, especially Ahmad Biqawi, Tania Hashem and Ihab Maharma. My greatest debt is to Laura Sayah who is always my first reader. Her constant encouragement and sustaining care during the difficult times made it possible for me to complete this work. Lastly, I am forever grateful to my parents for their unwavering support and for always believing in me.

Without this support and encouragement, I am fairly certain this work would still be in its early stages. I am, however, solely responsible for any flaws that remain.

To Azmi Bishara

INTRODUCTION
CENTRALISED STRUCTURES AND DECENTRALISED POLITICS: THE PROBLEM OF RESEARCHING AUTHORITARIAN LOCAL GOVERNANCE

It is rare to find in the literature an interpretation of the basic characteristics of the political, social and administrative frameworks of governance in Egypt that does not mention that the country has the longest tradition of centralisation in the world. Egypt was the perfect example of Karl Wittfogel's theory of hydraulic society.[1] For survival not only must a state be 'genuinely managerial',[2] but it must also be 'like the tiger',[3] monopolising all means of production, domination, intimidation and organisation in order to rule absolutely, with no local initiatives allowed to 'counterbalance and control the political machine'.[4] For Max Weber, Egypt is 'the historical model of all later bureaucracies'.[5] Its oldest bureaucratic administration was an inevitable consequence necessitated by an almost pure 'natural' economy[6] that called for unitary action in 'administrating the Nile waters and fighting the desert sands'.[7] Over centuries, centralism in Egypt was regarded as the *only* political order of things. It is, according to the Egyptian geographer Gamal Hamdan, 'the most distinct feature of the personality of Egypt':[8] deep-rooted, as old as the pyramids and lasting until today.[9]

However, over-centralisation is now considered the major reason for most failures in Egyptian local governance and it bears the responsibility for its various problems, such as poor performance, slowness and corruption at all levels. The predicament made various observers, researchers and politicians, including the Egyptian presidents themselves, consider a solution in some form of decentralisation reform that could politically empower local communities and change the status quo from the bottom up.[10] However, despite recognition of the need to decentralise the system of local administration (SLA), for decades the Egyptian regime had neither the desire nor the will to take any step towards implementation of such a measure. The explanation lies, by unanimous agreement among researchers, in the regime's ambivalence towards any kind of political mobilisation that could threaten the stability of its authoritarian control.

Since Nasser (1952–71), the Egyptian SLA has been characterised by a highly centralised top-down authority that gives a broad role to executive authorities, especially to the central government and the governor and his appointed executive councils, at all levels, including the local one.[11] This is despite the fact that the system, since the late Sadat/Mubarak era, has consisted of two branches: the first is executive and the second is elected. Nevertheless, elected local and popular councils (*al-majālis al-shaʿbiyya wa l-maḥaliyya*) have been endowed with only very limited consultative functions and, thus, they have always been subordinate to the central administration. In fact, it can be said that since the late 1970s, when the foundations of the contemporary SLA were laid and stabilised, it has barely been subjected to a noteworthy process of reform in accordance with the rapid social changes that local communities have undergone.

Currently, the country is divided into twenty-seven governorates (*muhāfazāt*). Each is like a small government administered by a governor, who is appointed by the president and serves at his discretion. The central ministries also have directorates (field-branches) in each governorate. Below the governorate level, there are two additional levels of local administration. The first is the district level (or metropolitan cities in urban areas), and the second is composed of local administrative units such as villages, towns and city neighbourhoods. Each level reports up to the next level, from which it receives its instructions and resources.

The over-centralised local bureaucracy in Egypt has been accused of stifling local agencies, leaving no room for community-based initiatives and no semblance of decentralisation. Therefore, with some exceptions, local elections have been marked by very poor popular participation and limited competition, whereby most victories have been declared by acclamation (*al-tazkiyya*), reducing elections in most cases to a mere façade. The fact that such a system has remained in place for decades with minimal changes, despite literally hundreds of reform initiatives introduced by various institutions (governmental, public, international and NGOs), seems paradoxical and challenging to 'authoritarian upgrading' literature, which basically assumes that authoritarian regimes resort to reforms to increase their resilience and consolidate their rule.[12]

This book's primary objective is to present an account of the strategies and mechanisms that over-centralised authoritarian regimes employ to upgrade their local governance without giving up their over-centralised authoritative character. Based on examining the Egyptian case, the study develops a theoretical framework and conceptual vocabulary that can help to understand decentralising politics and upgrading measures in centralised authoritarian contexts.

Decentralising Politics in Authoritarian Contexts: Lessons from Egypt

For decades, the study of centralisation and decentralisation processes has been largely dominated by public administration approaches, mainly derived from the western experience of governance. The concept of decentralisation has many distinct meanings depending on the period of history and the context in which it is used. Mainstream literature usually distinguishes between political, administrative and fiscal types of decentralisation. While administrative and fiscal forms are common in most political regimes throughout the world, the political one, which refers to the process whereby the power of political decision-making is transferred from a higher level of government to a lower one, is usually regarded as an essential element of democratic and 'good governance'.[13] Effective political decentralisation, thus, has been primarily associated with the process of democratisation.

In the past two decades, however, the study of centralisation–decentralisation has taken a neo-institutionalist slant after synthesising public administration approaches and historical institutionalism,[14] which has resulted in a shift from studying 'local government' to researching 'local governance'.[15] Much of the new focus has gone beyond the top-down and hierarchical options of a traditional public administration perspective,[16] to explore the greater use of informal networks and contracts on vertical and horizontal scales and local politics in general. From this perspective, a new understanding of political decentralisation emerged to question the assumed association between political decentralisation and democracy.[17] In this sense, even authoritarian regimes resort to various strategies of political decentralisation to enhance their resilience, durability and flexibility.[18]

One of the basic premises of the neo-institutionalist approach[19] of studying local governance is the post-Weberian theoretical distinction between authority and power. According to Michael Mann, the driving force of human society is not only institutionalisation, it also derives from 'restless drives' that constitute networks of extensive and intensive power relations.[20] Local governance, therefore, should not merely be conceived as the continuum of authority, but should also be widened analytically to include the continuum of power.[21] The first is hierarchical, often embedded in management structures and through official channels,[22] and the second is embodied in the informal means that may 'diverge from the formal structures of authority'.[23] Both formal and informal rules are interacting to constitute the system of local governance. Therefore, they should be brought together as one unit of analysis.

Accordingly, we may also identify two other general types of centralisation–decentralisation. The first is formal, in the sense that it appears on the structure of authority and, therefore, it can be approached through the domain of public administration literature. The second is informal, in the sense that it appears on the networks of power and, therefore, it should be analysed by an interdisciplinary approach that incorporates various theories from the different fields of social sciences. Thus, analysing the structures, processes and strategies of local governance requires a multi-research method and interdisciplinary approach.

Based on examination of the Egyptian case, it is my contention that it is common for centralised authoritarian regimes, in their endeavour to upgrade the system of local governance, to substitute informal decentralisation of the networks of power for formal decentralisation of the structure of authority to avoid – as much as possible – sharing power with wider segments of society. Informal political decentralisation is part and parcel of wider upgrading arrangements in Heydemann's sense. It is a path-dependent process induced by 'authoritarian learning'. It is, furthermore, an output of shifts in the political economy of authoritarianism and it entails – in the medium term – redefining the conception of local politics, which leads to a fundamental change between authoritarianism and its grassroots organisations.

Informal decentralisation benefits authoritarianism in three interrelated aspects. First, it grants the power-holder the ability to devolve power without abdicating legal authority, allowing authoritarian regimes to retain full control of local governance if things get out of hand. Secondly, it helps authoritarianism to minimise the costs of public service delivery and escape a fiscal crisis by shifting developmental missions to local communities without the need to reform the strong centralised structure of the government. Finally, it helps authoritarianism to manage and reorganise the huge patronage and neo-patrimonial networks at the subnational level, and to make them more effective, competitive and less costly. In sum, informal decentralisation endows authoritarianism with the privilege of being politically centralised and decentralised at the same time and, therefore, it expands its manoeuvring range.

This book aims to explore the political decentralisation strategies employed by the Egyptian regime to upgrade authoritarianism in its system of local governance without giving up power or democratising local governments. In order to achieve this objective, it primarily employs a historical institutional analysis to identify the authority–power reconfigurations that enabled the regime to dominate politics at the subnational level for decades. As will be shown, the upgrading process involved reconfiguring the relationships between the authority–power triangle of local governance, which under Mubarak was composed of the local bureaucracy, the ruling party and security agencies. The upgrading process helped the regime to be more effective in dominating local politics and to enhance its political control. However, its strategies failed to overcome the weakness of the system mobilisation functions, which reflect what this book refers to as the dilemma of authoritarian local governance.

Researching Local Politics: An Introduction to the Case Study

Unlike the study of local governments, where analytical frameworks are too dominated by a focus on formal institutional differences rather than by a concern with local politics, the local governance research stream still lacks a comparative typology.[24] This is simply because historically and across countries, and even within the same country, there are numerous different ways in which state–society relations and processes for public policy-making have been given shape. The fact that the field of local governance is increasingly tilting towards researching local politics (that is, patterns of political practices at the local level), including the role of informal and neo-patrimonial networks, makes it very contextualised. Analysis, therefore, should be based heavily on in-depth studies using process-tracing methods and interdisciplinary approaches to examine purposively selected field sites.[25]

Although this book draws upon a historical institutional analysis that focuses on the question of institutional change and evolution of Egyptian local governance, it is also supported by within-case analysis[26] based on extensive anthropological research in Kerdasa, a city and administrative centre located in the south-west of the Giza Governorate in the Greater Cairo peri-urban fringe. The Egypt 2006 census estimated the population of Kerdasa City to be 69,317.[27] If we take into consideration the annual growth combined with the inter-immigration rate to the peri-urban fringe of Cairo, which is about 3.4 per cent, we can estimate that the current population is over 100,000.

The fieldwork research aims at exploring and identifying evolutionary and systematic changes on the patterns of political practices and the roles of local political elites (or what I simply refer to as *local politics*), which cannot be observed by a macro institutional analysis. By local political elites, this book adopts a wide-ranging definition to include all individuals, organisations and opposition figures who could influence the political process or decision-making at the subnational level.[28]

The fieldwork interviews were conducted in December 2012 and October 2013 in Kerdasa, but most of the other interviews were held between March 2016 and January 2017 not only in Kerdasa, but also in Istanbul and Khartoum, to which many of Kerdasa's local Islamic figures and the revolutionary popular committee members fled after the military coup in July 2013. During that relatively long period, I had the opportunity to investigate a number of different aspects of local politics in the town. I interviewed townspeople, local figures and politicians with differing ideological backgrounds, which enabled me to examine the evolution of local political elites from contrasting slants.

The Greater Cairo peri-urban fringe refers to those areas where a rural–urban transformation is taking place. These localities, which surround the city of Cairo, are neither rural nor urban. Despite the process of urbanisation, their local communities are marked by a relatively strong social cohesion and a high degree of 'communityness'.[29] This region includes nine rural administrative zones (*marakiz*): Qaliub, Al-Khanka, Shibeen el-Qanatir, and El-Qanatir el-Khieriya in Qaliubia Governorate and in Giza Governorate: Imbaba, Ausim, Badrashain, El-Hawamidiya and Kerdasa. According to the 2006 Egyptian national census, the population of the nine peri-urban *marakiz* was estimated at 4.21 million inhabitants, representing 24.7 per cent of Greater Cairo's 17 million inhabitants.[30]

The population growth in these areas has been significantly above the prevailing natural increase rates, averaging 3.27 per cent per annum over the 1996–2006 period (during which Greater Cairo grew at an annual rate of 2.1 per cent, and the nation at 2.01 per cent). In the previous 1986–1996 period, growth in peri-urban areas was also strong, averaging annual increases of 3.3 per cent compared with 1.66 per cent per year for the Cairo Governorate and 1.9 per cent per year for the Delta governorates.[31] The fact that growth in these areas represents a significant proportion of Cairo's population growth and that they house large numbers of the city's inhabitants, made David Sims consider them in 'a real way, the future of the city'.[32] Needless to say, local politics can vary between one case and another in accordance with the variations in socio-economic contexts, but resorting to a case study is indispensable for researching the agency of local actors and their responses to institutional changes at the macro level.

In exploring local politics in Kerdasa, the book focuses its investigation on the changing patterns of political practice at the local level from the early 1980s to the eve of the January 25 Revolution (2011). In this respect, the role of the ruling party, the National Democratic Party (NDP), in the system of local governance is critical. This is because the party, as the largest institutional patronage machine, was one of the main vehicles through which the authoritarian regime not only intended to dominate local politics, but also, as contended here, contributed constantly to redefining it.

Under Mubarak (1981–2011), the strategies of informal political decentralisation shifted the political roles of the local leadership of the ruling party from being based on societal mediation among locals and keeping the 'domestic peace' (*al-silm al-'ahly*), to include navigating and exploiting the public service delivery system in favour of more authoritarian control. By upgrading its style of governance the regime was hoping not only to move a part of its developmental mission to local communities in order to reduce the cost of public expenditure, but also to manage local patronage networks and enhance their political efficiencies. Nevertheless, the upgrading strategies always faced a structural dilemma. While the regime was relatively able to manage the authority–power relations that constituted the system of local governance with minimal costs, it was unable to increase the system capacities of mobilisation (that is, popular support). This dilemma always created conditions for the emergence of alternative local politics, and especially the danger of the politics of identity and Islamic activism.

Although this study was not conceived with the Islamic movement at its core, the field research led to addressing the rise of Islamic activism in the 1980s to reflect on the authoritarian repressive measures against any alternative local politics that could challenge the authoritarian domination over constituencies. Since the foundation of the Egyptian republic in 1952, the Muslim Brotherhood (MB) has represented the most challenging opposition that the regime has encountered using various oppressive measures. Nevertheless, the relationship between the Islamic movement and the regime, in the era of Mubarak, fluctuated in accordance with the structural crises and economic swings that beset Egypt.

In the years of the 1980s, this relationship was, to some extent, smooth,[33] and across Greater Cairo mosques became an arena for populist sheikhs who evoked Islamic *da'wa* (preaching), and started gradually to challenge the regime's political domination over local politics. From the early 1990s, however, the regime launched successive campaigns that eradicated the *da'wa* movement. Furthermore, in the years that followed, new tactics were employed to extend the security agencies' domination to mosques by appointing new *imams* and *khatibs* who were loyal to the regime. By the late 1990s, the regime seemed to have gained the final triumph in the 'war of positions' over the mosques.

Thus, by the early 2000s, it became obvious that the authoritarian regime had conquered most aspects of local politics in the Cairo peri-urban fringe and wiped the floor of all potential opposition that could challenge the authoritarian domination. Local 'lesser notables'[34] became aware that there was no avenue for taking part in public work unless through the NDP and backed by the regime's informal networks. As Ismail Abu Musa, one of the leadership members of Kerdasa's NDP, said: '*kul al-balad kānat ḥizb waṭany*' ('everybody was [a member of the] NDP').[35] However, the NDP was unable to translate this domination into an electoral victory in the 2000 parliamentary elections without electoral rigging and fraud, and massive numbers of arbitrary arrests.

From September 2002, therefore, and in tandem with the rise of Gamal Mubarak's political profile, the subnational structures of the NDP were subjected to a thorough decentralising process, under the supervision of the State Security Investigations Service, to enhance the party's mobilisation functions and organisation. Nevertheless, after the setback of the 2005 general elections, new indicators showed that the authoritarian regime had reached the conclusion that modernising the subnational structures of the ruling party was just a waste of time: the regime, therefore, began to implement new configurations that marginalised the role of the NDP in the system of local governance.

Thus, the local leadership of the NDP, which was rooted in the communities, saw themselves replaced by parachuted 'arrivals', who came as a result of what has been known in Egypt as the 'money–power marriage'. On the eve of the January 25 Revolution, it had become apparent among the NDP's grassroots, in the towns of the Cairo peri-urban fringe, that the regime had turned its back on them. There is evidence to suggest that the regime resigned itself to the fact that although its system of local governance succeeded in dominating politics at the micro level, it showed a major deficiency in translating this domination into political hegemony, in the Gramscian sense, at the macro level. This study explores the different aspects of this dilemma.

The Structure of the Study

This monograph comprises five chapters, each of which addresses an aspect of the development of the system of local governance and the evolution of local politics in Egypt. Due to the complexity of researching local politics, each chapter draws on different theoretical premises that are built upon a broad range of literature from the diverse fields of public administration, politics, history, sociology and anthropology.

Chapter 1 serves as an introductory chapter that aims to clarify the research question and to explain the meaning of upgrading the authoritarian system of local governance. It also provides a brief but critical history of the development of the Egyptian system under three regimes, and introduces a conceptual framework to understand the logic of its institutional reconfigurations. Furthermore, it traces the historical development of local politics in the Cairo peri-urban fringe and the evolution of the political roles of the local leadership as a result of the process of upgrading. Moreover, it proposes a theoretical framework that can identify and explain the authoritarian dilemma in its institutional–mobilisation functions which prevented it from translating political domination into hegemony. However, it is not expected that this chapter will explain every argument in detail, but rather prepare the reader for the four subsequent chapters where each analysis will be expanded.

Chapter 2 is devoted to understanding the way that Egyptian authoritarianism upgraded its system of local governance. It starts by clarifying the shortcomings that could emerge if the analysis is restricted merely to addressing the over-centralised structure of local government. A weakness can lead to overlooking the structural bifurcation in the system, which allows authoritarianism to substitute informal political decentralisation for the formal one. Instead, I introduce a dual interpretive approach that utilises a process-tracing method to understand the Mubarak regime's strategies in decentralising its system of local governance, most importantly in this regard the role of elections. The decentralisation process under Mubarak did not, however, significantly affect the legal structure of authority but rather the regime's networks of power, leading to a fundamental change in the role of its grassroots networks and leadership.

Chapter 3 explores the political dilemma of the Egyptian system of local governance in its endeavours to counter the emergence of alternative local politics, namely, the challenge of Islamic activism, which proved to be more effective in political mobilisation compared with the local state inclusionary frames. Many dynamics contributed to making authoritarian institutions and networks inefficient in their mobilisation capabilities and organisation at the local level. Nevertheless, I stress the importance of considering the historical formation of the Arab state in general and the Egyptian state specifically, which made patronage politics a tool of political mobilisation, unable to combat the challenge of identity politics despite the regime's unceasing process of upgrading.

Chapter 4 sheds light on the strategies that were deployed by the regime's grassroots and rent-seeking local elites in their competition over positions that were seen as a route to political upgrading. While local leadership in Egypt used various strategies to upgrade themselves in the authoritarian political system, in the towns of the Cairo peri-urban fringe political clannism was the most prominent strategy used by lesser notables in this regard. Nevertheless, contrary to much received wisdom in the study of Middle Eastern social politics, I show that political clannism is a relatively modern phenomenon that was mainly motivated by the decentralising mechanisms that the Egyptian authoritarian regime employed to upgrade its system of local governance. Yet political clannism was only effective at the micro level and could not, by any means, counter the Islamic movement's sort of mobilisation, which was more efficient at the macro level.

Chapter 5 is dedicated to addressing the moment when the whole system collapsed after the January 25 Revolution, which led to the emergence of a new model of revolutionary local politics, led by popular committees (*lijān sha'biyya*) and backed by local communities. The new local leaders, who were mostly Islamists, had a greater capacity for political mobilisation and were, therefore, able to push the boundaries of local politics by assuming functions that had been historically cartelised by the government. However, the new model did not survive for long. In July 2013, a military coup took over Egypt and the authoritarian system of local governance was retained.

Theoretical Prospects of this Book

Although this study falls under the field of researching local governance, it is expected that the reader has only a basic knowledge of the theoretical framework of public administration since all related essential concepts and notions are clearly explained, namely, in the first two chapters. The reader, however, is required to have a good grasp of Middle Eastern politics and contemporary Egyptian political history. In all chapters, the analysis includes a historical background, but since the study covers a long period, it also refers to other contributions and literature in the notes.

As usual with the field of local governance research, the study heavily employs an interdisciplinary approach that borrows and synthesises many concepts and theories from different fields: public administration, politics, sociology and anthropology. At the macro level, this study conceptually draws on Heydemann's 'authoritarian upgrading' perspective, which is useful for examining the institutional reconfigurations inside the authoritarian regime in Egypt. At the meso level, it employs a historical institutional approach (Paul Hutchcroft et al.) to study the relationships between administration and politics in Egypt. At the micro level, the analysis resorts to historical sociology (Azmi Bishara and Nazih Ayubi) and anthrophony (Pierre Bourdieu et al.) to understand the metamorphosis of local politics in its different aspects. The book, therefore, offers a multi-layered perspective to understanding what I call 'the dilemma of authoritarian system of local governance in Egypt'. The main conceptual avenues utilised in this book are elaborated and defined in Chapter 1. But since it is impossible to explain everything in one chapter, many other theoretical premises are elucidated and integrated within the analyses in the subsequent chapters in a way that does not overwhelm the reader nor distract them from the main goal of the study, that is, understanding the upgrading process of the system of local governance in Egypt.

Lastly, although this study is on Egyptian authoritarian local governance, the results hold important lessons for scholars of public administration, local politics, social mobilisation, identity politics, patronage politics and authoritarian upgrading. Chapter 2, for example, develops an institutional methodological framework that helps to encompass the administrative structures of the state and its informal networks in one analytical unit. This framework is likely to be replicated and modified to understand local governance in other authoritarian settings. It shows scholars and experts of public administration that restricting the analysis to the administrative formal structures, without considering the role of informal networks, will definitely distort our knowledge on how authoritarian regimes actually rule. This implies reconsidering many of the 'good governance' international reports that suggest that the problem of local governance can be solved through increasing bureaucratic efficiencies and capacities (that is to say, reforming the system through apolitical agendas). This study shows that this is simply not possible. The problem with local governance in Egypt, for instance, is political not technical and it is structurally associated with the question of state legitimacy and democracy. There is no way that *apolitical* reforms will lead to 'good governance', because the problem of the system is *political.*

Later chapters could also be useful for scholars of local politics and political mobilisation at least in the Arab World. The historical empirical evidence suggests that no matter how authoritarianism improves its capacity to upgrade its control of extensive bureaucratic–patronage-based networks, it will fail to gain a robust base of local support unless it has other sources of legitimacy. This is simply because its huge quasi-structural informal networks share nothing except their closeness to the state. The absence of a state ideology renders the relationship between the authoritarian regime and its grassroots (and relations among the grassroots themselves) unreliable, unhealthy and characterised by mutual mistrust. The fact that the NDP, the entrenched ruling party, despite decades of upgrading and monopoly over local governance, failed to encounter the MB without the regime's coercion shows evidence of that. The MB, though subjected to continuous suppression, continued to win popular support that actually brought it to power after the first (and until now only) democratic elections in Egypt before the military coup prevented a democratic transition.

Chapter 4 offers a modest example of why we should not overstress the role of kinship networks in socio-political mobilisation. It questions much of the received wisdom that regards familial ethos and primordial attachments as an alternative western 'civil society' in the MENA. The chapter presents evidence that political kinship networks are sometimes important in local politics, but definitely not an automatic imperative for local communities. In the case of Kerdasa, political clannism was merely a strategy selectively employed by local notables who wanted to upgrade themselves in the networks of power of the system of local governance. It is better, therefore, to understand kin-based political mobilisation as a result of authoritarian governance rather than a genuine 'creation' of society. This methodologically requires shifting the focus from society to the interactions between society and the state. Kinship-based political mobilisation in the Cairo peri-urban fringe, however, was never efficient except on very micro scales. Yet further research is required to examine if it could go beyond that in other settings in Egypt or elsewhere in the Arab World.

Chapter 5 and the Epilogue are a token contribution to post-Arab Spring literature, namely, local politics during and after the 2010s revolutions. Given the difficulty of conducting safe fieldwork in most Arab countries, the academic contributions to understanding the transformations of local politics in the post-2011 era are valuable, but unsurprisingly rare. In Egypt, for example, we do not yet know how local communities throughout the country have been ruled since the fall of Mubarak in early 2011: who was in charge of local governance under the rule of the Supreme Council of the Armed Forces (SCAF) and the MB? What are the elements of continuity and change in local politics before and after the 2011 Revolution? The case of Kerdasa shows that the proliferation of new revolutionary organisations and protest movements after 2011, such as popular committees and community movements, marked not a break with past local politics but a continuation of it in new forms. However, further research is also needed to know for sure if this was also the case in other urban and rural settings.

It is not clear yet what impact the process of re-autocratisation that Egypt has experienced under al-Sisi has had on the system of local governance, and on local politics in general. An initial assessment in the Epilogue shows that the gap created after the dissolution of the NDP is now filled by coercive measures and brutal securitisation. The relationship between the regime and its grassroots is still ambiguous. Some indicators suggest that the regime has no clear strategy for managing the pre-2011 power networks.

Other indicators show that the new authoritarianism is in the process of developing mechanisms to create new reliable grassroots. Either way, resolving the dilemma of Egyptian local governance is unlikely to be an easy challenge.

Notes

1. Karl S. Wittfogel, *Oriental Despotism: A Comparative Study of Total Power* (New Haven, CT: Yale University Press, 1957).
2. Ibid., 49.
3. Ibid., 141.
4. Ibid., 49.
5. Max Weber, 'Bureaucracy', in Aradhana Sharma and Akhil Gupta (eds), *The Anthropology of the State: A Reader* (Chichester: John Wiley & Sons, 2009), 49–70 at 54.
6. Ibid., 57.
7. Nazih Ayubi, *Bureaucracy and Politics in Contemporary Egypt* (Oxford: Middle East Centre, 1980), 111.
8. Jamāl Ḥamdān, *Shakhsiyyat Miṣr: Dirāsa fy 'Abqariyyat al-Makān* (*The Personality of Egypt: Reflections on the Genius Loci*), 4 vols (Cairo: Dār al-Hilāl, 1967), 4:253.
9. Ibid.
10. Jorge Martinez-Vazquez and Andrey Timofeev, 'Decentralizing Egypt: Not Just Another Economic Reform', in Jorge Martinez-Vazquez and Francois Vaillancourt (eds), *Decentralization in Developing Countries: Global Perspectives on the Obstacles to Fiscal Devolution* (Cheltenham: Edward Elgar, 2011), 389–430; Sobhi Moharram, 'The Process of Controlled Decentralization in Egyptian Local Finance', *Developing Economies* 30(4) (1992): 450–81.
11. N. S. Fahmy, *The Politics of Egypt: State–Society Relationship* (London: Routledge, 2012), 179.
12. Steven Heydemann, 'Upgrading Authoritarianism in the Arab World', *Analysis Paper*, Saban Center for Middle East Policy at the Brookings Institution, October 2017.
13. John Loughlin, 'Decentralization', in Mark Bevir (ed.), *Encyclopedia of Governance* (Thousand Oaks, CA: Sage, 2007), 197–9, 196.
14. Paul D. Hutchcroft, 'Centralization and Decentralization in Administration and Politics: Assessing Territorial Dimensions of Authority and Power', *Governance* 14(1) (2001): 23–53.
15. Linze Schaap, '"Local Governance" Decentralization', in Mark Bevir (ed.), *Encyclopedia of Governance* (Thousand Oaks, CA: Sage, 2007), 532–4.

16. Anwar Shah and Sana Shah, 'The New Vision of Local Governance and the Evolving Roles of Local Governments', *Journal of Public Administration* 3(1) (2009): 2–15.
17. Allyson Lucinda Benton, 'How "Participatory Governance" Strengthens Authoritarian Regimes: Evidence from Electoral Authoritarian Oaxaca, Mexico', *Journal of Politics in Latin America* 8(2) (2016): 37–70.
18. Erik Vollmann, Miriam Bohn, Roland Sturm and Thomas Demmelhuber, 'Decentralisation as Authoritarian Upgrading? Evidence from Jordan and Morocco', *Journal of North African Studies* (2020): 1–32, 6.
19. Ellen M. Immergut, 'The Theoretical Core of the New Institutionalism', *Politics & Society* 26(1) (1998): 5–34.
20. Michael Mann, *The Sources of Social Power: vol. 1: A History of Power from the Beginning to AD 1760* (Cambridge: Cambridge University Press, 1986), 15.
21. Hutchcroft, 'Centralization and Decentralization in Administration and Politics', 26.
22. Ibid.
23. Ibid.
24. Gerry Stoker, 'Was Local Governance Such a Good Idea? A Global Comparative Perspective', *Public Administration* 89(1) (2011): 15–31, 20.
25. David Booth, 'Towards a Theory of Local Governance and Public Goods Provision', *IDS Bulletin* 42(2) (2011): 11–21.
26. The advantages of within-case analysis are numerous. For instance, it allows the examination of processes and organisational change over a long period in order to uncover the causal chain behind the outcomes. Since it is centred on '"process tracing', it helps researchers to identify the interaction between formal and informal rules as well as the influence of power networks on the process of decision-making. However, because it is heavily based on anthropological and ethnographic research, conclusions should be synthesised with cross-case examinations and a wider socio-historical analysis in order to avoid the risk of over-generalising knowledge developed in localised settings. On within-case methodology, see Barbara Paterson, 'Within-case Analysis', in *Encyclopedia of Case Study Research*, Vol. 1 (Thousand Oaks, CA: Sage, 2010): 970–3; and on process-tracing methods in social sciences, see Derek Beach, 'Process-Tracing Methods in Social Science', in *Oxford Research Encyclopaedia of Politics* (Oxford: Oxford University Press, 2017), last accessed 1 June 2020, available at: https://oxfordre.com/politics/view/10.1093/acrefore/9780190228637.001.0001/acrefore-9780190228637-e-176.
27. Egypt 2006 Census, data from Egypt's 2016 Census is not available yet.
28. Volker Perthes, 'Politics and Elite Change in the Arab World', in Volker Perthes

(ed.), *Arab Elites: Negotiating the Politics of Change* (Boulder, CO: Lynne Rienner, 2004), 1–32, 5–6.

29. The concept of 'community', like any broad concept such as 'society' and 'culture', has been widely employed in sociology although its variable meanings have continued to be an enduring enigma in social theory over time. However, the most current use of the concept has come to focus on networks of interpersonal interaction and the attachments, feelings or the attitudinal 'sense of community' existing among individuals. This made Albert Hunter conclude that 'it is overly simplistic to attempt to reach some summary "zero/one" judgment or determination as to whether something is or is not a community – better to ask about its degree of "communityness"'. Albert Hunter, 'Conceptualizing Community', in Ram A. Cnaan and Carl Milofsky (eds), *Handbook of Community Movements and Local Organizations in the 21st Century* (Cham: Springer, 2018), 3–23, 4.
30. David Sims, *Understanding Cairo: The Logic of a City Out of Control* (Cairo: American University in Cairo Press, 2011), 72–3.
31. Ibid.
32. Ibid., 270.
33. Hesham al-Awadi, 'A Struggle for Legitimacy: The Muslim Brotherhood and Mubarak, 1982–2009', *Contemporary Arab Affairs* 2(2) (2009): 214–28.
34. Hana Batatu used the term 'lesser rural notables' to refer to segments of the Syrian peasantry who had been marginalised before the Ba'ath rule and became the regime's grassroots afterwards. Hanna Batatu, *Syria's Peasantry, the Descendants of its Lesser Rural Notables, and their Politics* (Princeton, NJ: Princeton University Press, 1999). Salwa Ismail then used 'lesser notability' to refer to segments in the urban quarters who rose from *infitah* policies and became eligible to be mediators between their communities and the state. Salwa Ismail, *Political Life in Cairo's New Quarters: Encountering the Everyday State* (Minneapolis: University of Minnesota Press, 2006), 47–8. Mohamed Menza utilised the term later to understand clientelism in Cairo's urban quarters. Mohamed Fahmy Menza, *Patronage Politics in Egypt: The National Democratic Party and Muslim Brotherhood in Cairo* (London: Routledge, 2012).
35. Abu Ismail, *Interview*, 23 April 2016.

1

POLITICAL DECENTRALISATION IN CENTRALISED INSTITUTIONAL CONTEXTS: THE DILEMMA OF AUTHORITARIAN LOCAL GOVERNANCE IN EGYPT

The Question: Governance, Authoritarian Upgrading and Local Governance

Governance

The word 'governance' has had a somewhat obscure dictionary presence for a long time, but its extensive usage in academic literature occurred in tandem with its adoption in donor circles and policy-oriented discourse shortly after the fall of the Berlin wall (1991).[1] Yet the basic purpose of each use has been quite different. The notion of 'governance', in the donor-driven discourse, refers to the way in which countries, or provinces for that matter, were being 'governed', or were to be governed. The focus here is on formal state structures and intra-governmental relations.[2] By adding the adjective 'good' to it, 'good governance' has been ambiguously geared towards enhancing policy effectiveness, transparency, accountability, and conceptually preparing the terrain for policy intervention and encouraging public–private partnerships.[3] The guiding motive in this trend, according to Martin Doornbos, was to establish new global–institutional patterns of hegemony after the Cold War that entailed making the states apolitical.[4]

In contrast, the academic concept of 'governance', with which we are concerned, though also ambiguous, is primarily oriented towards better analysis of the institutional linkages between state and society contextually rather than intrinsically,[5] which requires in-depth case studies and thus cannot be limited to the formal–legal analysis of legislation.[6] It is largely concerned with developing a better understanding of the ways in which power and authority relations interplay to constitute or affect the process of decision-making.[7] In this regard, governance in a very general sense is defined as 'the formation and stewardship of the formal and informal rules that regulate the public realm, the arena in which the state as well as economic and societal actors interact to make decisions'.[8] The focus here is on the interaction between institutional changes, formal and informal, and the local social and political responses being engendered in various forms. However, although the term 'governance' is still debatable in its meaning, many social scientists today can hardly do without it.

Authoritarian Upgrading

In the past two decades, there has been another academic trend focusing on the ways and strategies used by Arab and Middle Eastern authoritarian regimes to 'upgrade' their governance in response to external and internal pressures and demands. Egypt has been a central example of how the implementation of political, economic and administrative reforms have breathed new life into the ability of authoritarian regimes to consolidate their grip on power rather than moving towards democratic transition. It has been academically established that economic and political liberation, which includes economic structural reforms and a limited transition to political pluripartism are necessary survival strategies in the aspiration to 'upgrade authoritarianism'.[9]

Steven Heydemann defines 'authoritarian upgrading' as 'reconfiguring authoritarian governance to accommodate and manage changing political, economic, and social conditions'.[10] The process of upgrading has made authoritarian regimes stronger, more flexible and more resilient, despite concerted pressure internally and externally to bring about sustained and systematic political reform and change. Authoritarian upgrading takes a variety of forms, each influenced by the particularity of individual regimes. Therefore, no single model could explain the path that Arab regimes follow in order to reconfigure themselves.[11] Furthermore, Heydemann stresses the importance of not overstating the capacity of authoritarian upgrading. He contends, instead, that the process is shaped by 'authoritarian learning', namely, 'lessons and strategies that originate within, and outside the Middle East, are diffused across the region, travelling from regime to regime and being modified in the process'.[12]

Authoritarian Upgrading in Local Governance

Authoritarian upgrading in the Middle East and North Africa (MENA) has been well addressed in the past two decades.[13] However, less research has been devoted to extending the analysis of upgrading measures to the field of *local governance*, which is considered a sub-theme of the field of governance in its general sense. The reason might be that both academic fields theoretically have suffered from a long history of what Paul Hutchcroft has termed 'division of labour'.[14] While the former has been dominated by public administration literature, the latter has been researched through more developed theoretical frameworks that belong to various fields of social sciences, such as politics, history, sociology and so on.

As discussed in the Introduction, however, from the 1990s a new institutionalist approach of researching local governance perceived institutions as political actors that not only respond to external changes, but also tend to dominate their environments.[15] The new approach, therefore, blended theoretical insights from the domain of public administration literature and others from different fields of social sciences. It opened the field of local governance to interdisciplinary views incorporating political and sociological theories to understand the development of different forms of domination over constituencies. The result has introduced the possibility of observing the historical development of the system of local governance, which entails an unceasing process of upgrading that does not only or even necessarily appear on the structure of authority, but does influence the informal networks of power that penetrate the layers of system.

This shift in focus from local government to local governance has had important consequences. It has helped to bring together 'regime theory, theories of the local state, and urban political economy into a broader analytical framework'.[16] In this respect, there are many definitions of the concept. It is conceptualised by Anwar Shah and Sana Shah as 'the formulation and execution of collective action at the local level',[17] or by John-Mary Kauzya as 'the exercise of authority [formally and informally] at the community level'.[18] Both definitions are neo-institutionalist, in the sense that they acknowledge, implicitly or explicitly, a sort of theoretical distinction between authority and power, making it necessary for any analysis to encompass the direct and indirect roles of formality (i.e., institutions of local government hierarchies) and informality (i.e., norms, patronage networks, community organisations, etc.) in pursuing collective action. The unit of analysis here is the pattern of political practices rather than technical capacities.[19]

In a further conceptual synthesis, it is my intention here to extend the question of 'authoritarian upgrading' to the field of local governance. Recent scholarship, with its main focus on hierarchical structures, suggests that authoritarian regimes can implement formal modifications to the existing system of subnational governance without ever endangering central control over decision-making within subnational institutions.[20] This principally involves a controlled top-down approach towards decentralisation. Existing literature adequately addresses the *why* question. Authoritarian regimes employ decentralising strategies to broaden their base of support,[21] improve power relations between the centre and the periphery,[22] reduce the cost of public service delivery by shifting developmental missions to local communities,[23] manage elite networks by promoting competitive clientelism,[24] and appease domestic society and international organisations.[25] Missing in the literature, however, is a thorough theoretical framework for understanding the question of *how*: how do centralised authoritarian regimes upgrade their system of local governance?

Based on the Egyptian case, and for the purpose of this research, this study defines *the authoritarian upgrading of local governance as the process of reconfiguring the relations between the continuum of authority and the continuum of power in order to consolidate the authoritarian rulers' domination over the ruled.* The continuum of authority here refers to the formal administrative hierarchical structures of local government, while the continuum of power refers to the informal networks inside and outside the administrative structures. The process of reconfiguration involves formal and/or informal centralisation and decentralisation strategies on a vertical and/or horizontal scale. As in the case of an authoritarian resilience thesis, the authoritarian upgrading of the system of local governance is also shaped by authoritarian learning.

In Egyptian local governance in the period under examination, I use authority to refer to the system of local administration (SLA), while I use power to refer to the local state–society patronage networks, which is best exemplified by but not restricted to the ruling party. Nevertheless, it is always important to remember that the authority–power distinction, though essential for understanding, is theoretical. That is, in reality, there cannot be any clearly defined line between authority and power. They are intertwined and integrated in a single matrix.[26] Thus, although the public administration framework is indispensable in analysing the centralised–decentralised mechanisms of administrative structures in local governance, it cannot alone understand how the process of decision-making actually works. Making sense of that also requires understanding the strategies of centralisation–decentralisation on the networks of power, which cannot be realised except through a parallel historico-sociological analysis of how the system was historically formed.

There are numerous ways in which authoritarianism could configure and upgrade its system of local governance. In the Egyptian case, the continuum of authority was historically subjected to an incremental process of centralisation that consolidated the centralist control, but the continuum of power, as I argue, was subjected to a process of informal centralisation and decentralisation that varied in its degree between one period and another. Under Mubarak, specifically, there is evidence that the process of decentralising power served as a sort of substitution for the process of decentralising authority to avoid the political risks of formal decentralisation. However, despite the continuous upgrading process, the system suffered from a serious 'dilemma' in its mobilisation functions, which threatened its political domination and stability.

In this introductory chapter, I utilise the conceptual synthesis developed above to provide a general overview of the history of the authoritarian upgrading of local governance in Egypt. Furthermore, I provide a brief history of the evolution of patterns of political practices at the local level, or what I simply call 'local politics'. Moreover, I identify what I mean by the 'dilemma' of the authoritarian governance in Egypt. However, because this is an introductory chapter, it provides only a brief discussion of arguments covered in the rest of the book and the links between them. My aim is to prepare the reader for the subsequent four chapters, to which I extensively refer where relevant.

The chapter, therefore, has three sections. The first, provides a brief but critical macro historical analysis of upgrading the system from the pre-1952 Revolution period to the January 25 Revolution, including a summarised chronological analysis of its institutional changes under three regimes (Nasser, Sadat and Mubarak). The second, utilises the fieldwork research to provide a micro historical analysis of the metamorphosis of local politics that resulted from the process of upgrading, namely, the transformation of the role of local political leadership and the historical change on their political practices. The third, resorts to Arab state-formation theories to propose a theoretical framework that can help in identifying and explaining the political dilemma of authoritarian governance in Egypt.

Upgrading the System of Local Governance in Egypt: A Critical View

Similar to the case of many post-independence states in developing countries, the contemporary system of local governance in Egypt was founded and created from the early 1960s within a period characterised by *étatisme*, whereby the state increasingly penetrated the society it ruled and extended its top-down control on everyday life. Prior to the Free-Officers Movement in July 1952, the village was the administrative unit, where the *umda*s (mayors) and *sheikh al-balad*s were the cornerstone on which 'the edifice of provincial society rests'.[27] They were rural intermediaries between the central government and villagers in an era that had been marked by a 'gap between ruler and ruled and between the various autonomous social groups among the ruled' that required 'the presence of a certain minimal social cohesion'.[28]

However, the role of rural intermediaries was subjected to a gradual decline from the late nineteenth century concurrent with the process of centralisation of power and bureaucracy. Along with this, monopolies were abolished and a capitalist mode of agricultural production emerged, which entailed a widespread conversion from sharecropping to money rents, especially after the Second World War.[29] The increasing privatisation of land led, on the one hand, to strengthening the landowner class and to increasing the number of *izba* owners,[30] and, on the other hand, to breaking the village community, which led to unprecedented rural–urban migration.[31]

On the eve of the toppling of the *ancien régime* (July 1952), the modern administration largely weakened the power of rural intermediaries, whose power, according to Gabriel Baer, 'waxed when centralised government waned'.[32] The SLA, instead, consisted of a network of municipal councils whose functions and allocations were greatly constrained and subject to central government control. The latter represented the interests of the landowner class.[33]

Local Governance under Nasser: The Foundations

Unlike other cases in the developing world in which local governance was demarcated by the interaction of a modern bureaucracy with pre-modern communal structures,[34] the Egyptian case represented a model in which the contemporary SLA had been merely an output of bureaucratic sprawl. A process that was to be intensified and, indeed, radicalised with the founding of the republic. The post-1952 version of developmentalism, led by Nasser (1952–71), aimed to keep the state autonomous in order to act unilaterally without bottom-up 'political mobilization of *any* kind' that could entail bargaining between rulers and the ruled, or the revival of potentially hostile elements from the remnants of the *ancien régime* in the countryside.[35]

The 1956 constitution, therefore, strengthened the grip of the central government on local units to such an extent that it made little provision for local autonomy or even initiative, thus, reflecting a historical tendency towards more centralist control. The Ministry of the Interior was responsible for appointing the directors (*mudirs*) of the directorates as well as for police and organisational administration. Major decisions were usually undertaken by the central ministry, the responsibilities of village councils being limited by rules and regulations, turning them into passive bodies.[36]

In 1960, the SLA was reorganised under Law 124, which divided the country into administrative units, namely, governorates, towns and villages, each of which had a separate legal identity. The central control was enhanced by the creation of a new Ministry for Local Administration for the supervision of local units. This new ministry assumed most of the pre-1960 responsibilities of the Ministry of Interior, leaving the latter with the responsibility for maintaining security – law and order.[37] Furthermore, the directors of provinces, who had been officials of the minister of interior, were raised in status to become governors of governorates, having the rank of deputy ministers responsible directly to the president of the republic.[38] In this period, a dual local government system (governors–ministers), under the president, was crystallising.

However, with the stipulation of Law 124 of 1960 and its subsequent amendments in 1962 and 1964, a new formula was introduced in local governance, paving the way for what was intended to be a 'collaboration movement'[39] to take part in politics at the subnational level. It was expected to be the political base of the regime and its local arm: local networks of notables working in parallel and side-by-side with the local bureaucracy. This movement was the ruling party: the Arab Socialist Union (ASU). The law and its amendments manifested the relationship between the ASU and local administrative units, and necessitated the election of members to the local councils from ASU membership within the relevant governorate, town or village. Each administrative unit (governorate, town, village) had to have a council comprising elected and appointed members empowered with broad authority and administrative responsibilities. The elected members were the same as those elected to the local committees of the ASU within the local units, and the appointed members were those active members of the ASU selected by the central authority, in addition to ex-officio members representing the different ministries in the local unit.[40]

The ASU was officially founded by a presidential decree in 1962 to be a mass party, although its structure and functions had been organised at least from 1959 under the name of the National Union.[41] The party was designed on the communist party model with its pyramidal shape and hierarchical order, and with commands flowing from top to bottom. However, as will be discussed in Chapter 2, the process of restructuring the party in 1965 made the relationship between the subnational levels of the party and the SLA more important than that with the national leadership of the party itself. The ASU, therefore, lacked any semblance of independence and was unable to function separately from the state.[42] This rendered the party–bureaucracy relationship in Egypt different from any communist pattern. Nazih Ayubi summarised the major difference by stating that, 'instead of a political party running a state, Egypt's state was trying to breathe life into a party'.[43] The ruling party in this sense was a subordinated institutional banner under which countless local state-society patronage networks functioned.

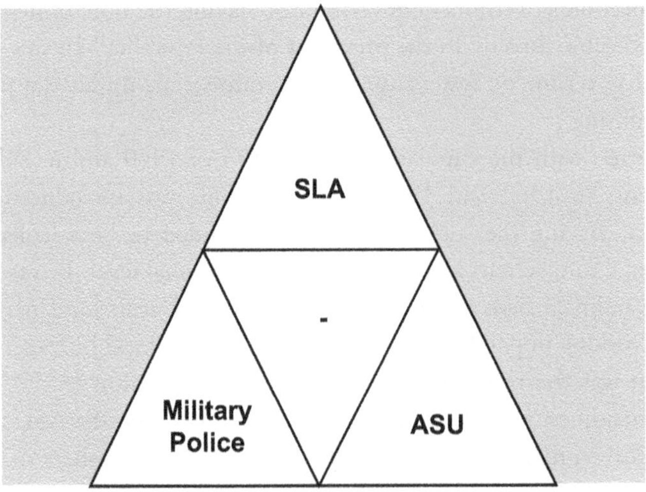

Figure 1.1 The system of local governance under Nasser

In sum, it can be said that under Nasser the system of local governance laid its foundations in which: (1) the SLA, or the local bureaucracy, had the upper hand, and (2) the ruling party emerged as a kind of collaborative movement consisting of a large number of state–society local patronage networks, while (3) the (military) police remained on the sidelines always ready to intervene. Those three elements (the SLA, the ruling party and security agencies) mainly constituted the authority–power triangle of local governance. As the subsequent chapters will show, relations among them were subjected to continuous reconfigurations under the rule of Sadat and Mubarak as a part of the process of upgrading.

Local Governance under Sadat: The Final Form

It is true that the foundations of the system of local governance had begun to take shape under Nasser, nevertheless, the system suffered from instability due to the struggle between rival powers in the regime (see Chapter 2). The system, therefore, would not acquire its final form until the end of the Sadat era (1971–81) after it had been subjected to a major comprehensive upgrade. This happened within the context of the country's political economy transition from 'populist' to 'post-populist' authoritarianism as a result of the failure of public sector capital accumulation.[44] The transition entailed a shift towards a controlled market-oriented economy and building new constituencies that consolidated the president's grip on power. The latter endeavour required the elimination of the rival power centres (*marākiz al-qiwā*) within the regime,[45] which largely left a deep impact on the development of the system of local governance.

Under Sadat, the tendency towards more central control on the structure of authority continued to prevail. In the later stages of his era, the authority of the governor was consolidated to such an extent that he had, until the second decade of Mubarak rule, become a representative of the president in his governorate. Sadat also reconfigured the horizontal links among the SLA, the security agencies and the ruling party. The new reconfiguration entailed disbanding the ASU and creating the National Democratic Party (NDP),[46] whose monopoly of the SLA was formally abolished. This step, however, did not remove the role of the ruling party from local governance, but rather, as Chapter 2 shows, integrated it into the SLA. This required increasing police intervention to guarantee the domination of the NDP.

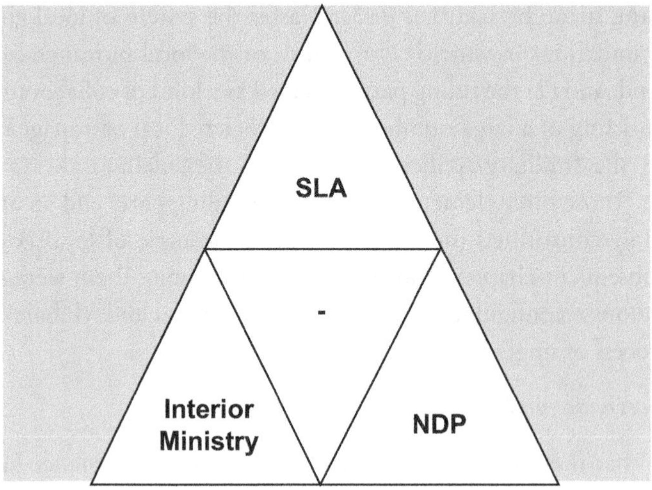

Figure 1.2 The system of local governance in the late Sadat/early Mubarak era

By late in the Sadat period, the role of the Interior Ministry was quickly expanded to replace that of the Military Police at almost all levels of politics, to extent that, by the early Mubarak era, it became difficult to determine the precise demarcation line that separated the ruling party from the security agencies.[47] The integration of the two organisations became more noticeable as both 'increasingly sought one another's support'.[48] The later development marked what Hazem Kandil has described as a metamorphosis from a coup-installed military regime into a police state:[49] 'while ASU leaders had come from a military background, the NDP elite was born under the watchful eyes of a police officer'.[50]

Overall, it can be said that the system of local governance under Sadat was subjected to two parallel processes. The first was a continuation of an incremental process of formal centralisation of the structure of authority, which crushed the possibility of any local entity or organisation acting independently of the state. The second was a process of informalising the relationships between the foundations of local governance. As will be addressed extensively in Chapter 2, Sadat's upgrading strategies granted the system of local governance the privilege of being centralised and decentralised at the same time. It was centralised on a vertical scale, whereby local units were overwhelmed by the control of the upper layers of the state pyramid, and it was also decentralised on a horizontal scale through fragmenting the process of decision-making among various formal institutions and informal networks of power, each of which was constrained by the other. This situation would greatly benefit his successor, Hosni Mubarak, and it would also endow Egyptian authoritarianism with the power to manoeuvre among the contradictions of the system until the current day.

Local Governance under Mubarak

Mubarak inherited the authority–power triangle of the system of local governance and made minor reforms to its structure of authority (the SLA). In fact, he consolidated its centralist control as the stipulation of Law 145 of 1988 suggests. In his thirty years of rule, furthermore, the power of the Ministry of Interior and its role in local governance constantly grew, formally and informally, reaching its peak in the 2000s with the rise of the Gamal Mubarak-led group on the political scene. However, the role of the ruling party in local governance experienced major reconfigurations that reflected an important aspect of the process of authoritarian upgrading. In this respect, the main strategy used by Mubarak to reconfigure the bureaucracy–party relationship was general elections, which served as a mechanism for centralising and decentralising the informal networks of power.[51]

We can chronologically divide the history of upgrading the system of local governance under Mubarak into three periods. The first was immediately after he rose to power in 1981; therefore, the process of upgrading was marked and motivated by the politics of succession. In this period, Mubarak aimed to pull the intentionally fragmentised strings of governance to consolidate his rule. He also had a negative attitude towards Sadat's legacy in the NDP. Therefore, he re-engineered electoral laws in a way that served to centralise the ruling party, namely, by reducing the number of electoral constituencies and banning independent candidates from running for elections. These measures empowered NDP centralist control, but, as Chapter 2 will show, they created a gap between the state and the regime's grassroots at the local level,[52] enabling the Islamic movement to fill it.

The second period started from the early 1990s, and was motivated by both the danger of the Islamic movement and the fiscal pressures that resulted from implementation of the Structural Adjustment Programme. Accordingly, the Mubarak regime again used elections to decentralise the ruling party. The number of electoral constituencies was increased, and independent candidates were allowed to run for election under the watchful eye of the State Security Investigations Service (SSIS), which increasingly became involved in the system of local governance. In this sense, elections served as a mechanism of outsourcing and updating the class of individuals who might be eligible for spoils in exchange for their support.[53] It helped the regime to reduce the costs of public expenditure by making the public service delivery system function selectively based on the elections results.[54]

However, it failed politically. The 2000 elections showed that the ruling party was ineffective in facing Islamists alone without coercion, most prominently electoral rigging and the security agencies' involvement. In the early 2000s, in the context of a fierce struggle between the 'old guard' and the 'new guard' groups inside the NDP and under the cloud of another fiscal crisis, a third epoch of the history of the system of local governance started. Further upgrading measures were taken to decentralise power networks, but this time through using elections to outsource power networks inside the ruling party itself in order to enhance its mobilisation functions.[55]

Consequently, a new system of electoral primaries was introduced in which members of the NDP secretly voted for the candidates of local and popular councils and also chose the candidate for the parliamentary elections. This reform movement caused a further weakening of NDP centralist control, but did not lead to democratising the party, nor did it enhance its mobilisation functions. Rather, it increased the role of the police in local governance

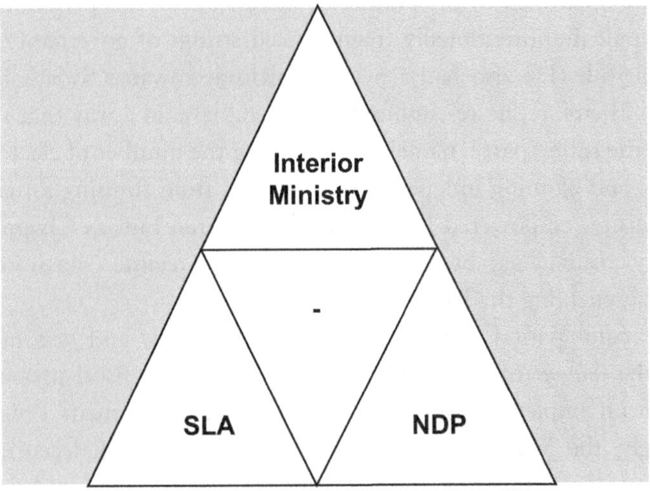

Figure 1.3 The system of local governance in the late Mubarak era

and turned NDP politics into chaos. The party was quickly consumed by endless struggles among power networks and the result was a political scandal and a major defeat in the 2005 parliamentary elections.

As the clock wound down towards the Egyptian revolution (2011), the NDP's role in the system of local governance was greatly marginalised and informally substituted with a new system in which security intelligence officers had the upper hand. As a result, a whole generation of local leadership found itself suddenly excluded from local politics and a new generation emerged with a fresh corrupted pattern of political practices. It was a reckless blunder that would partly lead to the collapse of the whole system, but as this study argues, it also marked the failure of the ambitions of Egyptian authoritarianism to translate its ruling party's political domination over local politics into political hegemony. I will return to discuss this idea extensively in the third section of this chapter and also in subsequent chapters, but for now, it is important first to provide a brief micro socio-historical analysis to show the implications of the upgrading process on local politics.

Metamorphosis of Local Politics: From Rural Intermediaries to Service Deputies

One of the most important outcomes of the process of upgrading the system of local governance in Egypt was the continuous change in the patterns of political practices at the local level, or what I simply call 'local politics'. However, distinct from researching the institutional reconfigurations of local governance, which requires analysis at the macro level, it is necessary for the purpose of examining the historical evolution of local politics to move the focus towards 'practices', which requires a micro anthropological investigation. In this respect, Pierre Bourdieu's very abstractive concept of 'field' has useful analytical value, since it allows investigation of the context within which the relations between agents and the structure are taking place.[56]

Bourdieu defines the field as a structured system of networks of social relations between the occupants of positions (individuals or institutions) that is constantly shifting throughout time and space.[57] It is a sort of socially constructed arena of struggles in which forms of capital (economic, cultural, social, symbolic) are employed and deployed by the occupants of positions to defend their ranks, and to impose principles of hierarchisation that favour them.[58] Each field is semi-autonomous, characterised by its own determinate agents, its own accumulation of history, its own logic of action, and its own form of capital. However, the degree of semi-autonomy of any field is constrained and influenced by its relation to other fields, therefore, it is subjected to a continued redefinition. A change in the semi-autonomous character of the field deeply influences their strategies.[59]

Bourdieu's concepts of field and capital are instructive in understanding the historical development of politics as a field of power on any level; therefore, it will be heavily utilised in this book to examine the micro aspect of local governance: local politics. As will be seen, the process of upgrading the Egyptian system of local governance, which involved strategies of centralisation–decentralisation, led to a continuous redefining of the boundaries of the political field at the local level. In this section, I employ Bourdieu's tool box to provide a brief but also critical historical background to the metamorphosis of local politics in Egypt, with a special focus on Kerdasa. However, this requires a penetrating exploration of the socio-political history of the town.

Kerdasa in the Pre-modern State Period

In his encyclopaedic work *Khiṭāṭ at-Tawfiqīyah al-Jadīdah* (1886), Ali Pasha Mubārak said that Kerdasa in the nineteenth century was a village in which 'sons of Mikkawi' were famous for their luxurious houses and orchards of fruits and palms.[60] The village was also known for planting vegetables, for its traditional weaving handicrafts and grain milling. Most importantly, the town was a caravan trading post for slaves and pilgrims travelling between Maghrebi countries and the rest of Egypt, and also to the east and south.[61] Thus, Kerdasa, like few other towns in the rural hinterland, was a merchant community, taking advantage of the communications network that linked Libya and the Kingdom of Wadai, through Cairo, with central Africa,[62] a station for slave brokering,[63] and a market for small-scale industrial activities such as cotton weaving and clothes' production.[64]

Being a trading post had consequences. It gave the town a continual need for strong local leadership that had ties to macro powers for protection. From the late eighteenth century to 1812, Mohammad Ali al-Mikkawi, a prominent merchant, filled this role backed by Murad Bey who was an influential Mamluki commander. Contemporary Mikkawis claim that their forefathers led an alliance with the Zumor family in Nahia, and other strong families in the surrounding towns.[65] They all enjoyed the privilege of being merchants in Ottoman Egypt.[66]

However, when Mohammad Ali Pasha came to power, he sought to consolidate power and wealth in the hands of his officials, who 'shared a lack of rootedness in local society'.[67] His modernisation project involved a process of deepening centralism and that was at the expense of local powers and compacts. In this respect, Kerdasa was no exception. In 1811–12, a series of battles took place between Murad Bey's allies and the pasha's troops, as al-Jabarti recounted in his history of Egypt.[68] The Mikkawis came to realise that they had backed the losing side. They found themselves refugees in the Libyan city of Tripoli and in Upper Egypt.[69] A few years later, they managed to obtain clemency through intermediaries, and returned to their hometown, but with minimal power.[70]

Bureaucratic Sprawl and the Decline of Rural Intermediaries

From the early twentieth century to the fall of the monarchy in Egypt (1952), there are several general observations that can be made about Kerdasa's local politics. First, unlike many villages in the countryside, especially in Upper Egypt,[71] villages in Lower Egypt witnessed a decreasing concentration of wealth among their elites.[72] In the first half of the twentieth century, many Kerdasian families could buy plots of land from the Mikkawis. Familial handicraft production prospered to meet the needs of urban centres. For example, a government survey in 1925 indicated that Kerdasa was 'quite a centre for weaving, apparently having 920 looms at work'.[73] Therefore, new families such as the Omars, Issas, Sheikhs and others, who had been socio-economically impoverished in the previous century, were now able to improve their standing to become the peers of many of the Mikkawis.

This is the context for understanding the rise of other families that challenged the Mikkawis' domination in Kerdasa. Although the Mikkawis seized the *umda* position, local notables from other families, such as the Omars, were able to occupy positions such as that of *sheikh al-balad*.[74] A consequence of this was the emergence of local disputes, especially when the ascendant families began to evoke the history of the Mikkawis' exploitation of their forefathers. What is important to stress here is that the role of local leadership after the British occupation was restricted to the settling of such local arguments (alongside other everyday disputes, of course).[75] This required the distribution of local positions to more than one family in order to maintain domestic stability. Thus, while local notables in the nineteenth century had been mediators between urban-based rulers and their local communities, in the following century they became mediators among the locals themselves.

This leads us to the second general observation, which concerns the continuous decline of the local leadership. In Kerdasa, at that time, the possession of social capital (that is to say, durable networks of relations) could not be translated into political capital (namely, power). Having a strongly rooted position in local society meant socio-economic security, but hardly more. This was mainly due to the political order in the monarchical era, in which political positions were appointed within very limited circles, mostly urban, or given to those in rural areas who had acquired the title of pasha, which could be hereditary or granted. It was also not unusual to find many members of the pasha's extended family impoverished or of modest socio-economic status.

In Kerdasa, only one branch of the landowning Mikkawi family had someone with a title. In the first half of the twentieth century, this was Mahmoud Fahmi Mikkawi (1918–82). He was the first one in his locality to gain the title of pasha, after his father and grandfather had the title of bey. However, he acquired it late in the 1930s, when expansion of the middle class pressurised the palace to upgrade a stratum of urban and rural notables from effendis to beys and from beys to pashas.[76] Thus, Mahmoud Pasha did not acquire the title because of his power, but rather due to the deterioration in the political status of the title of pasha over time. Nevertheless, he was ambitious to become involved in politics by running for parliament. Being a pasha at that time was not enough to become a politician. A member of parliament needed also to have the means to mobilise voters in his constituency. In most cases in rural Egypt, this was achieved through the pasha's clientelist lines, through *umdas* who distributed vote money to *fellahin*.[77] This was not applicable to Kerdasa, which possessed a relatively advanced market and a plurality of interest groups that could not simply be bought. Thus, Mahmoud Pasha invested heavily in the town in order to cultivate alliances across a broad local social base. In 1943, he founded an association for the textile industry that encompassed members of the various wealthy families who owned most of the textile workshops.[78]

In 1944, he established a cooperative society to provide local people with provisions. In 1946, he started another cooperative society to afford Kerdasa's housewives a source of income. In the late 1940s, he managed through his connections in the government to supply the town with a modern source of potable water, along with a public transport system and the establishment of a post office. Mahmood Pasha was elected in 1946, but this was only after selling more than half of his land to raise funds for his town projects. Nevertheless, as Chapter 4 will show, Mahmoud Pasha's motivations could not just be explained by politics, but also by the meaning of being a pasha in his time.

Mahmoud Fahmi Mikkawi left an impressive legacy not only in Kerdasa, but also in the surrounding towns. He was active in parliament, where he was a member of the legislative committee that proposed several laws. After the July 1952 coup, he was chosen by the revolutionary regime to become the secretary of the National Union, then the ASU, in Kerdasa, a base from which he continued to develop the town. In 1958, he founded Kerdasa's sports club. The case of Fahmi Mikkawi actually suggests that at least part of the traditional rural elite was revolutionary, therefore, enthusiastic to work with the new regime. Nevertheless, his model of local politics did not survive for long due to the intense process of centralisation and bureaucratic sprawl that Egypt experienced in the 1960s, which shifted the regime's bases from traditional rural notability to bureaucracy and led to the bureaucratisation of the ASU.

Although the reorganisation of the ASU in 1965 (see the previous section) allowed for larger numbers of lesser notables to take part in local politics, the semi-autonomous character of the political field at the local level shrank significantly, which left the role of local leadership until the late 1980s restricted to applying customary law, such as setting up reconciliation councils (*majālis al-ṣulḥ* or *majālis al-ʿarab*), and resolving disputes between townspeople, or leading self-help local initiatives. In Kerdasa, the rise of Sheikh Yousef Abdel Salam Saleh, who was *shaykh ʿarab* and the ASU local secretary general in the town after Mahmoud Fahmi Mikkawi, exemplified this trend. As a representative of the *first* generation of local leadership of the NDP in Kerdasa, Abdel Salam Saleh is a central figure in this study. His story will stay under examination in the next three chapters, but for now we will proceed with the transformation of local politics.

The Advent of Service Deputies

In the 1980s, the region underwent rapid socio-economic change due to the process of urbanisation. Urban growth left a deep impact on all aspects of life, from the transformation and diversification of domestic economies, which led to an increase in social mobility, to profound changes in family structures and even daily habits. One of the main consequences of this development on local politics was the increasing number of lesser notables from diverse families and different socio-economic backgrounds who accumulated social and economic capital that, theoretically, made them eligible to take part in local politics.[79] As will be addressed in Chapter 4, this made competition among them for positions in the political field intense compared with the previous era.

Nevertheless, the most important transformation in local politics occurred through the process of upgrading the system of local governance, which as discussed previously, involved strategies for decentralising the networks of power. The process started under Sadat, was then paused in the first decade of Mubarak's tenure as a result of the politics of succession, then resumed from the late 1980s under internal and external pressure. It made use of local and general elections to manage the competition among the increasing numbers of lesser notables who joined the NDP. Thus, various strategies were employed by local notables, most prominently the politicising of social capital which led to a revival of political clannism in Kerdasa.

The impact of decentralisation on the local leadership was twofold: it made local leaders more subordinate to the authoritarian system of local governance, whereby any local leader needed to be aware of his position within an informal network of power, from which he derived his chances to move on in the system. On the flip side, it expanded the role of the local leadership to assume the responsibility for mobilising local communities, especially local entrepreneurs, to allocate resources for urban development and public service. Thus, while the ASU local leaders, such as Sheikh Yousef Abdel Salam Saleh in Kerdasa, had been primarily social mediators among locals, the NDP local leaders, such as Haj Mohammad Abdel-Wahhab Mahjoub, became service deputies in their localities. Mahjoub represents the *second* generation of the NDP local leadership, and his story will be examined through the rest of this book.

Further Deterioration

Last, but not least, the role of local leadership would deteriorate from the 2000s, as a result of another phase of upgrading the system of local governance that entailed restructuring the subnational structures of the NDP and increasing the influence of the Ministry of Interior in local politics. The introduction of electoral primaries and the removal of the principle of formal nomination from September 2002 allowed various individuals, who lacked rootedness in their localities, to capitalise on their relations with corrupt police officers and to challenge well-established leaders.

This development had some contradictory consequences. It empowered the networks of power at the subnational level and increased their influence on the SLA. However, it amplified competitiveness in a way that led to the destruction of the party organisation through endless struggles at all subnational levels. The overall effect was to extend the influence of the Interior Ministry and marginalise the party role in local governance, which negatively affected the role of local leadership.

The fact that in the 2000s the police became the cornerstone of the system of local governance reflected two major aspects related to local politics. First, authoritarian overconfidence in the ruling constituencies with less need for established grassroots on the ground. This would lead to a power vacuum when the Interior Ministry was defeated by a popular revolution in January 2011. As will be discussed in Chapter 5, the whole system, consequently, would collapse leaving room for a revolutionary model of local politics to emerge, led by popular committees (*lijān sha'biyya*) and backed by local communities. However, the new model did not survive for long, since, in July 2013, the country experienced a military coup that immediately retained the authoritarian system of local governance.

Secondly, that Egyptian authoritarianism had reached the conclusion that the then established structures of the ruling party were unable to yield desirable political outcomes, especially when encountering the challenge of the Islamic movement. Therefore, the regime started to view them as a burden and, in the context of its fiscal crisis, other evidence suggests that the regime innovated new methods to exploit them.[80] But why was the NDP in particular (or patronage politics in general), despite a full authoritarian back-up and all upgrading arrangements, unsuccessful and ineffective in political mobilisation? There is no simple and quick answer to this question, but, as will be discussed in the following section, and extensively in Chapter 3, a key explanatory factor can be summarised in one short sentence: the absence of ideology.

The Dilemma of the Authoritarian Local Governance in Egypt: The Arab Question and the Problem of Macro–Micro Relations

Scholars of Arab state formation provide us with a broad macro-structural framework to understand the politics of authoritarianism. Perhaps one of the most daring attempts in the field of historical institutionalism to theorise the logic of Arab authoritarianism is Nazih Ayubi's derivative concept of corporatism. Ayubi's model of the Arab state was criticised, but is still influencing our understanding(s) of the trajectories of the Arab states, especially after the revolutions of the 2010s. In Egypt, the way that authoritarianism showed its ability to counter the January Revolution and to repress the democratic transition suggests that one of the core elements of corporatism is very relevant, that the Arab state tends to rule through quasi-structural social groups that are excessively dependent on it.[81] These corporatist groups are huge, and many of them, such as the army, judiciary and police, are very powerful, but some are also weak, such as the ruling party and syndicates. They are all, however, very costly because they exaggerate the role of the state,[82] leaving it trapped in a continuous economic crisis.

The main outcome of this situation is that the state can still rule, but with an eroded hegemony (in the Gramscian sense), which forces it also to be heavily dependent on coercion. The state, therefore, according to Ayubi, suffers from multiple, mutually reinforcing gaps: a 'demands–delivery gap' resulted from the economic stress, and a 'mobilization–institutionalization gap' resulted from the lack of hegemony.[83] To overcome both gaps, the state upgrades its style of corporatism by introducing limited and controlled political and economic reforms that do not aim to expand political participation, but rather minimise the cost of its inclusionary institutional frames. This attitude can be termed 'authoritarian upgrading'.

During my field research in Kerdasa, I had the opportunity to investigate major aspects of the historical development of the Egyptian authoritarian corporatist style, and the way it functioned on the micro level in the towns of the Cairo peri-urban fringe during the three decades of Mubarak's rule. Through examining the development of the system of local governance, I was able, first, to examine the capacity of the state inclusionary institutional frames that intended to incorporate social segments of local communities, and, secondly, to explore the regime security approach to liquidate local politics that was seeking genuine autonomy from the state. It is my contention that while Egyptian authoritarianism, during the examined period, was effectual in uprooting and liquidating any independent local organised politics, its inclusionary institutional frames had a major shortcoming in their mobilisational functions, and thus lacked popular support. The problem, as this book suggests, reflected the authoritarian dilemma in bridging the macro (the national) and the micro (the local).

Watched by security agencies, the NDP and the SLA were indeed the most prominent inclusionary institutional spheres that were employed to monopolise local politics and contributed continuously to redefine it in accordance with the state's changing economic and political agendas. Local notables, who accepted the logic of subordination, strived to compete for the existent positions by mobilising different kinds of social resources and entrenching themselves in the power networks that penetrated all layers of the structure of authority. On the flip side, those who dared to take part in independent local politics through joining formal political parties, such as the New Wafd party in the late 1970s, or informal movements such as the Islamic movement afterwards, were repressed by coercion.

At the lowest level of politics, the establishment of local branches of the NDP in the towns of the Cairo peri-urban fringe from the late Sadat–early Mubarak era was accompanied by the regime reconfiguring the system of local governance to overcome the problem of the numerous networks of power at the subnational level. The fiscal pressures pushed the regime to innovate methods that could outsource networks of power and make the system's inclusionary frames more competitive and effective. Thus, the institutional relationship between the ruling party and the SLA had to be informalised. Furthermore, general elections served as a 'market system' to regulate patronage politics and outsource the cost of political mobilisation and redistribution to the rent-seeking elite.[84] Involving general elections in the system of local governance saw the emergence of local political field(s), at each level of governance, with a limited number of positions and a large number of competitors. However, the degree of competitiveness was largely dependent on the regime strategies of informal centralisation–decentralisation, which varied between one period and another.

At the lowest level of local governance (namely, the village), lesser notables who competed in the local political field responded by politicising their durable social networks (explicitly, social capital). In the towns of the Cairo peri-urban fringe, the emergence of political clannism was one of the most prominent outcomes of this practice. Much received wisdom in the study of Middle Eastern social politics considers kinship structures and 'familial ethos', as a 'subaltern counterpublic' alternative to western 'civil society'.[85] It has been presumed that social identity in Egypt, and elsewhere in the MENA, has been closely linked to 'status in the network of kin relations'.[86]

The evidence presented in Chapter 4, however, shows that political clannism in the Cairo peri-urban fringe is a very modern phenomenon that was a result of authoritarianism developing mechanisms to manage its state–society patronage networks. This situation encouraged lesser notables to politicise kin-based networks in their struggle over the political field. Even so, the effectiveness of political clannism and kin-based political mobilisation was limited to the micro scale, and therefore could not, by any means, counter the Islamic movement sort of mobilisation, which was based on identity politics, and thus worked efficiently on the macro scale.

The weakness of the mobilisational capabilities of the system of local governance paved the way for the Islamic movement to challenge the regime's political domination over local politics. As Chapter 3 will show, Greater Cairo, starting from the early 1980s, experienced a rise of the *da'wa* movement that encompassed a variety of Islamic activism. This movement consisted of fast-growing local networks of devout youth led by populist sheikhs and newly graduated professionals, who quickly found themselves appealing to local communities by mobilisative Islamist rhetoric and public social work. The *da'wa* movement attracted thousands of local people who came in droves on a weekly basis to attend religious lessons for Islamic figures from the MB and a new Salafi movement. What marked this movement and made it a real challenge for the regime is that its political mobilisation was not based on patronage politics but rather on ideology, which proved to be more effective. Nevertheless, the life cycle of this sort of activism proved to be short. After the 1989 parliamentary elections, which witnessed the return of the MB to electoral politics, the regime launched successive waves of a security campaign that wiped out most of the *da'wa* networks. By the late 1990s, it became clear that local politics as a field was firmly dominated by the regime's inclusionary institutional frames and its networks of power, at its core the NDP networks.

Yet, despite all authoritarian measures taken to upgrade the system's inclusionary and exclusionary strategies at the micro level, the regime's inclusionary institutional frames failed to yield the desired political outcomes. Both the 2000 and 2005 parliamentary elections showed evidence of that.

Electoral rigging, arbitrary arrests and employing *balṭajiyya* (street criminals) were at an unprecedented intensity and scale to prevent an electoral landslide for the MB. The system was effective in dominating local politics at the local level, but it could not translate its domination into political hegemony on a larger scale (i.e., at the district and governorate levels). To put it differently, patronage politics, despite all its upgrading strategies over more than three decades, could not overcome the challenge from identity politics. The authoritarian dilemma was that regime strategies were effective on a micro rather than a macro scale.

The failure of the system of local governance to bridge the local (micro) and the national (macro) can be explained by Azmi Bishara's thesis of the *Arab Question*, which he has defined as the failure of the post-colonial Arab state to pursue the nation-building process. The process, if it had been completed, would have created a collective national 'we-ness' that would be responsible for bringing the fragmented society together, on the one hand, and connecting the state with society, on the other, thus producing a civil society capable of resisting as well as reifying state-sanctioned relations. The unfinished process, according to Bishara, has allowed Arab authoritarianism to become entrenched in the state apparatus, manoeuvring between formal and informal structures in order to pre-empt change. However, this has been at the expense of its political hegemony over society, which has been continuously eroded, leading to a constant conflict between state politics, on the one hand, and legitimacy, on the other.[87] The Arab Question, nevertheless, varies between one Arab state and another. Some states like Egypt and Tunisia are more legitimate than others such as Syria, Iraq and Libya. That explains why, when the 2010s revolutions erupted, their outcomes fluctuated between a democratic transition in Tunisia, military-based government in Egypt, and civil wars in Syria, Libya and Yemen. From the perspective of local politics, this study shows that the question of state legitimacy was also behind the failure of the Egyptian system of local governance and its collapse in the January Revolution.

The fact that the MB, despite all repressive measures and continuous authoritarian upgrading, could overcome the NDP on the macro scale shows the power of ideology that the regime never had. As Chapter 3 will show, although the Islamic movement in the towns of the Cairo peri-urban fringe lacked the rootedness, or social capital, that the NDP enjoyed on the micro level, it instead possessed symbolic capital. Symbolic capital, according to

Bourdieu, is a 'denied capital'; it disguises the underlying interested relations by showing it as disinterested pursuits, not as emanating from the pursuit of self-interest.[88] It is a form of power that is 'not perceived as power but as legitimate demands for recognition, deference, obedience, or the services of others'. It is a form of accumulation that seems to owe nothing to the logic of exploitation.[89]

Symbolic power enabled the Islamic movement to articulate its popular mobilisation with a broader collective 'cultural framework' that stresses the supranational Muslim community (*umma*), therefore, provoking religious emotions and identity politics. By contrast, lacking an ideological and cultural framework made the local branches of the NDP in the Cairo peri-urban fringe more like 'community organisations'[90] rather than branches of a political party. The NDP local leaders emerged from within local communities and were often perceived in their localities as clients of authoritarianism or, at best, as notables who provided direction and guidance in specific or varied areas of community life. From the late 1980s, they understood local politics as project-based work aimed at serving their localities and developing their amenities. This sometimes made them rooted, well-known and respected in their local settings, but unknown to other communities in the region or on a wider scale. It was, therefore, not possible for them to feel a sense of solidarity with other local NDP figures from neighbouring localities or even from the same town. In fact, they viewed them as rivals who competed with them on the political field and this rendered the party self-collapsing on the eve of any election. The reason was that the party's huge networks shared no ideology. They had nothing in common except their closeness to bureaucracy.

The evidence presented in the following chapters suggests that the Egyptian regime, from the mid-2000s, was resigned to this conclusion. Therefore, NDP local leadership in the towns of the Cairo peri-urban fringe observed the authoritarian regime gradually abandoning them. Their role in the system of local governance was greatly marginalised and substituted by a new informal system in which the SSIS had the upper hand, and in which bands of *balṭajiyya* frequently appeared to be on the side of the police. It seemed to most of them that the rules of the game had been changed forever and their lifetimes of political experience and of accumulating social capital were not respected. The old system of control was irreversibly dying and a new one was yet to be born.

Conclusion

This chapter has introduced a conceptual framework for studying the process of upgrading the authoritarian system of local governance in Egypt. It has also presented an overview of the history of its development and institutional reconfiguration since the time before the founding of the Egyptian republic. As observed, the process of upgrading the system reconfigured the relations between the formal structure of authority and the informal networks of power.

Under Nasser, the authority–power triangle of the system was established but suffered from instability due to the struggles inside the regime. Under Sadat, the system was stabilised after new reconfigurations among its components (the SLA, security agencies and the ruling party), but the relations among these were increasingly informalised. Under Mubarak, the upgrading was merely applied to the structure of power, mainly through elections. Each phase of upgrading was induced by fiscal crises and different domestic political challenges. Nasser's major concern was eradicating the hostile elements from the *ancien régime*. Sadat encountered the power centres inside the new regime, while Mubarak was influenced by the danger of the Islamic movement.

The process of upgrading, furthermore, led to redefining the relationship between the authoritarian regime and its networks of power, which entailed redefining the roles of local leadership in accordance with the regime's economic agendas. Nevertheless, the dilemma of the Egyptian authoritarian system of local governance, in the era of Mubarak at least, lay in its ruthless effectiveness in dominating and monopolising local politics, on the one hand, and to a large extent the futility of translating this domination into political hegemony, on the other. Thus, it worked on the micro scale, but failed on the macro scale. The following chapters discuss different aspects of this dilemma, but for the next chapter, more exploration of the Egyptian system of local governance is required.

Notes

1. Martin Doornbos, '"Good Governance": The Metamorphoses of a Policy Metaphor', in *Global Forces and State Restructuring*, (London: Palgrave Macmillan, 2006) 73–92, 74. See also Ved P. Nanda, 'The "Good Governance" Concept Revisited', *Annals of the American Academy of Political and Social*

Science 603(1) (2006): 269–83; Thandike Mkandawire, '"Good Governance": The Itinerary of an Idea', *Development in Practice* 17(4/5) (2007): 679–81.

2. Doornbos, *Global Forces*, 74.
3. Ibid.
4. Ibid.
5. Ibid., 77.
6. Vollmann et al., 'Decentralisation as Authoritarian Upgrading?' 6.
7. Doornbos, *Global Forces*, 77.
8. Göran Hydén, Julius Court and Kenneth Mease, *Making Sense of Governance: Empirical Evidence from Sixteen Developing Countries* (Boulder, CO: Lynne Rienner, 2004), 16. See also Jude Howell, 'Governance Matters: Key Challenges and Emerging Tendencies', in Jude Howell (ed.), *Governance in China* (Lanham, MD: Rowman & Littlefield, 2004), 1–18, 2.
9. Heydemann, 'Upgrading Authoritarianism in the Arab World'.
10. Ibid.
11. Ibid.
12. Ibid. On the emerging debate on the international trend of authoritarian diffusion, see Steven Heydemann and Reinoud Leenders, 'Authoritarian Learning and Authoritarian Resilience: Regime Responses to the "Arab Awakening"', *Globalizations* 8(5) (2011): 647–53; Thomas Ambrosio, 'Constructing a Framework of Authoritarian Diffusion: Concepts, Dynamics, and Future Research', *International Studies Perspectives* 11(4) (2010): 375–92.
13. See, for example, Eberhard Kienle, *A Grand Delusion: Democracy and Economic Reform in Egypt* (London: Bloomsbury, 2001); Joshua Stacher, *Adaptable Autocrats: Regime Power in Egypt and Syria*, Stanford Series in Middle Eastern and Islamic Societies and Cultures (Stanford, CA: Stanford University Press, 2012); Stephen Juan King, *The New Authoritarianism in the Middle East and North Africa* (Bloomington: Indiana University Press, 2009); Raymond Hinnebusch, 'Syria: From "Authoritarian Upgrading" to Revolution?' *International Affairs* 88(1) (2012): 95–113.
14. Hutchcroft, 'Centralization and Decentralization in Administration and Politics', 26.
15. Jon Pierre, 'Models of Urban Governance: The Institutional Dimension of Urban Politics', *Urban Affairs Review* 34(3) (1999): 372–96, 376. See also Chris Ansell, 'Network Institutionalism', in *The Oxford Handbook of Political Institutions* (Oxford: Oxford University Press, 2006), 75–89, 76–7.
16. Oliver D. Meza Canales, 'From Local Government to Local Governance', *Journal of Public Governance and Policy: Latin American Review* 1(1) (2015): 5–22, 16.

17. Shah and Shah, 'New Vision of Local Governance', 3.
18. John-Mary Kauzya, 'Strengthening Local Governance Capacity for Participation', in Vincente Fox (ed.), *Reinventing Government for the Twenty-first Century: State Capacity in a Globalizing Society* (West Hartford, CT: Kumarian Press, 2003), 181–93, 182.
19. Hydén, Court and Mease, *Making Sense of Governance.*
20. Vollmann et al., 'Decentralisation as Authoritarian Upgrading?'
21. Janine A. Clark, *Local Politics in Jordan and Morocco: Strategies of Centralization and Decentralization* (New York: Columbia University Press, 2018), 8. See also Rony Emmenegger, 'Decentralization and the Local Developmental State: Peasant Mobilization in Oromiya, Ethiopia', *Africa: The Journal of the International African Institute* 86(2) (2016): 263–87.
22. Pierre Francois Landry, *Decentralized Authoritarianism in China: The Communist Party's Control of Local Elites in the post-Mao Era* (New York: Cambridge University Press, 2008).
23. David Alan Craig and Doug Porter, *Development beyond Neoliberalism? Governance, Poverty Reduction and Political Economy* (New York: Routledge, 2006), 105–6.
24. Anoop Sadanandan, 'Patronage and Decentralization: The Politics of Poverty in India', *Comparative Politics* 44(2) (2012): 211–28.
25. Vollmann et al., 'Decentralisation as Authoritarian Upgrading?' 8.
26. Hutchcroft, 'Centralization and Decentralization in Administration and Politics'. See also Lloyd I. Rudolph and Susanne Hoeber Rudolph, 'Authority and Power in Bureaucratic and Patrimonial Administration: A Revisionist Interpretation of Weber on Bureaucracy', *World Politics* 31(2) (1979): 195–227, 198.
27. Earl of Cromer, *Modern Egypt*, 2 vols (London: Macmillan, 1908) 2:189.
28. Roger Owen, 'The Middle East in the Eighteenth Century: An "Islamic" Society in Decline? A Critique of Gibb and Bowen's Islamic Society and the West', *Bulletin (British Society for Middle Eastern Studies)* 3(2) (1976): 110–17, 113.
29. Iliya Harik, 'The Impact of the Domestic Market on Rural–Urban Relations in the Middle East', in Richard Antoun and Iliya Harik (eds), *Rural Politics and Social Change in the Middle East* (Bloomington: Indiana University Press, 1972), 336–37.
30. *Izba* system is a mode of agricultural organisation that oversaw a transitional stage from semi-feudal to capitalist modes of production. See Nazih Ayubi, *Over-Stating the Arab State: Politics and Society in the Middle East* (London: I. B. Tauris, 1995), 179.
31. Mostafa H. Nagi, 'Internal Migration and Structural Changes in Egypt', *Middle East Journal* 28(3) (1974): 261–82.

32. Gabriel Baer, *Studies in the Social History of Modern Egypt* (Chicago: University of Chicago Press, 1969), 60.
33. Fahmy, *The Politics of Egypt*, 183.
34. An example in the MENA is the development of the system of local administration in Morocco, see John R. Nellis, 'Tutorial Decentralisation in Morocco', *Journal of Modern African Studies* 21(3) (1983): 483–508. The Egyptian case can be also contrasted to the Thai case. In northern Thailand, the system of local governance was a sort of modernisation of the pre-modern structures of local organisation. See S. N. Eisenstadt and Luis Roniger, *Patrons, Clients, and Friends: Interpersonal Relations and the Structure of Trust in Society* (Cambridge: Cambridge University Press, 1984), 130–7; Andrew Walker, 'The Rural Constitution and the Everyday Politics of Elections in Northern Thailand', *Journal of Contemporary Asia* 38(1) (2008): 84–105. The Panchayat Raj system in rural India serves as another example of the same trend, see Subrata K. Mitra, 'Making Local Government Work: Local Elites, Panchayati Raj and Governance in India', *The Success of India's Democracy* 6 (2001): 103–26.
35. John Waterbury, *The Egypt of Nasser and Sadat: The Political Economy of Two Regimes* (Princeton, NJ: Princeton University Press, 1983), 311 (emphasis in original).
36. Fahmy, *The Politics of Egypt*, 184–5.
37. Ibid.
38. Iliya Harik, 'Mobilization Policy and Political Change in Rural Egypt', in Richard Antoun and Iliya Harik (eds), *Rural Politics and Social Change in the Middle East* (Bloomington: Indiana University Press, 1972), 287–314, 290.
39. Iliya Harik, 'The Single Party as a Subordinate Movement: The Case of Egypt', *World Politics* 26(1) (1973): 80–105.
40. Fahmy, *The Politics of Egypt*, 186. See also James L. Iwan, 'From Social Welfare to Local Government: The United Arab Republic (Egypt)', *Middle East Journal* 22(3) (1968): 265–77.
41. The National Union was formally announced in the 1956 constitution, but was not actually organised until 1959. On the history of the state's political organisations under Nasser, see Fahmy, *The Politics of Egypt*, ch. 4.
42. Ayubi, *Bureaucracy and Politics in Contemporary Egypt*, 441.
43. Ibid.
44. Raymond Hinnebusch, 'Towards a Historical Sociology of the Arab Uprising: Beyond Democratization and Post-Democratization', in *Routledge Handbook of the Arab Spring* (London: Routledge, 2014), 39–50, 45–6.
45. Hazem Kandil, *Soldiers, Spies, and Statesmen: Egypt's Road to Revolt* (London: Verso Trade, 2014), 297.

46. The NDP was officially established in 1978 and inherited the structure and functions of the ASU, which was disbanded by President Anwar al-Sadat (1971–81). The political bureau of the new party was headed by Sadat until he was assassinated in 1981, when former President Hosni Mubarak (1981–2011) became its next president. In the 2000s, the party also experienced an 'old guard–new guard' major division among its senior elites after the political ascendance of Gamal Mubarak.
47. Robert Springborg, *Mubarak's Egypt: Fragmentation of the Political Order* (Boulder, CO: Westview Press, 1989), 155.
48. Ibid., 156.
49. Kandil, *Soldiers, Spies, and Statesmen*, 322.
50. Ibid., 298.
51. In both 'authoritarian upgrading' literature in the MENA and 'competitive authoritarianism literature' in Latin America, elections are academically regarded as a mechanism of updating and outsourcing the authoritarian regime's clientelist lines. Chapter 2 will expand the analysis on the role of elections in Egyptian local governance.
52. Springborg, *Mubarak's Egypt*, 156–7.
53. Lisa Blaydes, *Elections and Distributive Politics in Mubarak's Egypt* (Cambridge: Cambridge University Press, 2010).
54. Ibid.
55. Stacher, *Adaptable Autocrats*, 99–100.
56. *Practices*, according to Bourdieu, are results of the interaction of *habitus*, *capital(s)* and *field*. *Habitus* is a set of deeply internalised dispositions that result from the process of socialisation. *Capitals* can be economic, cultural, social and symbolic, while the *field* is better understood as a conflictual context in which capitals are deployed. Further elaboration on Bourdieu's concepts is within the analysis in this chapter and later chapters.
57. Pierre Bourdieu and Loi'c Wacquant, *An Invitation to Reflexive Sociology* (Cambridge: Polity, 1992), 101.
58. George Ritzer (ed.), *Sociological Theory*, 8th edn (New York: McGraw-Hill, 2010), 532–4.
59. C. Calhoun, E. LiPuma and M. Postone (eds), *Bourdieu: Critical Perspectives* (Chicago: University of Chicago Press, 1993), 5.
60. 'Alī Pasha Mubārak, *Khiṭāṭ at-Tawfiqīyah al-Jadīdah. al-Matba'a al-Kubra al-Amiriyya* (Bulaq Masr [Cairo], 1886), 15:4–5.
61. Ibid.
62. Terence Walz, 'Libya, the Trans-Saharan Trade of Egypt, and 'Abdallah Al-Kahhal, 1880–1914', *Islamic Africa* 1(1) (2010): 85–107, 91.

63. Baer, *Studies in the Social History of Modern Egypt*, 425.
64. F. H. Lawson, 'Rural Revolt and Provincial Society in Egypt, 1820–1824', *International Journal of Middle East Studies* 13 (1981): 131–53, 139; C. V. B. Stanley, 'The Oasis of Siwa', *Journal of the Royal African Society* 11(43) (1912): 290–324, 305.
65. Mo'taz Mikkawi, *Interview*, Kerdasa, February 2017.
66. As Pascale Ghazaleh puts it, 'At the turn of the [nineteenth] century, then, being a *tajir* [= merchant] meant being able to mobilize men and merchandise, sometimes to assist rulers who did not have the means to do so. In the following decades, merchants lost many of their diplomatic, judicial, and military functions.' Pascale Ghazaleh, 'Trading in Power: Merchants and the State in 19th-Century Egypt', *International Journal of Middle East Studies* 45 (2013): 71–91, 77.
67. Ibid.
68. A. al-Rahman Al-Jabarti, *Aja'ib al-athar fi al-tarajim wal-akhbar* (Cairo: Ktab Inc, 2013), 1:252–3.
69. Ibid.
70. Ibid.
71. Mahmoud Abdel-Fadil, *Development, Income, Distribution and Social Change in Rural Egypt (1952–1970): A Study in the Political Economy of Agrarian Transition* (Cambridge: Cambridge University Press, 1975), 23.
72. Leonard Binder, *In a Moment of Enthusiasm: Political Power and the Second Stratum in Egypt* (Chicago: University of Chicago Press, 1978), 372–3.
73. '*Nubdha Sinā'iyya*', in *Sahīfa al-Tijāra*, 4 July 1925, 2. Cited by John Charlcraft, 'The End of Guilds in Egypt: Restructuring Textiles in the Long Nineteenth Century', in Suraiya Faroqhi and Randi Deguilhem (eds), *Crafts and Craftsmen of the Middle East: Fashioning the Individual in the Muslim Mediterranean* (London: I. B. Tauris, 2005), 338–76, 362.
74. Hussain Saleh Omar, *Interview*, 10 May 2016.
75. Baer attributes the decline of the importance of rural notability to the restrictions of administrative authorities of *umda*s under the British occupation, which prevented the appointed *umda*s from enriching themselves. As he concludes: 'the large landowning *umda*, so frequent in the days of Ismail, became a rare sight in mid-twentieth century'. Baer, *Studies in the Social History of Modern Egypt*, 53.
76. A historical account for these developments to be found in Lucie Ryzova, *Age of the Efendiyya: Passages to Modernity in National–Colonial Egypt* (Oxford: Oxford University Press, 2014).
77. For comprehensive details on electoral tactics in Egypt between wars, see James Whidden, *Monarchy and Modernity in Egypt: Politics, Islam and Neo-Colonialism between the Wars* (London: I. B. Tauris, 2013), 65–100.

78. Mohammad Khamis Abu Issa, *Interview*, Kerdasa, 12 April 2016; Mikkawi, *Interview*, February 2017.
79. Menza's study traces the socio-political transformation of the regime grassroots. He found that the segment of lesser notables, which flourished after the *Infitah*, became the new grassroots for the Egyptian regime. See Menza, *Patronage Politics in Egypt*.
80. Samir Sulayman, *The Autumn of Dictatorship: Fiscal Crisis and Political Change in Egypt under Mubarak* (Stanford, CA: Stanford University Press, 2011).
81. Ayubi, *Over-Stating the Arab State*, 25.
82. Ibid., 3 (emphasis in original).
83. Ibid.
84. Blaydes, *Elections and Distributive Politics*, 51.
85. Diane Singerman, 'Restoring the Family to Civil Society: Lessons from Egypt', *Journal of Middle East Women's Studies* 2(1) (2006): 1–32.
86. Eric Hooglund, 'The Society and its Environment', in Helen Chapin Metz (ed.), *Egypt: A Country Study*, 5th edn (Washington, DC: GPO for the Library of Congress, 1991), 91–154, 124.
87. Azmi Bishāra, *Fy-l-Mas'ala al-'Arabiyya: Muqaddima li-Bayān Dīmuqrāty 'Araby* (*The Arab Question: Introduction to an Arab Democratic Statement*) (Beirut: Center for Arab Unity Studies, 2007); Azmi Bishāra, *al-Mojtama' al-Madany: Dirāsa Naqdiyya* (*Civil Society: A Critical Study*) (Beirut: Center for Arab Unity Studies, 1998). Compare with Adham Saouli who argues that 'what emerged in the Middle East were not fully developed "states" as understood in Weberian terms, but social fields on which states form or de-form. Social fields are the territorial social arenas that structure relations among several social powers who interact in cycles of domination and resistance in attempts to establish hierarchical power (a ruling regime) as the first phase of state formation. Interactions within a social field generate path-dependent trajectories, memories, histories and identities that separate it from other social fields and give meaning to it.' Adham Saouli, *The Arab State: Dilemmas of Late Formation* (London: Routledge, 2012), 5.
88. David Swartz, *Culture and Power: The Sociology of Pierre Bourdieu* (Chicago: University of Chicago Press, 2012), 43.
89. Ibid.
90. On community organisations' frameworks, see Carl Milofsky (ed.), *Community Organizations: Studies in Resource Mobilization and Exchange* (Oxford: Oxford University Press, 1988).

2

CENTRALISED AND DECENTRALISED: THE AUTHORITARIAN UPGRADING OF THE EGYPTIAN SYSTEM OF LOCAL GOVERNANCE

In 2005, the prime minister and the governor of al-Giza issued two decrees stipulating that Kerdasa, a village that had been affiliated with the city of Ausim, would assume a new status as an independent city and administrative centre (*markaz 'idāry*) for twelve towns and villages, to the west and north of Greater Cairo. Within two years, several new government institutions had been established, such as a police station (*markaz shurṭa*) in the town centre, a city council (*majlis al-madīna*), and a popular council (*al-majlis al-sha'by*), among others. The decision increased the town's share of public expenditure and changed the legal status of many activities and transactions in the town. For example, all real estate properties, including land, residential apartments and commercial stores, automatically fell under a new tenancy law, which slightly benefited owners at the expense of their tenants. The decision also expanded the area that had been designated for urban development at the expense of agricultural land and improved the quality of services provided by the government.

Prior to this period, Kerdasa had administratively been considered a village with just one police post (*nuqtat shurṭa*), although its population, according to the 2006 Egyptian Census, had exceeded 60,000, and despite it being considered the centre of an electoral district (*dā'ira intikhābiyya*) in parliamentary elections, with two members in the People's Assembly. At that time, the town had formally been administrated by a local unit (*wiḥda maḥaliyya*) and a local council (*al-majlis al-maḥaly*). The first was an executive municipal apparatus that was responsible for most public services, while the second was a representative board elected by Kerdasa inhabitants, though its authority was extremely limited. Both institutions represented the municipal machinery in the town and were affiliated to the Governorate of al-Giza. They were intended, by virtue of their structure and existence, to comprise the local government in Kerdasa.

The transformation of Kerdasa from a village into a city was a formal recognition of its status that had transpired through a long historical process of urbanisation. However, this recognition came very late, since prior to that the town had, for the greater part, been urbanised from the mid-1990s, if not earlier. From the mid-1980s, Kerdasa has been a service centre for a large part of the surrounding area, embracing factories, clinics, many schools and hundreds of workshops.[1] By 1995, the town included a business college, hundreds of both formal and informal firms, and had become surrounded by a belt of informal housing. Its inhabitants had also started to become as familiar with *balṭajiyya* (street criminals) as those of any typical medium-sized Egyptian city. It was not only Kerdasa that experienced such a transition at this time. For example, its neighbouring 'village', Nahia, also made a significant advance towards urbanisation in the same period, but was not recognised as a city.

The Egyptian system of local administration (SLA) is notorious for being slow-moving and there is a firm consensus that its over-centralised command structure bears the main responsibility for failing to keep pace with the multifaceted transformations of local communities.[2] It is for this reason that the secretary general of the NDP in Kerdasa, Haj Mohammad Abdel-Wahhab Mahjoub, who worked hard on this issue, was extremely proud of his achievement (*injaz*) in convincing Egyptian local bureaucracy to upgrade his hometown to a city. But Mahjoub's achievement can also tell us about the way that local politics influenced the process of decision-making in Egyptian over-centralised local governance.

This chapter resumes and expands discussion on the Egyptian authoritarian system of local governance. It provides a broad perspective and dual interpretive approach that helps in understanding both the structure of the system and its historical formation, because both, as recent literature suggests, are not analytically separable.[3] For heuristic purposes, therefore, the chapter consists of two parts, each employing a different analytical approach. The first utilises public administration frameworks to deconstruct the authority structure of the system of local governance under Mubarak and to analyse its centralised and decentralised characters. This requires, however, reconsideration of the conceptual development of centralisation–decentralisation and their different forms.

As will be shown, restricting the analytical lens to the administrative and legal structures of the system of local governance can lead to overlooking its structural *bifurcation* between formality and informality, which is one of the most important characteristics that marks all systems and makes them amenable in practice. Therefore, another approach that builds on the state-formation literature should be incorporated simultaneously, to examine the informal aspect of system, which is an essential aspect in the workings of local governance.

Accordingly, the second part of this chapter explores the historical formation of the system to understand how power–authority was historically reconfigured in Egyptian local governance. The major focus, however, is on the changing role of the ruling party (the ASU, then the NDP) in local governance under three regimes (Nasser, Sadat and Mubarak). This is because identifying the change can reflect the pattern of the interactions between informal networks and the administrative structures of the state. It can also uncover to what extent patronage politics effectively influenced the process of decision-making.

It will be demonstrated that both authority and power structures were upgraded under Nasser and Sadat in a way that benefited authoritarianism. Under Mubarak, however, the process of upgrading took place informally on the power structure through decentralising the regime's informal networks. In this respect, Mubarak used elections, especially parliamentary ones, as a mechanism for substituting informal decentralisation for formal decentralisation to avoid sharing power with local communities. It was a strategy that benefited him in managing the regime networks of power when they became abundant in number at the subnational level. It also minimised the cost of the public service delivery system. However, Mubarak's informal decentralisation strategies failed to overcome the weakness of the party mobilisation functions, which made the regime, in the late Mubarak period and under fiscal and political pressures, reconsider its relationship with the party's established grassroots.

Vertically Centralised: The System of Local Administration in Mubarak's Egypt

According to a study by the World Bank, Egypt is ranked 114 out of 182 countries on decentralisation and the closeness of government to the people, which categorises it as a highly centralised country.[4] The country is governed by a premier–presidential system. Below the central government level, there are twenty-seven governorates. Each is like a small government led by a governor who enjoys the same status as that of a minister. He is appointed by the president and in practice is mostly drawn from the Ministry of the Interior or the military. Nevertheless, the central ministries have directorates in each governorate, and they share the responsibilities of governance with or under the governorates.

Below the governorate level (the first level), there are two additional levels of local administration. The second is the district level (or metropolitan cities in urban areas), and the third is composed of local administrative units, such as villages, towns and city neighbourhoods. Each level reports up to the next level, from which it receives its instructions and resources. There are about 300 districts (*markiz* in rural governorates and *aksam* in urban governorates) at the second subnational level, and over 200 cities (*mudon*) and over 1,000 villages (*qura*) at the third subnational level. There are also thousands of unincorporated settlements without a council. The population size of administrative units at the district level (*marakiz* and *aksam*) in the era of Mubarak varied over time between 50,000 and 500,000, and their jurisdictions should have been large enough to provide public services, such as water treatment plants and hospital facilities. The average population size of cities and villages, on the other hand, could reach more than 20,000 and they should also have had local units that provided most local services in a manner responsive to local needs.

In practice, however, there have been significant deficiencies in administration capacity especially at the third level.[5] There has also been vagueness in the criteria for the upgrading of a village into a city. Various informal pressure networks could influence the governorate or the ministries to issue a decree to upgrade a village into a city, regardless of its ambiguous urban character or the predominance of a certain type of economy.[6] For example, until 2005 Kerdasa was defined as a village although its average population, according to the 2006 census, exceeded 65,000. This was also the case for many towns and cities in the Greater Cairo peri-urban fringe.

At its second and third levels, the local government for any municipal unit comprises two separate bodies: executive and elected. At the third level, the executive body is the local unit (*wehda mahalliya*), which enjoys as much possible authority as any municipal institution; all of its staff, including its chair, are appointed by either the governor or the prime minister. On the other hand, the elected body of the smallest unit (the village) is represented by the local council (*al-majlis al-mahalli*). The elected branch of a city and capital of its district (*markaz wa-madīna*) (from the second level) should also have a popular council (*al-majlis al-sha'bi*), alongside the local council. In general, each local executive institution should be paralleled by an elected local institution. However, although higher-level elected councils (popular councils) have supervisory authority over the lower-level elected councils (local councils), they have no authority over the executive branch at the same level.[7]

Since their foundation by Law 52 of 1975, elected councils, which should reflect the spirit of representative decentralisation, have never been endowed with any important constitutional authority, except for the right of *istijwāb* (monitoring and questioning). Nevertheless, this right is advisory rather than mandatory, since there has always been an executive institution responsible for mediating between both branches of local governance. Prior to 1988, the governorate took this role according to Law 43 of 1979, although its regulations stipulated that local councils had the right to monitor and question (*istijwāb*) the governorate itself.

In 1988, an amendment was introduced giving the Ministry of Local Development the final decision in such disputes. In 2008, a new and improved bill was discussed in the People's Assembly but was never adopted. This situation led public administration researchers to consider that the Egyptian local government system could actually be characterised as a form of de-concentration rather than one of devolved local self-government. The Egyptian public administration system is equipped with an elaborate system of de-concentrated field offices of line agencies, and service delivery decisions are made by the central government or governorates.[8]

This was despite the fact that reaching some balance between the local executives and local elected councils was always on successive presidential manifestos of reforms and the NDP annual conferences.[9] Suffice it to say that from 1956 until the early 1990s, 156 separate reform proposals were submitted, but they seldom found a listening ear.[10] Dozens of other initiatives were introduced afterwards,[11] but also failed to materialise.[12] James Mayfield in summarising the life cycle of every ambitious agenda to reform the SLA, states:

> at first the new ruler/regime takes considerable interest in local government and seeks to invigorate and even democratize it. The enthusiasm gives away,

> however, first to caution, then to backtracking, as central control is asserted once again and access to local government by contending elements of civil society is increasingly restricted.[13]

A historical review of the Egyptian legislature also shows that the SLA, since the late 1970s, has been subjected to several laws that did not make any significant changes to its structure. Table (2.1) shows the main laws that affected the SLA legal structure functions and flow of commands. As can be noticed, most of the important laws were issued under Nasser and Sadat while those laws issued under Mubarak had minor effect. Furthermore, most laws, in all periods, were intended to deepen the tendency towards more centralist control mainly by broadening the authority of the governor, as Law 52 of 1975 and Law 34 of 1979 suggest, or the central government as Law 145 of 1988 indicates. The historical development of the SLA, therefore, can be summarised in two idioms: more centralism and less democracy.

The reluctance to reform the structure of authority in the system of local governance by some form of democratic decentralisation has been largely attributed to authoritarianism, and the unwillingness of the ruling caste to share power with wider segments of society: which is true. However, it seems somehow contradictory to the academic trend of 'authoritarian upgrading' in the MENA region.

As discussed in the previous chapter, for more than two decades Egyptian authoritarianism has been a prominent example of the 'authoritarian upgrading' literature trend. The Egyptian regime, until the January 25 Revolution (2011) at least, has shown an outstanding ability to capture the benefits of selective economic and political reforms, such as economic liberalisation and moving towards multipartism and sponsoring semi-official civil society sectors, to structurally transform itself in a way that reinforced authoritarian control.[14]

However, the Egyptian SLA, which has been one of the most important tools of deploying power from the central level to the subnational level, appears in mainstream scholarship to be immune from reform and excluded from authoritarian flexible arrangements. There is a firm consensus that the strict hierarchy and over-centralised local government has made no room for any meaningful political decentralisation. Local communities have no financial and decision-making autonomy from centralised state directives,[15] which has therefore limited the ability of local initiatives to act as a vehicle of development.[16]

Table 2.1 The legislative development of the legal structure of the SLA

Law	Most important legal and political effects
124 of 1960 (under Nasser)	• The creation of the contemporary Egyptian SLA. The country was divided into three levels: governorates, centres or districts, villages or neighbourhoods. • Governors of provinces were raised in status from officials of the Ministry of the Interior to the rank of deputy ministers responsible directly to the president of republic. • The law was amended in 1962 and 1964 to establish the relationship between the ruling party (the ASU) and the SLA (see later in this chapter).
57 of 1971 (under Sadat)	• Consolidating the governor authorities. • The creation of two kinds of council in each governorate working parallel with each other. The first was elected but with minimal authority, and the second was the executive council, vested with comprehensive power.
52 of 1975 (under Sadat)	• Consolidating the governor authorities. • The introduction of a dual-branch council system at all subnational level, the first being executive and vested with most authority, the second being elected but with minimal authority. • The active membership of the ASU as a requirement for the candidature of the local councils was dropped.
43 of 1979 (under Sadat)	• Made the governor like a 'little king' in his province.
145 of 1988 (under Mubarak)	• The law replaced the title 'Local Government' with the title 'Local Administration'. • The law made minor changes to the status of governor, making him the representative of the highest executive authority in his governorate, instead of being the president's representative. In return it empowered the central government authorities. • The law deprived elected councils of some of their authority. • The law was amended a few times in the 1990s to avoid being declared unconstitutional by the Supreme Constitutional Court.

Yet the system of local governance does not consist solely of the SLA. The SLA only represents its structure of authority, while there is also its structure of power, which comprises various informal networks and power centres that influence the process of decision-making. The later structure was also subjected to other forms of political centralisation–decentralisation. However, understanding their logic requires reconsideration of the conceptual development of the process of centralisation and decentralisation.

Reconsidering Centralisation and Decentralisation

Why should the concept of centralisation–decentralisation be considered? As shown in the previous section of this chapter, is not difficult, in the light of the formal structure of the system of local governance, to conclude that the system had no semblance of political decentralisation. To become an elected member of a local council was not worth the trouble, as this post was honorary and practically unpaid.[17]

Even in the last decade of the Mubarak era, when the Egyptian media and many civil society organisations continually attacked corrupt practices in the SLA, they rarely targeted its elected branch. They reprehended the executive branch specifically, and especially the *wiḥdat maḥaliyya* (local units), which were theoretically authorised to use part of local resources (most importantly, land and real estate) for the public good rather than for private gain. Those who occupied the highest ranked posts in this institution were often not actually 'locals', but rather were executive chiefs often appointed from the army and the Ministry of the Interior.[18] In short, they belonged to the state itself and not the local representative bodies. Therefore, local council elections should theoretically have no importance.

However, the Mubarak regime never allowed any margin of flexibility to local elections compared with the parliamentary elections, although the latter were far more important in all aspects. This can be observed, for instance, in a report that documented a number of incidents that took place in the local council elections of March 2008. The report noted countless violations of the electoral law, including fights between candidates and police involvement to prevent certain candidates from campaigning. The security forces were accused of tampering with ballot boxes. They were also witnessed turning a blind eye to *balṭajiyya*, who were hired by many candidates to prevent their opponents' voters from reaching voting stations.[19] This was all in the context of an election that few people cared about and its electoral turnout, as a percentage, barely reached double digits.

Really? It is not rational that authoritarianism would deploy so much power and embroil itself in criminal acts to dominate positions that were not influential or did not affect its political control. The reason behind this analytical shortcoming, as discussed in the previous chapter, lies in the 'division of labour' that has long 'separated analyses of administrative and political structures' and, therefore, has 'developed the basic distinction between authority and power'.[20] In the real world, however, there is a constant interaction between them, whereby 'administrative structures can be conceived of in formal terms, for heuristic purposes, but it is clear that they are always – albeit in varying degrees – imbued with informal networks that display their own dynamics'.[21]

This separation has affected many public administration studies and reports on Egyptian local government – including reports sponsored and guided by various international organisations, which have focused on the formal system that has been detailed briefly above. As observed, if this system were isolated and examined separately, it would be intuitive to assume that representative local bodies had almost no role. That assumption, however, undermines the role played by the informal networks of power, which could make insignificant positions significant.

To overcome this shortcoming, Hutchcroft alternatively proposes a neo-institutionalist theoretical model that develops two distinct continua of administrative and political centralisation–decentralisation. The first continuum is concerned with centralisation–decentralisation of authority and builds on the foundations of public administration literature. The other continuum is related to the centralisation–decentralisation of power and draws upon scholarship on state formation and politics. Combining the administrative–authority continuum and the political–power continuum into a single matrix allows for analysis of the complex interplay that exists between the two realms.[22]

The combination of both continua, furthermore, can help in identifying practices of centralisation–decentralisation beyond their classical definitions. From a traditional public administration perspective, it was often assumed that centralisation–decentralisation was primarily a vertical phenomenon, whereby the 'centre' is 'higher', on some vertical scale than the actors to whom the packets of centralised or decentralised authority are distributed. In this sense, the most abstractive definition of decentralisation has been that of 'authority being spread out from a smaller to a larger number of actors'.[23]

Recent scholarship, however, also considers it on a horizontal scale, in which horizontal centralisation–decentralisation refers to the extent to which non-managers, especially informal networks, affect decision processes.[24] In this regard, three points should be taken into consideration while assessing the politics of local governance:

1. That the authority structure of the system of local governance might be strictly centralised on a vertical scale, but it could also be marked by degrees of informal decentralisation on a horizontal scale whereby the process of decision-making depends on the basis of cooperation, loyalty and trust among networks at the subnational level rather than hierarchical diktat.[25]
2. That it may be an oversimplification to content ourselves with a generalised enquiry into centralisation–decentralisation. Instead, the notion should be disaggregated to examine which step in the decision-making process is centralised and which decentralised, and what 'overall effects this pattern seems to have on the final actions'.[26]
3. Unlike vertical hierarchies, which are rigid and static because they are handed down by legislation, horizontal links are fluid and flexible and, therefore, could be subjected to continuous reconfigurations that serve the will of dominant groups. In this sense, the overall picture of any system of local governance is complex, in which the horizontal links are 'layered on the top of vertical hierarchies, rather than replacing them'.[27]

For these reasons, it is better to view any system of local governance as structurally bifurcated between the realms of formality and informality, which makes grasping the system dynamics, though possible, challenging and but never comprehensive. This is because whatever the basic character of the structure of authority, there are always informal networks – hidden by its nature – that penetrate the system, influence the flow command and divert the process of decision-making. In this sense, public administration frameworks only serve as the starting point.

The Effect of Bifurcation

To understand the importance of power networks in limiting the centralised character of the continuum of authority, we must re-examine the Egyptian SLA from a bifurcated point of view. Figure 2.1 gives a basic outline of the SLA in Egypt from 1988 until now. As can be seen, the system roughly consists of three levels. Each chief in level 1, such as the members of the governorates' executive councils, is appointed either by the governor or by the prime minister.

Usually, each executive council consists of members that represent all directorates (*mudīriyyāt*). The directorate is an institutional unit assigned

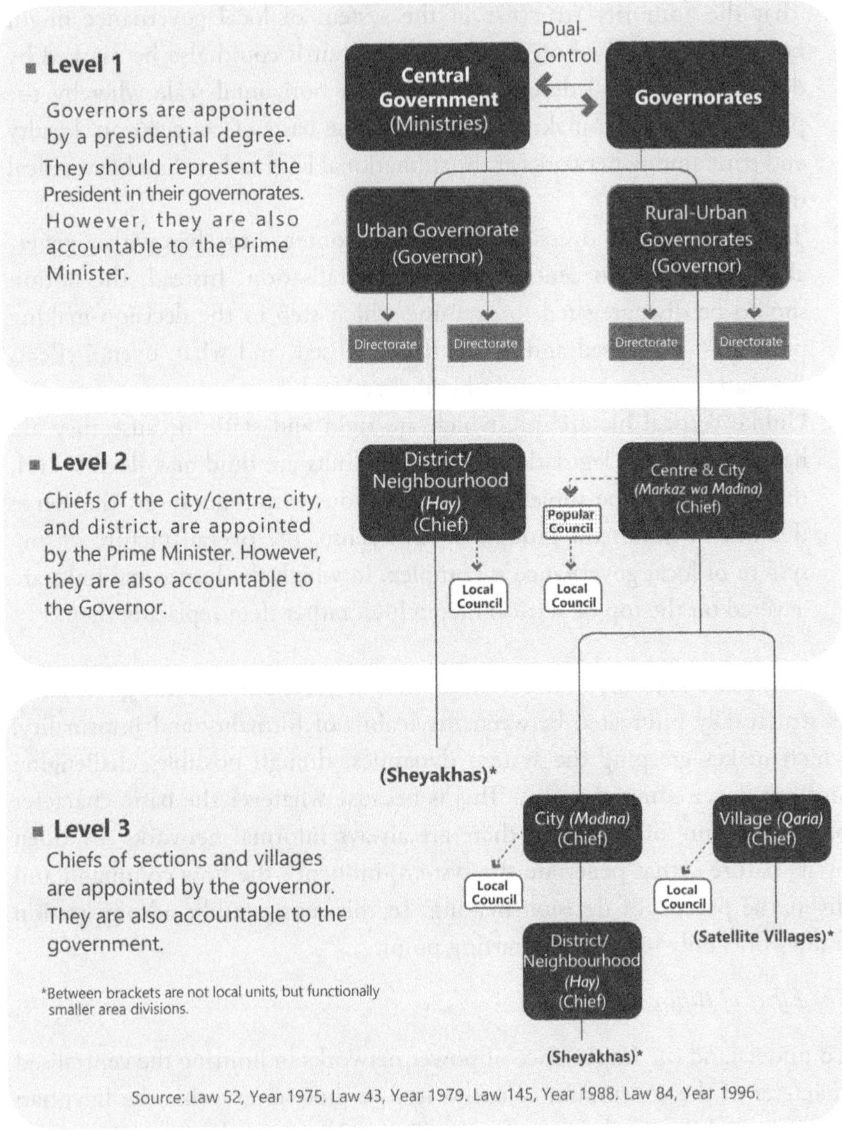

Figure 2.1 The structure of the Egyptian SLA

by its ministry but taking orders from both the governor and the ministry. Theoretically, the governor has constitutional power over the directorates. Appointed by presidential degree, the governor should represent the president in the executive council, but he is also accountable to the prime minister. As mentioned earlier, the governor is the most powerful man in his jurisdiction especially since the stipulation of Law 43 of 1979. This assumption is correct in theory, but in practice, however, that power depends on the governor's personality and the extent of the real power held by ministries and the chiefs of directorates over a given period. Generally speaking, the position of governor from the early 1990s almost became a retirement gift for retired/former generals from the armed forces.

The system itself allows for the shifting of power from one entity to another, because its most fundamental characteristic is the dual control principle: an insistence that 'central ministries will still have significant technical and professional supervisory powers and responsibilities over their staff assigned to governorates'.[28] This principle is also applied to the other levels of the system. For example, chiefs at level 2 are appointed by the prime minister, although they also take their orders from the governorate, whereas chiefs at level 3 are assigned by the governorate, but could also be accountable to directorates (in level 1), which are accountable to both the central government and the governorate.

The same principle is applicable to the distribution of responsibilities, which makes expenditure accountabilities at different levels of government, for the most part, unclear. On many occasions, moreover, the legislation assigns the same function to several levels of government. It could be assigned to the village council, neighbourhood council, city council and governorate council. Then, 'which of the four authorities is in charge? Saying that all the four are responsible may simply imply that nobody is responsible in particular.'[29]

Since each position inside the system is accountable to multiple institutions, and takes orders from different entities, many administrative chiefs at each level become reluctant to take developmental initiatives in their localities. This is due to the difficulty they face in convincing more than one manager at the upper level to approve their ideas, or to provide support if plans go wrong.[30] It is, therefore, an administrative problem that cannot be resolved except through a sort of political accommodation among many parties. The result as Sobhi Moharram puts it:

> Irrespective of what the law provides, most processes involve to a great extent informal, personal interactions. These personal relations are far more important in determining what is achieved, and what is not achieved

> than the prescribed formal linkages between the different levels of bureaucracy. This aspect of informality . . . introduces arbitrary elements into the decision-making process of local government.[31]

This situation has led to a normalising of contradictions in the process of decision-making among many entities, which induce informal networks to fill in the voids left by weak capacities of the system.[32] Because each executive official had multiple loyalties to numerous institutions in the SLA, the system not only reinforced a struggle for power and fragmentation within this structure, but actually produces it.

This can explain, from an administrative point of view, why the era of Mubarak was marked by fierce contestation among groups of cronies (*shilal*, sing. *shilla*) who competed for power.[33] According to Robert Springborg and Clement Moore, *shilal* established a shadow 'patrimonial rule' through which these groups would compete to exploit public spoils that they could not access legally.[34] However, I would suggest that the *shilal* might be the natural outcome of a system that was historically designed to constrain every official, except the president, through a network of power centres. It is an outcome of a historical tendency of simultaneously centralising and fragmentising the decision-making procedures of local government to make it difficult for 'any political figure or group to generate substantial or potential political opposition'.[35]

One consequence of this was the importance given to factors other than the position of chiefs in the structure of authority: most importantly, the chief's position in the informal network of power and his ability to manoeuvre and cultivate connections within the system, as well as his ability to lobby and put pressure on decision-makers. In other words, it did not only matter where you were in the system, but also who you were. It is therefore better to understand the chief's position in the structure of authority as bifurcated, in terms of it belonging to two realms simultaneously: the formal realm of authority and the informal realm of power. The interplay between both realms constitutes a mechanism of horizontal decentralisation that determines the actual influence of the chiefs in the system of local governance. This process is fluid and hidden and cannot simply be measured by the public administration frameworks.

Because of the bifurcated character of the system of local governance, we can understand why the Mubarak regime was reluctant to liberate the local council elections, despite their very limited constitutional authority. Being an elected member in a local council might be symbolic, but it might also offer access to power networks on the ground, thus, giving an important role to someone capable of an 'out of the box' political initiative. This was particularly true if someone with a local council position was shrewd enough to realise the map of power that is articulated within the structure of bureaucracy.

In fact, as will be discussed in the second part of this chapter, members of the local councils in the towns of the Cairo peri-urban fringe, especially the heads of councils, and who usually were the NDP local secretaries, often utilised the gaps in the SLA in ways that benefited them politically. Due to the fragmented nature of the SLA, the heads of the local councils were sometimes able to acquire influence through using the contradictions within the system. In a system where all executive units at the lower level took orders from different units of the upper level, local council members, who theoretically enjoyed nominal authority, could possibly move between units and thereby lobby, pressure and drive inactive administrative units to pay some attention, at least, to their local communities' demands and needs. The same logic could also be applied to other chiefs in the various subnational units of the SLA.

This is why any interpretation of the Egyptian system of local governance should not be restricted to analysing the administrative continuum embodied in the SLA, but it should also include its power continuum represented by power networks (or *shillas*) that was articulated with the institutionalisation of authority. However, the problem that the Mubarak regime faced, from the late 1980s at least, was that these networks became too abundant in number, and therefore it became impossible to please all. Under fiscal pressures, there had to be a way of outsourcing them to minimise their cost to the regime. Hence, an election was needed.

In order to understand how elections, in this context, served as a mechanism of informal decentralisation, the analytical lens should be moved to examine the informal aspect of the system of local governance. This is, nevertheless, a challenging task and needs a different approach to analysis.

Horizontally Decentralised: Upgrading the Egyptian System of Local Governance

At first glance, study of the informal structure of the Egyptian system of local governance seems unpromising. Unlike the formal structure represented by the SLA, which is easier to identify, informal power networks, by their definition as interpersonal, are harder to grasp analytically. They are fluid and subjected to continual reconfigurations, making the shift in power often unexpected and dependent on the political context.[36] Furthermore, their hidden characters make measurement problematic and research focus has to be on practices and on the process of decision-making rather than institutional frames.[37]

Therefore, understanding the workings of informality requires, first, employing a process-tracing approach and, secondly, relying on case study research, which in turn increases the degree of uncertainty and indeterminacy.[38] Yet the level of uncertainty that results from case study and process-tracing investigation can be substantially reduced if the analysis also incorporates cross-case comparisons and a wider socio-historical consideration.

According to Hutchcroft, one way that can help in understanding the informal aspect of any system of local governance is to examine the historical formation of the relationship that was developed between the administrative structures and patronage-based political organisations. To what extent do patronage politics effectively permeate administrative structures of the local state?[39] Tracing the historical development of this relationship allows us to uncover the informal decentralisation strategies that political regimes employ to keep pace with challenges at the subnational level in a way that could not be concluded by approaching the formal structure of authority alone.[40]

In Egypt, for decades the ruling party represented the major institutionalised patronage machine. Nevertheless, the relationship between the local state and the ruling party was subjected to major developments from the foundation of the republic based on the regime strategies of horizontal centralisation–decentralisation.

The NDP and the Local State in Egypt: What was the Relationship?

As has been concluded based on the earlier part of this chapter, each administrative position in the SLA was bifurcated in terms of having formal and informal sides. The NDP, nevertheless, was the only institutional sphere in the system of local governance that belonged to the informal realm. By its definition as a political organisation, the NDP was not technically part of the state, but its members acquired their influence from being in the state or at least in close contact with it. Thus, it might be better to understand the NDP subnational structures as an informal extension of the state domain, in which the party had a foothold in bureaucracy and another in local communities.

Similar to the case of many ruling parties, the general structure of the NDP was designed on the same footing as the electoral map and to a great extent was similar to the hierarchy of the SLA. From 1990 to 2005, Egypt was divided into 222 electoral districts, each of which elected two members of the People's Assembly – one had to be a professional (*fi'āt*), and the other a worker or *fallāḥ*. The president appointed an additional ten members, bringing the total to 454.[41] In the NDP structure, each electoral district was represented by a secretary general (*'amīn 'ām*), usually (but not always) from among the elected MPs who gained the highest votes in their constituencies. To become an MP (a district's secretary general), members should have entered at the lower level (level 3-A or B in Figure 2.2) as part of a patron–client relationship and incrementally upgraded themselves.

While the district's secretary general was accountable in the party to the governorate's secretary general, he was also responsible for the local secretaries beneath him, all of whom were accountable to him. Figure 2.2 shows a branch of the NDP's structural tree. As will be noted in Figure 2.2, the NDP consisted of two bodies: the national body (level 1 in figure); and the lower body or the party subnational level (2 and 3 in figure). Figure 2.2 summarises the chain of ranks and shows the basic characteristics that marked each level from the late-1980s to the early 2000s.

Most studies and analyses on the politics of the NDP have been preoccupied with understanding what was played out at the upper levels (1+2 in Figure 2.2), and less concerned with understanding what was going on at the party's grassroots (3 in Figure 2.2), except during election periods when the entire party was under the pressure of voter mobilisation. While the upper and lower bodies theoretically seemed to form a coherent and unified organisation, they were, in reality, two different and almost separate entities. The situation was inherited from the structure of the ASU in the late 1960s, which was marked by a remarkable gap between the national and the subnational levels as will be discussed later in this chapter.

The fact that the general structure of the NDP was roughly identical to the general structure of the SLA made the former often act as an informal arm of the local government. Since the SLA was marked by bifurcation and fragmentation in its command and control structure that frequently led to functional paralysis, the NDP local secretaries, until the early 2000s, frequently performed a central role in negotiating the system and optimising it.

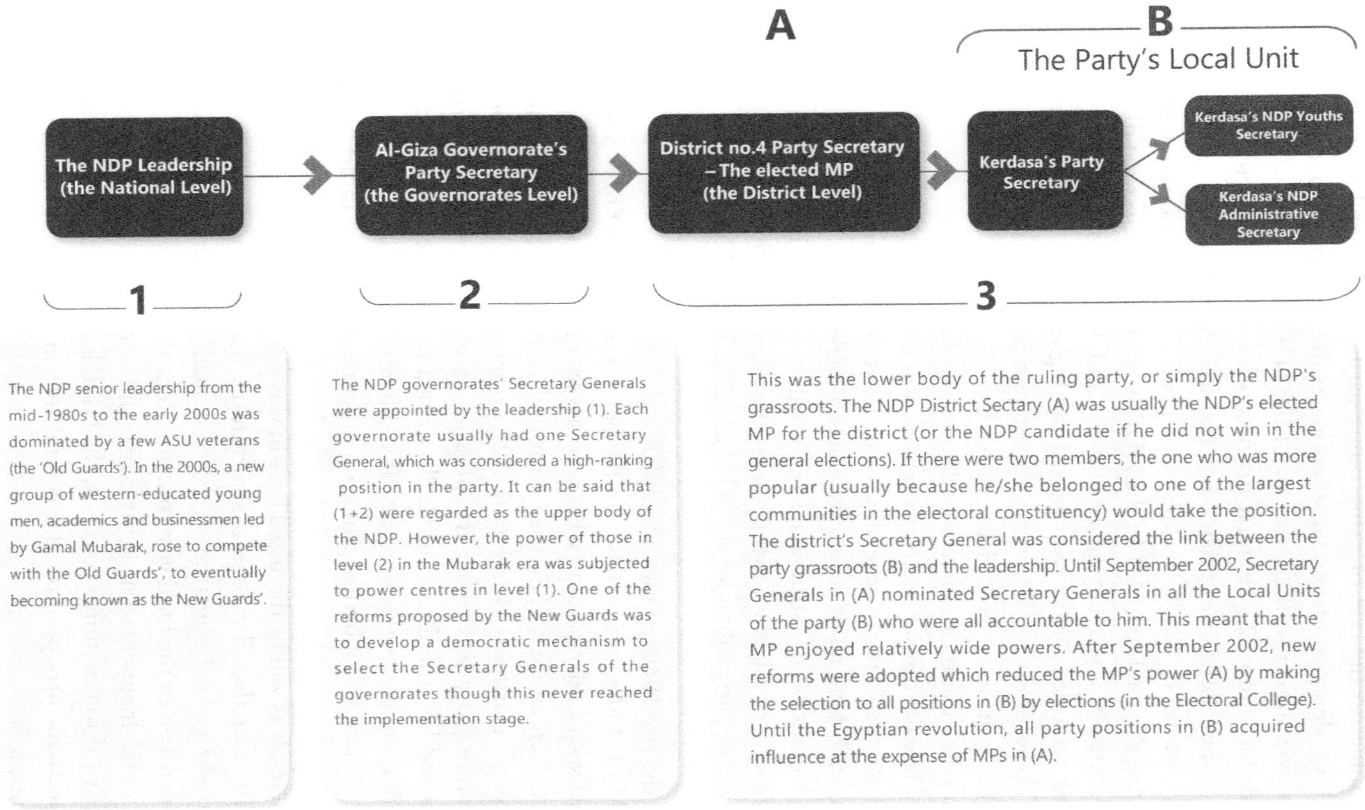

A
B
The Party's Local Unit
The NDP Leadership (the National Level)
Al-Giza Governorate's Party Secretary (the Governorates Level)
District no.4 Party Secretary – The elected MP (the District Level)
Kerdasa's Party Secretary
Kerdasa's NDP Youths Secretary
Kerdasa's NDP Administrative Secretary
1
2
3
The NDP senior leadership from the mid-1980s to the early 2000s was dominated by a few ASU veterans (the 'Old Guards'). In the 2000s, a new group of western-educated young men, academics and businessmen led by Gamal Mubarak, rose to compete with the Old Guards', to eventually becoming known as the New Guards'.
The NDP governorates' Secretary Generals were appointed by the leadership (1). Each governorate usually had one Secretary General, which was considered a high-ranking position in the party. It can be said that (1+2) were regarded as the upper body of the NDP. However, the power of those in level (2) in the Mubarak era was subjected to power centres in level (1). One of the reforms proposed by the New Guards was to develop a democratic mechanism to select the Secretary Generals of the governorates though this never reached the implementation stage.
This was the lower body of the ruling party, or simply the NDP's grassroots. The NDP District Sectary (A) was usually the NDP's elected MP for the district (or the NDP candidate if he did not win in the general elections). If there were two members, the one who was more popular (usually because he/she belonged to one of the largest communities in the electoral constituency) would take the position. The district's Secretary General was considered the link between the party grassroots (B) and the leadership. Until September 2002, Secretary Generals in (A) nominated Secretary Generals in all the Local Units of the party (B) who were all accountable to him. This meant that the MP enjoyed relatively wide powers. After September 2002, new reforms were adopted which reduced the MP's power (A) by making the selection to all positions in (B) by elections (in the Electoral College). Until the Egyptian revolution, all party positions in (B) acquired influence at the expense of MPs in (A).

Figure 2.2 The structure of the NDP, 1990–2011

In Kerdasa, the NDP local leaders understood their roles in harnessing the system to develop their town as a means of gaining political capital and popularity. In return, the NDP local leadership, from the late 1980s, was assigned the role of mobilising its local communities in order to reduce governmental expenditure on urban development. The NDP's local and district secretaries helped to organise the collection of various kinds of donations from locals to develop local amenities, facilities and infrastructure, such as roads, sewage networks, schools, mosques, cemeteries, services centres and so on.

Theoretically, it seemed to be a collaborative win–win relationship, but in practice, as will be shown later in this chapter, it was not. Therefore, not only did the regime from the early 2000s reconsider its relationship with the party's grassroots, it also turned its sights on them in order to exploit them. However, before showing why this relationship with the subnational structures of the ruling party did not work for the Egyptian regime and why it had to be changed, first, we have to dig deeper into history, from its beginnings, to understand how it was established.

The Beginnings: The Ruling Party as a Collaboration Movement

As was briefly discussed in Chapter 1, the system of local governance since the July 1952 coup has experienced several stages of evolution: the first stage lasted until the late 1950s. It was characterised merely by bureaucratic de-concentration, establishing field branches of central ministries controlled by the central government through the directors of provinces who served at the pleasure of the Interior Ministry. At the time, the system at the lower level consisted of municipal and village councils in major towns and villages. Local positions were occupied by traditional rural intermediaries who served as *'umad* and who derived their power from the dominance of their families in the local economy. This stage can be considered a continuation of the style of governance that had functioned before the toppling of the *ancien régime.*[42]

The second stage with which we are concerned, started approximately from the early 1960s in tandem with two processes that were taking place. The first entailed a deepening centralism and bureaucratic sprawl through the investment of greater powers in the governors of provinces who were, by Law 124 of 1960, raised in status from officials of the Ministry of the Interior to the rank of deputy ministers responsible directly to the president of the republic. Not only did this change bring authority to bear on the governors, but also it 'brought the government closer to the ordinary citizen'.[43]

The second process entailed the creation of the ASU, the single political party that was created by presidential decree in 1962, by Nasser, as a means of gathering mass support and nurturing a new stable middle class 'without which the rulers cannot rule'.[44] The aim of founding the party, according to Leonard Binder, was to shift the bases of power 'more completely from traditional social structures to bureaucratised, government and military structures'.[45] The ASU was expected to be the vehicle that was responsible for economically mobilising Egyptian society.

The role of the ASU in local governance reached its peak with a package of reforms supervised by the then national secretary general of the party, Ali Sabri (1962–71). The Sabri group, which represented the leftist wing of the post-revolutionary ruling coalition, sought to establish the political legitimacy of the regime in the ASU. The regime, according to this perspective, must be based on the masses from which the vanguard would spring, following the Leninist structural model, in which the Communist Party is superior to the state administration.[46] However, due to the struggles inside the regime, Sabri's ambition to establish the ASU over the state had been thwarted. He was purged from the ASU in 1971, but his reform movement, though it was not fully applied, left an important impact on the ruling party–bureaucracy relationship.

It enabled a close association between the party's subnational secretaries and the SLA, but the party on the national level remained static, lacking an independent voice of its own.[47] The ASU subnational secretaries acquired their power not from their ranks in the party but through the governors, who during the party reorganisation were informed of the regime's desire to see the party advance its programme in the provinces.[48] Eventually, an Institute of Local Administration was established in Cairo in 1968 to train local personnel and councillors and make the relation between executive bureaucratic units and the ASU more obvious.[49]

The result, therefore, was not a hegemonic party, but rather a new 'collaboration movement'[50] between the bureaucracy and a segment of lesser notables who rose to prominence due to the transformation of Egyptian society in the post-revolutionary era and who, prior to that, had lacked a political base. This movement acquired some mobilisational characteristics at the local level and de-mobilisational characteristics at the national one.[51] It allowed for larger numbers of lesser notables to take part in politics at the community level through joining the ASU, but it degraded the semi-autonomous character of the political field at the local level, by making it more subordinated to bureaucracy than at any period before.

By breathing life into this movement, it was aimed, under the eyes of the Military Police, to create grassroots for the regime, to be involved in their communities' developmental affairs but without extending that to affect politics at the national level.[52] The gap between the national and subnational levels of the ASU, according to Ayubi, explains why, when Sadat eliminated the rival power centres within the state in May 1971, the small apparat that was heading the party was easily removed: 'The whole organisation almost collapsed and ceased to function, for it had no organic or political life of its own that would have enabled it to sustain and outlive its immediate masters.'[53] The ruling party would at least keep its main character as collaborative at the local level, but static and bureaucratic at the upper level until its collapse after the 2011 Revolution.

This was the historical context in which a generation of ASU local leaders (who would later become the *first* generation of the local NDP) gradually came to replace the roles that had been assumed by traditional notability represented by *'umad* and *shaykh al-balad.* Prior to these developments in Kerdasa, as discussed in Chapter 1, local politics had largely been dominated by local notables from the landowning family, al-Mikkawi, who for a long time had seized the *'umda* position. Nazmi Mikkawi was the last *'umda* of Kerdasa and Mahmoud Fahmi Mikkawi, who had been a member of parliament in the royal era, became the local secretary general of the ASU and the head of the local council. As a result of the Nasserist social policies, by the end of the 1960s, the whole region had experienced a rise of new lesser notables from other families, challenging the local domination of the traditional notability through joining the local branches of the ASU.

One of those was Yousef Abdel Salam Saleh from the Omar family, who worked with Fahmi Mikkawi and then succeeded him as the local secretary general of the town and the head of the local council. Therefore, members of al-Mikkawi family, who had owned significant tracts of land prior to the 1980s, extensively moved away from the town after selling most of their land to other families. Nevertheless, due to the lack of semi-autonomy, the definition of local politics in this period did not exceed collaboration with the government and solving local issues especially by mediating between locals. This was best exemplified by the emerging status of *shaykh 'arab*, who was a very respected man in his locality and so was trusted to solve local hostilities and mediate between locals. Therefore, the influence of local leadership on the local bureaucracy was limited. Later in Chapters 3 and 4, we will comprehensively reflect on the practices of social mediating in local politics, but for now, the chronological examination of the role of the Egyptian ruling party in local governance will be resumed.

The Ruling Party in Local Governance under Sadat

Although the foundations of the Egyptian system of local governance had been laid under Nasser, the current system owes much to Sadat who re-engineered it. This was in the context of a comprehensive reconfiguration inside the authoritarian regime in the 1970s that involved a fundamental change in Egypt's political economy to controlled economic and political liberation, including reintroducing multipartism. The new developments were induced by external and internal influences that were widely researched.[54] Internally, Sadat sought to build a new constituency that 'owes nothing to Nasser'.[55] He was also preoccupied by consolidating presidential power and eliminating rival powers (*marākiz al-qiwā*) within the regime; one of which was the ASU, led by Sabri. In 1971, therefore, Sabri and his colleagues were purged, and in 1978 the ASU itself was disbanded and replaced by the NDP.

However, the change was not only restricted to the party's name and its leadership, but was also a fundamental transformation of the state–ruling party relationship. Under Nasser, the ASU was seen as a vehicle for modernising Egyptian society and achieving economic growth. Therefore, it was made supreme in the parliament; a fact that was reflected in the party secretariat's major function of screening parliamentary candidates, all of whom had to establish positions within the ASU before they could run for election. Therefore, elections themselves had little importance.[56]

Sadat, in contrast, advocated a market economy to achieve economic modernisation instead of depending on the ruling party, which led to depriving the ASU of this role.[57] In practice, this entailed the shifting of power from the ruling party to the parliament and abolishing party superiority in the elected councils at all levels, including the subnational ones. Thus, while the ASU senior leaders had constituted an apparat and a power centre inside the regime that had constrained Nasser himself, the NDP senior leaders became a group of parliamentarians working under the president on assigned tasks, and their main role was largely restricted to guaranteeing, by any means, a super majority in the People's Assembly. Ever since, the role of the ruling party has increasingly dissolved in electoral politics.

The same measures were taken at the subnational level. The promulgation of the Local Government Law 52 of 1975 and its subsequent amendment in 1978, consolidated centralist control of the SLA and dropped the ruling party's formal monopoly of local councils.[58] It also reorganised the SLA to comprise two branches. The first, as mentioned earlier, is executive representing bureaucracy and has most authority, while the other is elected by popular election but with no power at all.[59] Law 52 of 1975 has been regarded by many accounts as a positive step towards political decentralisation, but in its essence it aimed to accommodate the subnational structures of the ruling party in the SLA, making the latter superior to the former. This in fact led to more integration between both organisations compared with the previous era to the extent that, by the early Mubarak era, it became hard to determine the precise demarcation line that separated the ruling party from the local government.[60]

Sadat's overall measures led to further vertical centralisation of the system mainly by empowering the SLA, but the process of integrating the ruling party and the SLA made the system on the horizontal scale bifurcated and informally decentralised, in the sense that the process of decision-making at the subnational level became shredded among various power networks. This is simply because Sadat's intentions were not to reform the system, nor to increase its efficiency, but rather to fragment it, in a way that granted him, as president of the republic, unexceptionable power and more room for manoeuvring. Ironically, he did not live long enough to enjoy the authoritarian gains of such a policy; but Mubarak did.

Nevertheless, Sadat's measures also created undesirable political outcomes. The liberation of parliamentary elections allowed rival movements at the subnational level to challenge the ruling party even in what were supposed to be its traditional bases; the rural areas. In the late 1970s, the New Wafd Party, the major political party of the interwar era that had recently been allowed to return to the political scene decades after the abolition of all political parties by Nasser in 1954,[61] sought to utilise the reforms to make a base for the re-established party by attracting followers who were popular in their localities, regardless of their cultural and ideological backgrounds.

It was claimed that the then newly established party succeeded in attracting '10,000 followers cutting across all social categories in a short four months, but the 1200 members included in its general assembly probably reflected its active membership'.[62] The regime responded by tightening control through a security approach. In the towns of the Cairo peri-urban fringe, as will be discussed in the next chapter, local arms were used to suppress the New Wafd candidates, among whom was Mohammad Sayed Ghizlani, who was physically suppressed by figures from the Mikkawi family in 1979.

On the other hand, the process of shifting power from the subnational structures of the ruling party to the SLA weakened the local secretaries which, therefore, made the system of local governance suffer from a fragility in its mobilisation functions. Political participation in the local elections was very low compared with Nasser's time, and those who were elected to local councils lacked the motivation even for regular attendance at the councils' meetings. In Kerdasa, a governmental study on the work of one committee clearly shows this tendency. This study, based on a survey conducted in 1982, examined the minutes of twenty-one meetings of the Consultative Committee for Population and Development (CCPD), from October 1978 to May 1980. The committee was established pursuant to Law 52 of 1975 and consisted of thirty-two members from both the elected and executive branches. Twelve of them were elected members in Kerdasa's local council, five were appointed and fifteen were employees in the local unit. The study noticed that regular attendance rates were high at all meetings, with an average of 87 per cent.[63]

However, the survey noted that regular attendance among the elected members (who were the local leaders of the NDP in Kerdasa) was very low, at approximately 22 per cent. The study attributed the low attendance of elected members to the poor motivation among locals, due to the 'old history' that had established a sense among them that 'popular work is not effective'.[64] Furthermore, the study revealed that the value of all projects implemented by the CCPD 'was L.E. 65,480, out of which a total of L.E. 15,300 was paid by the people of Kerdasa' while the rest was funded by the government. The money contributed by Kerdasians went mainly towards the repair of mosques (L.E. 10,800, or 70.59 per cent of the total donations), while the rest of this money went towards education, water, electricity and other small projects.[65]

In sum, it can be said Sadat's upgrading measures on the system of local governance consolidated the authoritarian control over the state, but they also had negative political outcomes that threatened the authoritarian political domination over local communities. Nevertheless, the integration of the ruling party and the SLA paved the way for new strategies in reconfiguring power–authority relations at the subnational level without the need for restructuring the SLA. In this period, the regime began to realise the potential benefits of elections in doing so. For the parliament, Sadat tended to conduct elections on an individual basis, allowing a relatively large number of independent candidates for many reasons, most importantly as a way of mobilising rural support and also to weaken the central control of the ruling party to prevent the emergence of a strong party leadership.[66] However, it was under Mubarak that elections were utilised into maximum extent.

The Ruling Party in Local Governance in Mubarak's Early Tenure: The Role of Elections

The Mubarak era can be considered as one of continuity during which the upgrading strategies on the system of local governance introduced by Sadat were crystallised. Mubarak inherited a system that was vertically overcentralised but at the same time was able to be centralised–decentralised horizontally. From then on, the main strategy that would be used to reconfigure the authority–power relationships was not restructuring the structure of authority, but rather centralising–decentralising networks of powers. This was managed through elections.

After he rose to power, Mubarak was preoccupied by consolidating his rule. Springborg points out that Mubarak had an ambivalent attitude towards Sadat's legacy of fragmentation, especially the NDP, which was compromised by contradictory directions, making it difficult to manage.[67] But at the same time, he lacked the power and legitimacy to offer alternatives.[68] In the first decade of his rule, therefore, he tried to pull the strings of governance by re-engineering electoral laws and legislations in a way that retained centralist control by the NDP.[69]

Thus, in 1983, the 'first-past-the-post' electoral system was changed. Instead, a new law mandated a party-list proportional representation system and reduced the number of constituencies from 176 to 48, with independents banned from offering their candidacies.[70] The change was meant, first, and above everything else, to secure a vast majority for the NDP in the People's Assembly, and, secondly, to exert the influence of the party structure and ensure its centralised control behind a new party leadership loyal to the new president.[71] Centralising measures were also taken regarding local elections. An amendment to the Local Government Law 50 of 1981 was passed in the parliament stipulating that local elections should be held based on the voting lists of constituencies, where the party that wins the majority acquires all the seats of the local council. In practice, the amendments drained the liberation efforts taken by Sadat from its content.

However, Mubarak's moves proved to have devastating consequences on the NDP rank and file. As Springborg puts it:

> The new electoral law destroyed the bargaining power of notables with the ruling party, for not only could they not run as independents, but the constituencies now so large that those whose power bases virtually guaranteed success in the old, relatively small ones now had to sail in broader, uncharted waters and in competition with other local notables. Those in charge of selecting candidates to serve on the NDP's lists, which included the party [senior] leaders, representative of the security agencies, the President himself, and various ministers, could, once they resolved their conflicts, impose their choices on constituencies.[72]

The process of centralisation meant giving the NDP senior leadership a formidable power even in deciding the lowest appointments such as the membership of local councils. It was a strategy which largely undermined the role of NDP local leadership compared with any period before, since it practically led to degradation of the semi-autonomous character of the political field at the subnational level. The outcome of such a development was further weakening of the party mobilisation function at the local level, therefore affecting authoritarian political domination.[73]

Local politics in the towns of the Cairo peri-urban fringe was greatly affected by these developments. A gap created between the regime and its local networks of power led to many lesser notables refusing to take part in public work, which significantly affected the horizontal relationships between the pillars of the system of local governance. However, this did not mean the demise of local politics, but rather the emergence of alternative local politics that challenged the regime's political domination and filled the resultant gap. In the years of the 1980s, the region experienced the revival of the Islamic movement whereby *ahli* (communal) mosques became a platform for populist sheikhs who publicly criticised the regime's political and social policies. The *da'wa* movement attracted thousands of local people who came in droves on a weekly basis to attend religious lessons from Islamic figures from the MB and a new Salafi movement.

From the eve of the 1988 parliamentary elections, the regime was alarmed and, until the mid-1990s, launched successive waves of security campaigns aimed at crushing the movement and arresting its influential leaders. We will return to discuss the regime's approach towards this movement in the next chapter, to show how a security approach was applied to thwart any arena of local politics that could challenge the domination of the system of local governance, but for now it is enough to analyse the upgrading measures the regime undertook to overcome the failings of its system.

The 1990s: Back to Decentralisation

Under pressure from the Supreme Constitutional Court (SCC), which ruled that elections on party lists were unconstitutional, and in tandem with compacting the Islamic movement, the regime in the 1990s introduced new reforms on both electoral legislations of the People's Assembly and local councils that involved decentralisation measures. The reforms were also induced by the implementation of the Structural Adjustment Programme, which made the state gradually abandon its duty to provide basic services, such as education and health, to the citizenry. The regime, therefore, sought to utilise elections as a way of reducing public spending.[74]

With regard to parliamentary elections, the number of electoral districts was raised from 48 to 222, and the electoral system was returned to an individual candidacy system of two-round electoral rule. Those candidates who received an absolute majority of votes in the first round were elected. If no candidate made it, a second round of voting took place to determine the winner. The move away from party lists breathed life into local politics, boosting the number of independent candidates who reached the 1990 election to more than 2,000 compared with only 589 official party candidates. The number of independents in the 1995 election rose to more than 3,000, compared with 739 who were formally nominated by their parties.[75] The same trend continued in the elections of 2000, 2005 and 2010.

Although the new electoral system harmed the central control of the ruling party, it benefited the regime in terms of allowing it to 'cultivate and enlarge a constituency on which it could rely and which, despite its limited size, served as its social base'.[76] For this reason, from the 1990 election the NDP introduced a new practice in which the idea of political partisanship (*al-iltizām al-ḥizby*) was abandoned. No dissident was to be expelled or punished, and no member was to be frozen if he decided to run for election as an independent. Furthermore, the winning independent candidates were invited to join the party and be reintegrated within its ranks.[77]

Local council elections are far less important than parliamentary elections, but due to the large number of candidates, they were harder to manage and control, therefore, the Mubarak regime was more hesitant in extending decentralisation measures to them. This process theoretically started in 1988 with a very minimal amendment to the Local Government Law 50 of 1981, allowing for one independent candidate, whose name did not appear on a party list, to be elected to any one council. All remaining seats continued to go to the list that obtained most votes.

The new, very limited, reform intended to avoid a declaration of unconstitutionality by the SCC.[78] However, although it was declared unconstitutional by the SCC in June 1988, the law governed both the 1988 and 1992 council elections. Thus, the results of these elections reflected the domination of lists, favouring the formal nomination of the NDP. Most victories were declared by acclamation (*al-tazkiyya*).[79] Eventually, it was only in 1996 that Law 84 stipulated that the election of local councils was to be entirely based on majority vote for individual candidates, but after depriving the local councils of even the minimal authority they had.

Both packages of liberative reforms on local and general elections revolutionised local politics and made the local political field(s) more competitive, leading to the emergence of a *second* generation of ambitious NDP local leaders who assumed new roles compared with their predecessors. While the first generation of NDP leaders had been expected to solve local hostilities and to mediate between local people, the new local leadership, in contrast, was brought closer to the local bureaucracy to reduce the cost of public expenditure, by mobilising local communities to fill the gap left by the state withdrawal from certain areas of urban development projects as a result of accelerating the neo-liberal policies.

Furthermore, elections served as a disciplinary mechanism in rechannelling public spending to the areas that were supportive of the regime, based on the election results. Supported by statistical analysis, Lisa Blaydes has found that during the 1990s, voting for opposition candidates in the parliamentary elections reduced a district's access to public funding for infrastructural development, while voting for the NDP parliamentarians helped in negotiating services and infrastructure improvements, including roads, hospitals and schools. These parliamentarians were often referred to as 'service deputies' (*nuwwāb al-khadamāt*).[80]

In this sense, elections emerged as an 'even-handed mechanism'[81] and a 'market system' for managing competition between members of Egypt's ruling party and party-affiliated independents. It was a 'decentralised distribution mechanism that aids authoritarian survival by regularising intra-elite competition, while at the same time outsourcing the cost of political mobilisation and redistribution to the rent-seeking elite'.[82]

From the early 1990s, the NDP became more attached to the system of local governance. Its vision was based increasingly on 'servicing local people' (*khidmat 'ahl al-balad*). This slogan became central to candidates' electoral campaigns for parliament or local councils in the Mubarak era. Ever since, local figures in general, and members of parliament above all, have frequently used this slogan in their day-to-day activities: in their statements to the media, their meetings with local people or public functionaries, and even in their private lives. As Marie Vannetzel has put it, the concept of politics has been dissolved into the idea of public 'services', and the definition of 'the good representative' has altered to 'the one who serves people', an idea that has been strongly 'anchored in the political imaginary'[83] (see Chapter 3). In Kerdasa, it was the rise of Haj Mohammad Abdel Wahhab Mahjoub in local politics following Sheikh Yousef Abdel Salam that exemplified this shift.

Abdel Wahhab Mahjoub was one of those local notables who was ambitious to rise in NDP politics. He was one of the first local figures to realise the potential in being the head of the local council in Kerdasa. After being elected to this position in the late 1980s, he was able to convince the head of the city of Ausim, and later the governor, to allocate funds to expand Kerdasa's main streets.[84] In the first half of the 1990s, he was able, through his connections with the al-Giza Governorate, to allocate resources for the development of new entrances to the town, opening new roads, extending the sewage network and improving street lighting. During his tenure, moreover, the name of the street in which textile stores were located was changed from Market Street to al-Siyahi Street ('Tourism Street'). He also worked hard to convince the governorate and the central government to reclaim nine feddans that had been illegally seized by a private factory in the town. Later, this land would be designated for projects such as a school complex, a vehicle-licensing agency and a youth centre.[85]

In my interview with Abdel Wahhab Mahjoub, he stated that prior to his term, the head of the local council was expected only to keep what he called the 'domestic peace' (*al-silm al-ʾahly*). The head was expected to resolve hostilities between townspeople, to lead reconciliation efforts and settle disputes before the police became involved. In his term, the role of the head of the local council significantly evolved to include the lobbying of public institutions and the mobilisation of local people to develop Kerdasa's amenities. Mahjoub, of course, tried to convey this development as a purely personal achievement.[86]

Mahjoub's claims, however, were not wholly without foundation. As indicated in Chapter 1, the role of local notables in rural settings had declined since the late nineteenth century. During the tenures of Nasser and Sadat, local notables were expected to apply customary law. They were required to be 'mediators', settling disputes between two or more kin groups, between one village and another, or resolving conflicts at marketplaces. They were trusted to resolve disputes over land and inheritance or even within the same household.[87] Mahjoub did indeed introduce a new model. He worked hard, and his ambition can partly explain some of his achievements in Kerdasa. However, his accomplishments were also in tandem with the changing conception of local politics as a result of the process of upgrading that reconfigured the relationship between the SLA and the ruling party.

In 1996, Abdel Wahhab Mahjoub was upgraded to become a member of the Governorate Council (*majlis al-muḥāfaẓa*). His successor as the head of the local council, Mohammad Hasanin Mikkawi, continued to represent the interests of the people of Kerdasa. Hasanin Mikkawi, with Mahjoub's support (in al-Giza Governorate), was able to convince the governorate to invest more in Kerdasa's infrastructure, such as the sewage network, the lighting system and street paving.[88] Furthermore, they worked together with the local unit to convince the governorate to invest in public transportation. In 2000, Mahjoub tried to utilise his achievements politically by running in the parliamentary elections as an independent, but he was unable to make it. As we will see in Chapter 4, other power networks from the town of Nahia thwarted his attempt.

Mahjoub's bid to run for the People's Assembly in 2000 was blocked but his ambition was not yet curtailed. He continued through his position in al-Giza Governorate to provide the town with public buses, connecting Kerdasa with the al-Haram area as well as other surrounding towns and villages.[89]

During Mahjoub's term, the decision to transform Kerdasa from a village to a city was made; it was only a matter of time. This meant, as mentioned in the introduction to this chapter, that the town had a larger budget from which it was able to spend more on public amenities. It also meant that the town became a centre and city *(markaz wa-madīna)*, with its own independent resources such as billboard revenues and local taxes.

How did Kerdasa's local NDP succeed in convincing the state to upgrade their town? It did this primarily through two strategies. The first was by employing contradictions among the SLA and manoeuvring between power centres in the Egyptian bureaucracy; the second strategy was to entice the state to establish local institutions by contributing to them from local community resources. Donations from politicians, entrepreneurs and local people in general were collected at different times as contributions, in order to convince the government that the town deserved better public institutions.[90] Nevertheless, although this collaborative relationship between the subnational structures of the NDP and the SLA was useful for the regime at the micro scale, it was not politically useful at the macro scale.

In this respect, elections proved to be an effective mechanism for mobilising the regime's patronage networks and the NDP local leadership who helped in reducing the cost of public services. However, it failed to mobilise local communities politically. In local council elections, the authoritarian restrictions and the absence of real symbolic and material rewards made local agents reluctant to mobilise their economic and social resources in order to compete over the positions. The lack of a genuine role ensured that the seats on the local councils were virtually designated for local notables who were chosen based on their social status (not to mention their security records), and this, of course, was reflected in local participation at the meetings and committees that were supposed to discuss local issues. In early April 1997, therefore, local elections were held but did not mobilise candidates, nor did they mobilise voters, as may be gauged from the turnout which varied between 4 per cent and 20 per cent.[91]

The dilemma of the NDP was clearly apparent in the parliamentary elections. It is true that competition among the regime's networks was high, driving local leaders (who for various reasons were ambitious to be elected to the People's Assembly),[92] to mobilise their grassroots or work hard for their home towns. Nevertheless, the party's failure in the 2000 election, in which the regime was obliged to enforce rigging to prevent a disaster in front of the

MB, suggested that it was out of touch with local communities. This led the regime, under pressure from the Gamal Mubarak-led group, to conclude that restructuring the NDP was unavoidable.[93]

The Rise of Gamal Mubarak: Too Much Decentralisation

By the early 2000s, the regime had become more experienced, confident and effective in managing elections. Therefore, what had begun in the 1990s as a hands-on approach to managing the NDP grassroots turned into, in the 2000s, a strategy for exploiting them. This new development was a result of another shift in the political economy of authoritarianism, in which the decline of external rentier revenues transformed the state from a rentier state to a predatory one. According to Samer Soliman, the regime first forced unconstitutional taxes on sections of the Egyptian population, and, secondly pressured its 'loyal base in the business community' to fund many projects in the state's welfare system.[94] Thirdly, it turned its sights to the Egyptian people, setting income-generation above all other considerations 'regardless of whether that necessitates unconstitutional means and even if it wreaks havoc on the economy'.[95] Inevitably, this required more involvement of the police in the everyday life of Egyptians.

In tandem with this transition, the NDP in September 2002, for the first time since its foundation, began a serious internal reform process by modernising its platform and electoral protocols for nominations of local, district and governorate positions. Formal nomination was removed and electoral primaries (*al-mugam'at al-intikhabaya*) were introduced to decentralise the subnational branches to the maximum extent. Open nominations were called to choose members for local councils and for the People's Assembly, which significantly increased the competition among the regime's patronage networks.

The new reforms further weakened the central control of the party, thereby allowing more interaction between the local state and the party's grassroots. This led to the emergence of a *third* younger generation in local leadership who had previously been unable to work within the NDP fold because its structure could not accommodate them. However, contrary to their predecessors, the newcomers parachuted into the political field as result of what was known in Egypt as the marriage of money and power, thus, they lacked rootedness in their localities. Yet they had a greater influence on the local state bureaucracy.

Whilst it is true that the new decentralisation measures enhanced the semi-autonomous character of the political field, making local politics more competitive, it also made it more chaotic. In the period between the application of the new reforms and the 2005 election, the NDP experienced major cleavages in all leading layers. The so-called 'old guard' wing of the party was subjected to a gradual process of marginalisation which coincided with the incorporation of a new elite bloc called 'the new guard' led by the President's son, Gamal. At the subnational level, the political field(s) witnessed the emergence of innumerable *shillas* wrangling over almost every available position: from the posts of local secretary general to the nominations for both local councils and the People's Assembly.

For the local secretary general positions, the party allowed for any NDP member to be a local secretary if he collected 200 powers of attorney (*tawkīlāt*) from other local members. This led to the possibility of creating many secretaries in the same locality. For parliamentarians, they now had to 'work harder than ever before to extract any kind of development assistance from the government'.[96] Thus, the path was steered towards the emergence of what Blaydes calls the 'super-MPs', who used their personal wealth to pay ministries to build infrastructure in their districts.[97]

The 2005 parliamentary election, therefore, witnessed a dramatic rise in the number of independents who ran on their own. There were nearly 4,300 candidates who ran without the support of any party in 2005, compared with the 444 on the official NDP list, the fewer than 300 from the 'formal' legal opposition, and 150 from the MB (though nominally they also stood as independents).[98] The result was that although the NDP won a 74 per cent majority in the People's Assembly, out of the party's 444 official candidates only 145 gained seats (32 per cent of the vote). The rest were, as usual, reintegrated into its ranks.

Thus, the new measures indeed made the political field at the local level very competitive, but the results of the 2005 parliamentary election showed that the new system failed to translate that into a politically desirable outcome at the national level. Final results indicated that the MB, despite extensive repression and electoral fraud, was able to raise its share in the parliament from seventeen seats in the 2000 election to eighty-eight in the 2005 election. In short, the NDP was consumed at the subnational level by eternal struggles among various local power networks. The system proved to be self-collapsing.

It was after these new indicators began to emerge that the authoritarian regime gradually and informally started to implement a new configuration, mainly by augmenting the role of the police in the system of local governance at the expense of the NDP. An informal rule emerged in which the State Security Investigations Service (SSIS) (*'amn al-dawla*) had the upper hand. A security approach was applied to alienate the second generation of NDP local leaders who had resisted the change. The authoritarian regime no longer viewed the local structures of the ruling party as a collaborative movement; instead, transformed elections into an exploitative machine.

In Kerdasa, Mahjoub started to realise that the system that he had for long time invested in was changing. A new development materialised when the NDP local leadership started to bypass their superior cadres and to contact, or even to complain to, the higher levels of the NDP. The reforms brought new competitors into political field. In 2003, Mahjoub knew that he would be excluded from the position of local secretary of the party. Therefore, he set out to reach and appeal to the NDP's Secretary General of al-Giza Governorate, Kamal Abu al-Kheir.

In his analysis, Mahjoub said that Abu al-Kheir was assigned by Gamal Mubarak to hold internal elections to elect secretaries to the party's local level. Mahjoub claimed that he and his nephew broke into a meeting between Abu al-Kheir and the NDP's MPs from al-Giza. To become a local secretary general, the new party protocols required 200 endorsements from any members of the NDP. Mahjoub brandished more than two thousand NDP membership endorsements from Kerdasa, to prove that he was capable enough to remain in his position.[99] As a result, Abu al-Kheir divided the position of party secretary of Kerdasa into two posts. The first was called the NDP's Secretary of Kerdasa (*'amānat* Kerdasa) headed by Mohammad Hasanin Mikkawi, and the second the NDP's Secretary of New Kerdasa (*'amānat* Kerdasa *al-jadīda*) assigned to Mahjoub. However, Mahjoub's efforts to cajole the NDP to install its 'own secretary' in the town was considered by the other local secretary, Hasanin Mikkawi, as a 'consolation prize'.[100]

Hasanin Mikkawi claimed that the local secretary general became less important in local politics. He stated that although he was the NDP local secretary of Kerdasa from 1996 to 2010, he was aware that this position, especially after 2002, was less central than it had been before. Mikkawi said that it was not unusual for many towns to have more than one local secretary following the NDP reforms in the early 2000s. He said that by the late 2000s, the city of Ausim, for example, had four local party secretaries who competed for positions such as the heads of local and popular councils and who had ambitions beyond that.

The NDP leadership, according to him, started to grant any NDP member the status of local secretary once he had secured written endorsements from 200 NDP members, and his political record was proven clean (*naẓīf 'amniyyan*).[101] This was, he said, because the NDP had no interest in turning down any figure in any locality and knew that many minor notables in villages and towns would seek out any position that might satisfy or enhance their prestigious status within their community.[102] According to Hasanin Mikkawi, this was at the expense of the local secretary general, which became more of a ceremonial position.

Mikkawi agreed that the power of the NDP's district secretaries was declining in the 2000s. However, this was not to the advantage of local secretaries at the lower level, but rather for those who had positions on the local councils. In al-Mikkawi's words:

> When I decided to work in the public service, I was not particularly worried about the NDP's local secretary position. I was actually interested in running for the local council presidency, where I could serve Kerdasa. The NDP's local general secretary position was not important in itself. It was only a foothold from which the candidate could mobilize his supporters to elect him to the local council.[103]

From the mid-2000s, however, it become obvious to many in local leadership from the second generation of the NDP, in the towns of the Cairo peri-urban fringe, that they were gradually being marginalised. As Chapter 5 will show, many of them observed new SSIS-backed competitors, who brought their own money with them, joining the political field. A new and final chapter of party politics began, but it was destined to be short.

Conclusion

This chapter has shown that examining the 'formal' aspect of local governance separately, without considering the 'informal' one, can help in identifying the characteristics of the authority structure of the system of local governance, but cannot help in understanding the system dynamics which are largely dependent on the informal networks of power. Analysis, therefore, should not only assess the formal parameters of the administrative centralisation–decentralisation, but should also widen its focus to include informal networks. The authoritarian upgrading of the system of local governance, as this chapter suggests, is the process of reconfiguring the relationships between authority and power. It is a hands-on approach, whereby it learnt from the lessons and crises the regime faced at the local level.

Under Nasser and Sadat, the system of local governance was subjected to comprehensive phases of upgrading that affected both the structure of authority (the SLA) and the structure of power, however, the upgrading process under Mubarak did not significantly affect authority, but rather the power networks, in a manner that served both the authoritarian control over local politics and the country's political economic agenda. The process involved strategies of informal horizontal centralisation–decentralisation that was induced by authoritarian learning, therefore, its strategies varied between different phases. Nevertheless, the main strategy used by the Mubarak regime in order to control the process of centralisation–decentralisation was re-engineering electoral legislation, which led over time to altering the relationship between the authoritarian regime and its grassroots, therefore, changing the role of the ruling party's leadership in local governance.

Nevertheless, despite all the upgrading measures taken, the system suffered from a major deficiency. While it was effective in monopolising local politics, it failed to mobilise local communities and was incapable of translating its domination over local politics into a political hegemony on the macro scale. This was embodied in the failure of the NDP to make considerable advancements in the general elections without employing a security approach and electoral rigging. The next chapter will propose an explanation for the reasons behind this failure, especially when it comes to encountering the Islamic movement.

Notes

1. Mohammad Moustafa Habashi, 'Social Values and its Impacts on Rural Development: A Field Study in the Village of Kerdasa in al-Giza Governorate', PhD dissertation, University of Asyut, 1982, 306–10.
2. Jorge Martinez-Vazquez and Andrey Timofeev, 'Decentralizing Egypt: Not Just Another Economic Reform', in Jorge Martinez-Vazquez and Francois Vaillancourt (eds), *Decentralization in Developing Countries: Global Perspectives*

on the Obstacles to Fiscal Devolution (Cheltenham: Edward Elgar, 2011), 389–430; Sobhi Moharram, 'The Process of Controlled Decentralization in Egyptian Local Finance', *Developing Economies* 30(4) (1992): 450–81.

3. The dual approach used in this chapter is influenced by Paul D. Hutchcroft, whose contribution developed conceptual vocabulary for describing and analysing the complexities of centralisation and decentralisation in both administration and politics. See Hutchcroft, 'Centralization and Decentralization in Administration and Politics'.
4. Maksym Ivanyna and Anwar Shah, 'How Close is Your Government to its People? Worldwide Indicators on Localization and Decentralization', *Economics: The Open-Access, Open-Assessment E-Journal* 8(2014/13 (2014): 1–61.
5. Martinez-Vazquez and Timofeev, 'Decentralizing Egypt'.
6. Moharram, 'The Process of Controlled Decentralization', 452.
7. Martinez-Vazquez and Timofeev, Decentralizing Egypt', 421.
8. Mehmet Serkan Tosun and Serdar Yilmaz, *Centralization, Decentralization, and Conflict in the Middle East and North Africa* (Washington, DC: The World Bank, 2008).
9. Martinez-Vazquez and Timofeev, 'Decentralizing Egypt'.
10. Moharram, 'The Process of Controlled Decentralization', 464.
11. Soraya M. El Hag, 'A Review of Decentralization and Local Development Initiatives in Egypt between the Years of 1994 and 2011', MA thesis, American University in Cairo, 2014, available at: http://dar.aucegypt.edu/handle/10526/4136.
12. Martinez-Vazquez and Timofeev, 'Decentralizing Egypt'.
13. James B. Mayfield, *Local Government in Egypt: Structure, Process, and the Challenges of Reform* (Cairo: American University in Cairo, 1996), xiii.
14. Heydemann, 'Upgrading Authoritarianism in the Arab World'.
15. Tamir Moustafa, 'The Dilemmas of Decentralization and Community Development in Authoritarian Contexts', *Journal of Public and International Affairs* 13 (2002): 123–44, 131.
16. Nazih Ayubi, *The State and Public Policies in Egypt since Sadat*, Political Studies of the Middle East Series, No. 29 (Reading: Ithaca Press, 1991), 138; Jamie Boex, 'Democratization in Egypt: The Potential Role of Decentralization', Policy Briefing, Urban Institute Center for International Development and Governance, Washington, DC, February 2011, 3; Tosun and Yilmaz, *Centralization, Decentralization, and Conflict.*
17. A member of the local council was paid 10 LE monthly.
18. Zeinab Abul-Magd, *Militarizing the Nation: The Army, Business, and Revolution*

in Egypt (New York: Columbia University Press, 2017), 117–18.

19. More details can be found in the EACPE's report: 'Local Councils Elections in Egypt', EACPE, April 2008. See also: Mohammad Egati et al., 'Popular Participation through Local Councils in Egypt', *Arab Forum for Alternatives*, Cairo, 2011.
20. Hutchcroft, 'Centralization and Decentralization in Administration and Politics', 25.
21. Ibid., 27.
22. Ibid., 25.
23. Christopher Pollitt, 'Decentralization: A Central Concept in Contemporary Public Management', in Ewan Ferlie, Laurence E. Lynn Jr. and Christopher Pollitt (eds), *The Oxford Handbook of Public Management* (New York: Oxford University Press, 2005), 371–97, 373.
24. Ibid., 376.
25. Ibid., 385.
26. Ibid.
27. Ibid., 389.
28. Mayfield, *Local Government in Egypt*, 89. See also Moharram, 'The Process of Controlled Decentralization', 477.
29. Martinez-Vazquez and Timofeev, 'Decentralizing Egypt', 401.
30. Mayfield, *Local Government in Egypt*, 118.
31. Ibid.
32. As Thomas Demmelhuber, Roland Sturm and Erik Vollmann put it: 'the impact of decentralization is heavily reliant on informality and its framing by neopatrimonial networks'. Thomas Demmelhuber, Roland Sturm and Erik Vollmann, 'Decentralization in the Arab World: Conceptualizing the Role of Neopatrimonial Networks', *Mediterranean Politics* (2018): 1–23, 2.
33. Robert Springborg, 'Patrimonialism and Policy Making in Egypt: Nasser and Sadat and the Tenure Policy for Reclaimed Lands', *Middle Eastern Studies* 15(1) (1979): 49–69; Clement Moore, 'Clientelist Ideology and Political Change: Fictitious Networks in Egypt and Tunisia', in Ernest Gellner and John Waterbury (eds), *Patrons and Clients in Mediterranean Societies* (London: Duckworth, 1977), 255–74.
34. Ibid. See also Waterbury, *The Egypt of Nasser and Sadat*, 346–7.
35. Moharram, 'The Process of Controlled Decentralization', 477.
36. Laura Ruiz de Elvira et al., 'Introduction: Networks of Dependency: A Research Perspective', in Laura Ruiz de Elvira et al. (eds), *Clientelism and Patronage in the Middle East and North Africa: Networks of Dependency* (London: Routledge, 2018).

37. Alena Ledeneva, 'Informality and Informal Politics', in Graeme Gill and James Young (eds), *Routledge Handbook of Russian Politics and Society* (London: Routledge, 2013), 383–93, 376.
38. On case study research and the problem of indeterminacy, see Jorge Sousa, 'Indeterminacy', in Albert J. Mills, Gabrielle Durepos and Elden Wiebe (eds), *Encyclopedia of Case Study Research, Volume 1* (Thousand Oaks, CA: Sage, 2010), 454–6.
39. Hutchcroft, 'Centralization and Decentralization in Administration and Politics', 36.
40. Ibid.
41. For the 2010 elections, the last to be held under President Hosni Mubarak, an additional 64 seats were added, all reserved for women, bringing the seat total to 518.
42. Moharram, 'The Process of Controlled Decentralization', 480; Binder, *In a Moment of Enthusiasm*, 26. On the rise and the decline of the *'umda* in local politics, see Baer, *Studies in the Social History of Modern Egypt*, 46–7.
43. Harik, 'Mobilization Policy and Political Change in Rural Egypt', 290.
44. Binder, *In a Moment of Enthusiasm*, 20, 26.
45. Ibid., 327.
46. Amos Perlmutter, *Egypt: The Praetorian State* (New Brunswick, NJ: Transaction Publishers, 1974), 167–75.
47. Ayubi, *Bureaucracy and Politics in Contemporary Egypt*, 307–8.
48. Harik, 'Mobilization Policy and Political Change in Rural Egypt', 307.
49. Ayubi, *Bureaucracy and Politics in Contemporary Egypt*, 210–11.
50. Harik, 'The Single Party as a Subordinate Movement: The Case of Egypt'.
51. Ibid.
52. Ibid.
53. Ibid., 450.
54. Raymond A. Hinnebusch, *Egyptian Politics under Sadat: The Post-Populist Development of an Authoritarian-Modernizing State* (Cambridge: Cambridge University Press, 1985).
55. Hazem Kandil, *Soldiers, Spies, and Statesmen: Egypt's Road to Revolt* (London: Verso, 2014), 158.
56. Fahmy, *The Politics of Egypt*, 61–2.
57. Ibid.
58. Sadat's reforms in 1975 dropped active membership of the ASU as a requirement for candidature of the local councils, allowing any Egyptian, who is more than twenty-five and registered on the voters' list at a specific local unit, to run to the local elections.

59. Moharram, 'The Process of Controlled Decentralization', 481.
60. Springborg, 'Patrimonialism and Policy Making in Egypt'.
61. For further details on the context of the re-emergence of the Wafd Party, see Raymond William Baker, *Sadat and After: Struggles for Egypt's Political Soul* (Cambridge, MA: Harvard University Press, 1990), 63–6.
62. Raymond A. Hinnebusch, 'The Reemergence of the Wafd Party: Glimpses of the Liberal Opposition in Egypt', *International Journal of Middle East Studies* 16(1) (1984): 99–121, 114.
63. Ibid.
64. Kadry Hefny, 'Content Analysis for Counseling Meetings Committee in the Local Unit of Kerdasa, Giza-Egypt', *Population Studies* 10(66) (1983): 41–58, 49–50.
65. Ibid., 57–8.
66. Hisham Aidi, *Redeploying the State: Corporatism, Neoliberalism, and Coalition Politics* (London: Springer, 2008), 78.
67. Springborg, 'Patrimonialism and Policy Making in Egypt', 156–7.
68. Ibid., 43–4.
69. It has been academically established also that authoritarian regimes need elections to manage and outsource rent-seeking elites. In the authoritarian upgrading literature stream, elections can be an upgrading strategy that makes authoritarianism more flexible and resilient. For comprehensive analysis of the Egyptian case, see Blaydes, *Elections and Distributive Politics.*
70. Blaydes, *Elections and Distributive Politics*, 41.
71. Ibid.
72. Springborg, 'Patrimonialism and Policy Making in Egypt', 160.
73. Ibid., 44.
74. Blaydes, *Elections and Distributive Politics*, 44–5.
75. Numbers of independent candidates vary between different sources. The reason for the confusion is that the MB candidates nominally stood as independents.
76. Kienle, *A Grand Delusion*, 5.
77. Jamāl Zahrān, 'Independents and Dissidents' ('*al-Mustaqilūn wa l-Munshaqūn*'), in 'Amru Hāshim Rabīʿ et al. (eds), *The 2005 Elections of the People's Assembly* (*Intikhābāt Majlis al-Shaʿb 2005*) (Cairo: Al-ʾAhram Center for Political and Strategic Studies, 2006), 171–98, 182.
78. Kienle, *A Grand Delusion*, 74–5.
79. Ibid.
80. Blaydes, *Elections and Distributive Politics*, 56, 76.
81. Ibid., 63.
82. Ibid., 51.

83. Marie Vannetzel, 'The Muslim Brotherhood's "Virtuous Society" and State Developmentalism in Egypt: The Politics of "Goodness"', in Irene Bono and Béatrice Hibou (eds), *Development as a Battlefield*, International Development Policy Series No.8, (Geneva: Graduate Institute Publications, Brill-Nijhoff, 2017), 225.
84. Abdel-Wahhab Mahjoub, *Interview*. I was able to verify Abdel-Wahhab Mahjoub's claims from different parties.
85. Ibid.
86. Ibid.
87. Ahmed Zayed, 'Culture and the Mediation of Power in an Egyptian Village', in Nicholas S. Hopkins and Kirsten Westergaard (eds), *Directions of Change in Rural Egypt* (Cairo: American University in Cairo Press, 1998), 368–9.
88. Mohammad Hasanin Mikkawi, *Interview*. I was able to verify Mikkawi's claims through many sources.
89. Ibid.
90. Almost all the local NDP leaders interviewed by me have stressed the importance of local donations in convincing the local unit or Giza Governorate to support their efforts to provide Kerdasa with more services (electricity, street paving, etc.) and facilities (youth clubs, school complexes, a vehicle-licensing agency, etc.).
91. Ibid.
92. On the benefits expected as a result of being a member of parliament, see Blaydes, *Elections and Distributive Politics*, 53–8.
93. Stacher, *Adaptable Autocrats*, 99–100
94. Sulayman, *The Autumn of Dictatorship*, 127.
95. Ibid., 97.
96. Blaydes, *Elections and Distributive Politics*, 76.
97. Ibid., 76.
98. Zahrān, 'Independents and Dissidents', 180.
99. Mahjoub, *Interview*.
100. Mikkawi, *Interview*.
101. Ibid.
102. Mikkawi, *Interview*; Ismail Abu Musa, *Interview*, Kerdasa, 25 December 2016.
103. Mikkawi, *Interview*.

3

ALTERNATIVE LOCAL POLITICS: THE RISE AND THE FALL OF THE *DA'WA* MOVEMENT

In the 1980s, the towns of the Greater Cairo peri-urban fringe experienced the rise of what can be described as a *da'wa* movement. Mosques, whose numbers grew exponentially, embraced a new generation of Islamists who for the first time since the mid-1950s enjoyed a space of political tolerance as a result of the authoritarian upgrading arrangements of the late Sadat–early Mubarak era. Mosques, therefore, became platforms where political, social and cultural policies of the government were publicly condemned, and there was a proliferation of consumerism and western lifestyle practices that stemmed from Sadat's *infitah* social and economic policies. Thousands of Egyptians from the region attended religious lessons that were offered by renowned sheikhs from different Islamic currents, discussing a wide range of social and political topics. It was a '*da'wa* revolution' according to Khaled Sa'd, one of the adherents of Ali Qinawi; a Salafi scholar from Kerdasa.

The previous chapter examined the authoritarian approaches to upgrading the Egyptian system of local governance, which involved strategies of informal centralisation and decentralisation that aimed, among other things, to dominate local politics and to manage the regime's power networks at the subnational level. Yet the subordinated institutional frames, which were intended to contain the regime's networks, suffered from a structural dilemma: an inherent weakness in their mobilisation functions. Nevertheless, this did not mean that local communities were averse to politics, but rather it led to the emergence of alternative local politics. This chapter is devoted to examining the rise of the *da'wa* movement in the towns of the Cairo peri-urban fringe as an expression of this phenomenon. It will try to provide an explanation for the weakness of the authoritarian mode of political mobilisation compared with the Islamic one. In one sentence, it is true that the former was backed by the authoritarian regime and attached to the state public-service machine, but compared with the latter, it lacked the capability of extending *general trust* beyond the immediate circles of the clientelist lines.

Different dynamics resulted in the lack of 'general trust' between the state and local communities. Of those dynamics, the chief causes were the dysfunctional government institutions and the neglectful rule that marked Egyptian local governance due to the acceleration of neo-liberal policies. However, as the first section of this chapter will show, other dynamics related to the historical formation of the Arab state in general and the Egyptian state specifically contributed to making the regime's networks inefficient in their mobilisation capabilities and organisation at the local level.

The second section of this chapter will examine the evolution of the relationship between the NDP and the *da'wa* movement. This relationship went through two phases between two generations of NDP local leadership. While the first generation (the ASU veterans) showed sympathy to the movement and provided protection and support for it, the second generation collaborated with the security agencies and helped the authoritarian regime to obstruct its social activism. The change in attitude reflects the change of roles that were assigned to the local NDP leadership between the two generations as a result of upgrading the system of local governance, as discussed in the previous chapters.

The third section this chapter will investigate the competition among Islamists over communal (*'Ahlī*) mosques. Compared with the authoritarian institutional spheres that were subordinated to the system of local governance, mosques, which embraced the *da'wa* movement, proved to be more competitive and capable of mobilising a wide segment of devout youth who joined different Islamic organisations that challenged the regime in the early 1990s. The reason behind this lies in the ability of the Islamic mode of political mobilisation to articulate its discourse within a cultural framework. Therefore, despite the security approach that was employed by the regime to encounter the Islamic movement and obstruct its social activism, the latter possessed a sort of capital that authoritarianism lacked: *symbolic capital*. Thus, although the Mubarak regime, by the late 1990s, was able to suppress the movement, arrest its influential members and dominate mosques, it was unable to eradicate its political influence.

Trust is Missed: The Limits of Patronage Politics

The previous chapter identified the dilemma that was faced by the system of local governance during the era of Mubarak. Despite the upgrading strategies, the ruling party, which represented the main institutional patronage machine, was characterised by weak mobilisation functions and organisation. This dilemma was reflected in poor political participation and in the NDP's failure in the general elections. Consequently, the system was unable to translate its domination over local communities into hegemony, in the Gramscian sense, which meant the continuous need to employ security measures and electoral rigging to guarantee the authoritarian domination over local politics. But why was the NDP, in spite of all the upgrading measures, unable to enhance its mobilisation functions? Different historical and structural dynamics played key roles in limiting the effectiveness of Egyptian patronage politics, causing the failure of the system of local governance and its networks in generating *general trust* among local communities, which consequently affected its mobilisation functions.

There is a wealth of scholarship that shows that trust is associated with many desirable social, economic and political outcomes, such as economic growth,[1] political stability,[2] as well as political participation.[3] Bernard Barber defines trust as composed of 'socially learned and socially confirmed expectations that people have of each other, of the organizations and institutions in which they live, and of the natural and moral social orders that set the fundamental understandings for their lives'.[4] Studies on trust stress a 'fundamental ethical assumption: that other people share your fundamental values', and the necessity of having 'positive views of strangers, of people who are different from ourselves and presume that they are trustworthy'.[5]

Relations of trust are distinguished from relations of confidence. The latter are based on 'objective information, external regulations over conduct, contractual agreements, rational and informed decisions'. Relations of trust, on the other hand, 'tend towards subjective perceptions, moral sanctions, gentlemen's agreements, non-rational choices'.[6] Scholarship also differentiates between kinds of trust, among them the broader distinction between generalised and particularised trust. Generalised trust extends beyond an individual's immediate circle of friends and family and underpins cooperation among strangers. It is often associated with collective identities or the existence of a common cultural framework that provides a sense of belief that reduces the 'felt experience of vulnerability associated with extending trust to others'.[7]

In contrast, particularised trust (or intra-group trust) refers to trust that exists among limited social units such as kinship and friendship networks or even among ethnic and religious groups.[8] Due to its 'narrow radius', particularised trust produces a 'two-tier moral system', with good behaviour reserved to limited circles, and a 'decidedly lower standard of behavior in the public sphere'.[9] According to Francis Fukuyama, 'this serves as a cultural foundation for corruption, which is often regarded as a legitimate way of looking after one's family'.[10]

In the towns of the Greater Cairo peri-urban fringe, one of the major shortcomings of the system of local governance was its failure to gain general trust among local communities. Although the NDP leadership was often rooted in its home towns, at least in the first two decades of Mubarak's rule, many factors resulted in its social status deteriorating among local communities. One of the main factors that was widely researched was the eroding of the state public-service system at the metropolitan level due to accelerating neo-liberal policies, which made public service delivery selective and discriminatory.[11] This deepened the sense of marginalisation among citizens who observed the unfair urban planning agendas of the state, by allocating resources to develop new desert towns while neglecting their localities.[12] In this regard, literature also stresses a causal mechanism between the efficiency of the administrative machinery of the state and generalised trust.[13] The existence of the latter has also been associated with political mobilisation.[14]

The Arab Question and the Historical Formation of the State in Egypt

However, neo-liberalism alone is not enough to understand the inherent weakness of mobilisation functions. There are also other dynamics that are related to both the *Arab Question* (that is to say, the historical formation of the Arab state in general), and the historical formation of the Egyptian state in particular. As discussed in Chapter 1, the failure of the post-colonial Arab state to pursue the nation-building process ensued from its inability to produce a collective identity that could reify state-sanctioned relations. One of the results of this was that the regime and its ruling party had no ideology or a national project to appeal to the general population. This situation has made the Islamic movement, whose popular mobilisation was based on religious sentiments and identity politics, a real challenge for the regime since 1952.

While the *Arab Question* is common for most Arab countries, there is another factor specific to the historical formation of the Egyptian state per se. It is the relative timing of bureaucratisation and mass political participation. According to the seminal theory of Martin Shefter, determining the relative effectiveness of a 'constituency for patronage' depends on the timing of its historical formation. If a 'constituency for bureaucratic autonomy' or the process of bureaucratisation has preceded the emergence of mass mobilisation, it is unlikely that patronage politics would be effective in mass mobilisation. Instead, 'externally mobilised parties', whose appeal is based on external symbolic and cultural resources such as ideology, would emerge. If the timing is reserved, that is, mass politics preceded the formation of a modern bureaucracy, the outcome is more likely to be a patronage-ridden bureaucracy, facilitating the creation of 'internally mobilised parties' that tend to establish a linkage with its popular base through clientelist networks.[15]

It is clear that the Egyptian state fits into the first category in terms of the historical formation of its bureaucracy. The modern Egyptian bureaucracy is one of the oldest in the MENA and its origin can conservatively be traced to the nineteenth century with the rise of Mohammad Ali Pasha's modernisation project,[16] a long time before the emergence of any popular politics.[17] However, one may also notice that the NDP can be defined as an 'internally mobilised' party that obviously fits into the second category. It lacked a concrete ideology, programme or symbols that might endear it to the public. Instead, it had patronage as a tool for mobilising its constituency. But as Asef Bayat notes:

> In much of the Middle East (except in Lebanon and in the case of Istanbul's street car parkers' 'mafia'), patronage seems to work more through individual channels and rarely leads to group activities. Favours are granted more to individuals or families (in getting the security of tenure or jobs, for instance) than groups who then can bargain with their patron in exchange for his support.[18]

Shefter's theory can partly help us to identify the dilemma that Egyptian authoritarianism has had with its relation to its ruling party which, as discussed in the previous chapter, for decades made it innovative in upgrading mechanisms that involved decentralisation processes to re-engineer this relationship. From a comparative politics perspective, the Egyptian regime type is more compatible with an 'externally mobilised' organisation in order to be able to diffuse its control effectively. Ironically, the only such type of organisation in Egypt that could fit this profile is the Islamic movement, which has never been given the opportunity to do so. In fact, this also explains the bitter and longstanding struggle between the MB and the regime. In brief, the former had what the latter lacked: ideology, therefore, was aware of its danger.

However, instead of conducting a historic reconciliation with the Islamic movement (similar to other cases in the MENA),[19] the Egyptian authoritarianism preferred to upgrade its system of local governance to quash any opposition to its control. As the previous chapter elaborated, in the Mubarak era the process of upgrading were implemented on the power structure represented by the regime's networks, rather than on the structure of authority. During his tenure, Mubarak's strategies in upgrading the system of local governance experienced major shifts. In the 1980s, he used parliamentary elections to centralise the networks of power, while in the 1990s he reintroduced many of Sadat's strategies of decentralisation. In the last decade of his rule, the decentralisation process reached its maximum extent with restructuring of the NDP under pressure from the Gamal Mubarak-led group. In each period, the upgrading strategies led to fundamental changes in the relationship between the authoritarian regime and the local leadership of the NDP. Nevertheless, they failed to revitalise the NDP to overcome the MB without employing a security approach, nor did they succeed in mobilising local communities to achieve the desirable economic outcomes.

The NDP was the party of locals. This was both its strength and weakness. While the party was rooted locally in almost every town in Cairo's peri-urban fringe, it failed to translate its local strength to the district and governorate levels. In fact, it is more accurate to understand the NDP subnational branches as a sort of community organisation in Egypt, rather than as one unified national party. The local NDP figures, especially in the 1990s, were sometimes successful and often well-known in their localities, but they were barely known in the neighbouring towns and villages. This was because they lacked the means to extend their influence beyond clientelist and patronage networks, which could work efficiently on the micro scale but not on the macro scale. Hence, it is better to think of the problem of the NDP not in terms of structure, but rather in terms of the limits of the idea of patronage politics as a tool of political domination in Egypt and perhaps in the MENA.

This is what rendered the NDP impotent in its competition with the MB on Cairo's peri-urban fringe and elsewhere in Egypt. The former did not lack rootedness in local communities in general, especially among the clans (*'ā'ilāt*), and was backed by the state and attached to its public-service machine. Therefore, it found little difficulty in monopolising community politics. For many lesser notables, in fact, joining the NDP was viewed as following 'the order of things'; it was an essential step for any individual who wanted to have a say in local politics. In the words of Ismail Abu Musa, a veteran member of Kerdasa's NDP: '*kul al-balad kānat ḥizb waṭany*' ('everybody was [a member of the] NDP').[20] However, because it was socially constructed to resemble a community organisation, the NDP struggled to forge a large-scale campaign to convince people who belonged to surrounding towns and villages. In a large-scale region that consisted of many local communities, patronage politics did not work; here, it was the politics of identity that flourished. This is why the MB, by contrast, was able to defeat the NDP in a region where most local politics were historically subordinated to the state.

The weakness of mobilisation functions of the authoritarian system of local governance and the lack of political participation through its subordinated spheres did not mean that local communities in the towns of the Cairo peri-urban fringe were averse to politics. Rather, it led to the emergence of informal arenas that embraced a new trend of political mobilisation. From the late 1970s, the region experienced an unprecedented wave of communal (*'Ahlī*) mosque building. Unlike governmental mosques, which were funded by the state and staffed by government-appointed imams, *'Ahlī* mosques were self-constituted organisations, financed through donations and staffed by imams from the local communities. According to one estimate, the number of *'Ahlī* mosques in Egypt increased from 20,000 in 1970 to more than 46,000 in 1981. Of those, only 6,000 were directly administered by the Ministry of Religious Endowments.[21] Mosques became centres for what became known as the *da'wa* movement, which presented another model of local politics with a different logic and greater mobilisation capacities. The movement was nurtured under the eyes of the Sadat regime. It was hoped that it would be one of the key cultural–organisational ideological pillars of the post-Nasserite order.[22] However, it ended up being one of the most challenging threats that the Mubarak regime would encounter.

The NDP and the *Da'wa* Movement

It is widely agreed that the Nasser regime was relatively successful in uprooting the MB by the end of his era. The old structure of the organisation, which had been urban-based, had been atrophied by that time after two huge military crackdowns in the 1950s and 1960s. However, from the mid-1970s, a new chapter of the Islamic movement started when Egyptian authoritarianism started to search for new legitimacies in the post-1967 war era. The Egyptian political and economic turn was to be accompanied by a new moral discourse that stressed 'village morals' (*qiyam al-qarya*),[23] the role of the family instead of class, as well as the centrality of faith (*al-'īmān*) instead of emancipation. The new discourse also entailed 'the creation of an objectified and functionalised Islamic tradition' to serve the new political arrangements inside the regime.[24] By reinventing the traditions,[25] the regime paved the way for political Islam revivalism and the rise of mosques as an arena for political mobilisation.

In the 1980s, the towns of the Cairo peri-urban fringe, similar to many other localities in rural and urban settings in Egypt, experienced the rise of a *da'wa* movement, which was a contemporary piety movement requiring 'all adult members of the Islamic community to urge fellow Muslims to greater piety, and to teach one another correct Islamic conduct'.[26] According to Saba Mahmood, this movement encompassed a range of practical activities, including 'establishing neighbourhood mosques, social welfare organizations, Islamic educational institutions, and printing presses, as well as urging fellow Muslims toward greater religious responsibility, either through preaching or personal conversation'.[27]

In the past decades, a lot of ink has been spilled on the dynamics that led to the rise of political Islam in Egypt and elsewhere in the MENA. Scholarship has stressed the role of the ruralisation of cities associating it with conservatism;[28] the decline of Arab nationalism after the Arab defeat by Israel in 1967, leaving an ideological vacuum that was filled by a new supra-state revisionist Islamic ideology;[29] the Iranian revolution and the spread of a revolutionary Islam model;[30] the negative side- effects of state-building;[31] the corruption and inequality exacerbated by oil remittances from the Arab Gulf which 'turned those who felt excluded to political Islam as an ideology of protest';[32] and the global shift towards re-traditionalisation and the flourishing of identity politics.[33] It is not my aim here to re-establish what has been established, but rather to examine the development of early Islamic activism at the local level and its relationship with the subordinated arenas of local politics.

As a part of authoritarian upgrading arrangements, President Sadat, in his early tenure, criticised Nasser's security apparatuses' repression of their opponents, including the practice of torture against Islamists.[34] He released thousands of MB members in the early 1970s and allowed them to work on the ground, though informally. This was an attempt to use their influence (especially at the 'grassroots' level) to work against the leftist wing of the Egyptian coalition government and to support his radical policy changes to the economy, which required a shifting of alliance from the USSR to the United States.[35] Sadat won the battle against 'power centres' (*marākiz al-qiwā*) in the state. He radically changed Egypt's foreign orientation. However, he also opened the way for the Islamisation of society. In 1981, he paid for this with his life.[36]

On the morrow of their release, the MB organisation's leaders found themselves alone with almost no grassroots support. The northern branch of *al-Jamā'a al-'islāmiyya*,[37] one of the largest semi-organised *da'wa* networks, decided to 'pledge' itself to the MB leadership in the late 1970s, giving the organisation a new impetus, which led to a revival of the MB. One such member of *al-Jamā'a al-'islāmiyya*, Abdel Moneim Abou-el Fotouh, later to become a prominent political Islamic figure in Egypt, was the Student Body President of al-Qasr al-Aini College, which embraced a vigorous Islamic activism that was encouraged by Sadat's divide-and-rule policy. In his memoirs, Abou-el Fotouh recalled how he discovered the prohibited organisation. When he attended the college, he had a vague image of the MB that was distorted by the Nasser regime propaganda.[38] According to him, Sadat's policies of enabling freedom of speech gave a new generation of devout youths in universities a golden opportunity to reconnect with the Islamic movement as it then existed. The MB at this time represented the historical legacy and *al-Jamā'a al-'islāmiyya* represented the grassroots.[39]

Many of Abou-el Fotouh's peers and contemporaries in the 1970s and 1980s shared elements of his experience. Abdel Salam Bashandi, who was one of the prominent local leaders of the MB in Kerdasa, and its candidate in the parliamentary election for the district in the 2000s, also said that he learned properly about the MB only when his father was released from political imprisonment in 1971.[40] Prior to then, Bashandi's awareness of the MB had been distorted by Nasserite propaganda. From the early 1970s, Ikhwani political prisoners were gradually released. Therefore, many of Bashandi's peers started to contact the Brothers. Ikhwani doctrines such as Banna's teachings (*Rasāʾil Ḥasan al-Banna*) were circulated among a new generation, and were amplified by a deep social, cultural and ideological wave that hit most Arab countries.[41]

Bashandi was involved in Islamic activism before he joined the MB. He describes how he managed with his friends in the late 1970s to hold events in Kerdasa such as conferences, seminars, religious book exhibitions and holding Eid prayer in public. To these events, *ulama* and sheikhs from all over the country were invited, including those of the MB. Bashandi was also among a group of Kerdasian youths involved in charitable events such as organising markets for household goods to support low-income families, as well as offering free after-school tutoring sessions.[42] These activities, as I was informed by many Kerdasians, were remembered by a whole generation in the town.

The first generation of Islamic activists, as Bashandi and others who witnessed this period tell us, made efforts to change the names of streets and neighbourhoods in Kerdasa to Islamic names. At that time, all of these activities were held under the slogan of the Muslim Youth of Kerdasa (*Shabāb Kerdasa al-Muslim*).[43] It was a collective act involving the identification and objectifying of social space aimed at 'the control of space and at the investment of space with a particular moral outlook'.[44] At the time, this practice was novel, but it was also perceived as part and parcel of community activism: a practice that reminds us of Salwa Ismail's findings that the Islamic movement's mobilisation of activists was anchored in the socio-spatial organisation of urban settings that 'undergird collective action and opposition'.[45]

In the towns of the Greater Cairo peri-urban fringe, this kind of Islamic activism was not initially perceived as political by the first generation of the NDP leadership (the ASU veterans). Sayed al-Zinnari, who was one of the organisers, has confirmed that the local Kerdasian NDP figureheads supported their initiatives by facilitating their use of the town's amenities for their charitable and religious activities. Sheikh Yousef Abdel Salam Saleh, who had been a prominent local member of the ASU in the Nasser and Sadat periods, and became in the early 1980s the head of the local council and the local NDP's secretary general, had opened the doors of Kerdasa schools, mosques, sports club, as well as familial social houses (*dūr al-Munāsabāt*) to them.[46]

Zinnari described the relation between the first generation of the local NDP leadership and Islamic activism as a cooperative and supportive one. Until the late 1980s, those in charge of the NDP in Kerdasa, according to Zinnari, 'were good men'. They viewed Islamic activists like Bashandi and Zinnari as 'devout youths whose activities were useful to the town'.[47] Local figures such as Abdel Salam Saleh and Mohammad Abu Taleb, who were the NDP cornerstones in Kerdasa at this time, made serious efforts to 'support our activities because they represented Kerdasa not the NDP'.[48] In this period, there was 'a real sense of belonging to Kerdasa among everyone' (*kān fī ḥāga ismaha Kerdasa*).[49] Nevertheless, it should be also observed that 'there was a division of roles'. Islamic activists were responsible for charitable work and *da'wa*, while the then local NDP leaders (the ASU veterans), who were much respected, were responsible for the town's public affairs, such as resolving local disputes.[50] At that time, as was elaborated previously, the main role assumed by the local NDP leadership was to keep the domestic peace (*al-silm al-'ahly*) and solve local disputes. The definition of local politics had not yet been expanded to include charitable work and public service. Therefore, both Abdel Salam and Abu Taleb did not see any problem in Islamic activism. On the contrary, they encouraged it.

Islamic activists never imagined that they could do what the ASU veterans did, because the former were too young. The nature of the public work for which the then NDP local figures were responsible could be handled competently only by veterans with years of experience. On the other hand, nobody expected Abdel Salam Saleh and Abu Taleb to do what the Islamic activists did, because the latter's activities were presumed to be a form of youth action – activities that were 'organized by boys'.[51] In short, there was an age gap that prevented any competition, and thereby any collision or confrontation. Even in parliamentary elections, Zinnari states, local people did not care about the candidates' ideological orientation, whether they were Ikhwan or NDP members; they voted for the candidate who was from Kerdasa. This was the sole principle.[52]

It is also worth noting that from the early 1980s, right after Mubarak ascended to power, the local NDP leadership was subjected to a deliberate marginalisation as a result of the regime's strategies of centralising its networks of power. As addressed in the previous chapter, the changing of the electoral system from individual to a party-list representation consolidated the central control of the party at the expense of the local structures, effectively destroying the bargaining power of local notables and undermining their political roles, which became restricted to applying customary law. This also facilitated the *da'wa* movement to bring forward new personalities who gradually came to take part in local politics, albeit only for a while.

The Case of Mohammad Sayed al-Ghizlani

In this context, Mohammad Sayed al-Ghizlani had the opportunity to become involved in 'public work' and to gain experience that would make him a role model in the town. Sayed al-Ghizlani was born in 1952, and from the mid-1970s he was involved in activities organised by the *da'wa* movement in Kerdasa. In particular, he was known for organising after-school sessions in Kerdasa mosques for students from low-income families. He was also active in many charitable events, especially in the holy month of Ramadan. Sayed al-Ghizlani graduated from al-Qasr al-Aini College as a doctor. From the late 1970s, he became known for offering free medical services to poor people, alongside his job in the Ministry of Health. In 1979, Sayed al-Ghizlani was the first person in his town to try to utilise his reputation politically. He was convinced by Sheikh Salah Abu Ismael (see later) to run on the New Wafd Party list for the parliamentary election. As discussed in the previous chapter, the New Wafd Party, led by Fuad Siraj al-Din, sought to make a base for the re-established party by attracting followers who were popular in their localities.

Al-Ghizlani was one of those followers, but he failed to be elected. He was prevented by Nazmi al-Mikkawi, the formal candidate of the NDP in Kerdasa. In the 1979 electoral campaign, which was based on the individual system, members of the Mikkawi family physically assaulted Sayed al-Ghizlani and prevented him from campaigning in Kerdasa.[53] However, this repression, through the regime's local arm, was not motivated by fear of the rise of Islamists. It was too early for that. Islamists had not yet manifested the sort of threat they would in later decades. Such acts of repression as were carried out against the New Wafd should rather be viewed as a reflection of Sadat's decision to alienate the newly legalised party and thwart its re-emergence, out of his fear that it would 'rally all those dissatisfied with the regime for whatever reason'.[54]

The New Wafd was the first political entity outside the regime's umbrella to be aware of the rise of a new segment of local notables in such localities as Kerdasa that would compete with members of the ruling party. On Cairo's peri-urban fringe, those who ran on the Wafd list in 1979 were mostly religious and involved in the *da'wa* movement. In Nahia, a neighbouring town to Kerdasa, Issam al-Aryan, who later became one of the MB's most prominent leaders, ran on the Wafd list, but he was also physically attacked by the al-Zumor family, the local arm of the regime there.[55] Another Islamist-linked candidate, in the village of Hormus (near Imbaba), was Salah Abu Ismail, an Azhari sheikh who had relations with many entities in the Gulf States, who thereafter became involved in charitable and *da'wa* work.

Abu Ismail was one of the few candidates to win a seat in the parliament. He would later become a leading figure in the MB (though informally) and a prominent Islamic scholar, who would have a great influence on the Islamic movement, at least in Lower Egypt.[56] His son, Hazem Salah Abu Ismail, would lead a new Salafi movement after the January 25 Revolution, and try to run in the presidential election of May 2012, but the electoral commission, under the influence of the Supreme Council of the Armed Forces (SCAF) had him disqualified. The failure of the *da'wa* movement leadership to participate in politics within the scope of formal political entities pushed them to abandon formal politics and to restrict their activism to charities and *da'wa* on the local level, thereby investing in their personal status. Nevertheless, even this pattern of local activism could not have survived without protection from the then ASU veterans who regarded themselves responsible for community politics.

Until the late 1980s, as discussed previously, charitable initiatives were regarded by the first generation of NDP local leadership veterans as complementary to their role and necessary, since these activities were in the interests of their localities. Consequently, in Kerdasa, Yousef Abdel Salam Saleh and Mohammad Abu Taleb, who were the ruling party representatives, provided cover for youths such as Sayed al-Ghizlani. For this reason, in the middle of the 1980s al-Ghizlani quit his job in the Ministry of Health in order to establish, with the support of his brother, a clinic that had a dual purpose. On the one hand, it was a business project from which he could earn his living, taking advantage of the deteriorating conditions of the public clinic in Kerdasa. Simultaneously, it was a charitable institution through which he was able to provide many low-income patients with proper treatment. Through his behaviour as a 'good doctor', al-Ghizlani became a much-respected notable in his town, which would later be translated into political capital as will be discussed in the next chapters.

There was another reason why the NDP elite was able to embrace the emergence of Islamic-oriented local personalities such as Sayed al-Ghizlani. At that time, to be an 'Islamic' was not to be considered 'politically Islamic', as the politics of identity was still nascent. In other words, having an Islamic orientation was not taken to mean support for the MB. In fact, the MB lacked any method for contacting those young devout men who had emerged from *da'wa* networks. Other Islamic groups, such as the Jihad Organisation, were minor and secretive in character, and therefore had no interest in establishing social bases. In short, those involved in the *da'wa* movement had no established connections with any existing Islamic organisation in the late 1970s and early 1980s.

Sayed al-Zinnari and Abdel Salam Bashandi articulated this point. They recalled that they did not have the opportunity to get to know Kerdasa's 'old local leaders' of the MB, such as Gaber Rizq and Sayed Nizili, until the middle of the 1980s. When they finally met, it was not in Kerdasa.[57] As stated by al-Zinnari:

> When we reached puberty in Kerdasa, we did not find Sayed Nizili and Gaber Rizq or any other *ikhwani*. We heard about them, but we never met them. Actually, they did not know that we existed because they were not based in the town, but rather in the City of Cairo. Gaber Rizq had an office in el-Tawfikiyya. We started to visit him to receive blessings from him (*nākhod il-baraka*). In other words, we went to *al-ikhwan*, they did not come to us.[58]

Thus, the absence of any connection with the MB, or any other Islamic organisation, made the local NDP leadership on Cairo's peri-urban fringe determined to provide the Islamic activists with protection from the regime's security apparatus. In the second half the 1980s, all interviewees who later became Ikhwani figures in Kerdasa said that local NDP figures intervened to prevent their arrest by the security forces. For example, Sayed al-Ghizlani's son, Mohammad, stated that on the eve of the 1985 parliamentary election, Yousef Abdel Salam Saleh intervened to release his father from detention.[59] However, the state of tolerance that the *da'wa* movement leadership enjoyed would not last for long. From the late 1980s, a new, younger local leadership of the NDP emerged with a new pattern of local politics.

Patronage Politics vs Identity Politics

From the early to the late 1980s, the MB enjoyed relative toleration from the Mubarak regime. Although the organisation was denied legal recognition, it was not subjected to repressive measures, and so had greater leeway to agitate. The MB was also allowed to pursue its activities, though with certain restrictions, and permitted to move back into its downtown headquarters.[60] Furthermore, its alliances with the Wafd in the parliamentary elections, especially in 1984, gave its leadership a chance to re-emerge in the media and to reconnect with its potential grassroots, which mainly consisted of educated youths in universities, city suburbs and the arena of civil society. In this period, Mubarak did not see the return of the Ikhwan as a threat to the regime. It was assumed that their limited participation in the parliament and professional syndicates would curtail their underground expansion, making their movement visible and absorbed into the regime's subordinated spheres.[61]

From 1987 onwards, however, the Mubarak regime became alarmed by the MB's electoral successes. Their growing presence was also paralleled by a shift in their attitude, as 'the group moved from portraying itself to be a potential counsellor to the state to now decidedly step up as political opposition'.[62] The MB challenged Mubarak by running in the 1987 election in alliance with the Socialist Labour Party (SLP). They achieved, at the time, their highest representation in parliament (thirty seats), increasing the share of the SLP from twenty-seven to fifty-seven seats.[63] The shift provoked the state to 'disseminate a tarnishing image of the Brotherhood in the media' based on a narrative portraying the Brotherhood as 'the enemy of the nation'.[64]

At the subnational level, the regime, in response, chose to implement new upgrading strategies on its system of local governance, introducing decentralisation measures on the networks of power. The process of upgrading led to the emergence of a new generation of local NDP leaders, who were assigned new developmental roles accompanied by the swing towards neo-liberalism. This included making the electoral system candidate-centric and increasing the number of electoral constituencies, which consequently stimulated the regime's local patronage networks, giving them further impetus in the competition over the political field.

Local politics in the towns of the Cairo peri-urban fringe were greatly affected by these developments. As discussed in the previous chapter, the concept and the definition of public work changed. The 'politics of goodness',[65] which was introduced to local communities by Islamic activists from the *da'wa* movement, became the fundamental practice for all local political elites. On the micro level, the 'division of roles' principle, which had been implied previously between the first generation of the NDP local leadership (the ASU veterans), on the one hand, and the *da'wa* movement activists, on the other, was over. With the emergence of the second generation of local NDP men (Abdel Wahhab Mahjoub, Mahmood al-Mikkawi, Moustafa al-Gabiri, etc.), the 'age gap' became irrelevant and Islamic activism was seen politically.

In Kerdasa in this period, the first generation of the local NDP leadership, which was the same generation that took charge of the local ASU, had started to fade out. Nazmi Mikkawi, who was the last *umda* of Kerdasa, retired at this time and his close family lost any interest in politics.[66] Sheikh Yousef Abdel Salam Saleh was replaced by Haj Mohammad Abdel-Wahhab Mahjoub, a young NDP member who realised the new rules of the game.

Mahjoub understood that local politics had become more central to the state's developmental vision than it had been in the time of his predecessors, especially the problem related to the distribution of scarce resources designated for public-service delivery. Therefore, he cultivated connections with the head of the Local Council of Ausim, personnel from the Governorate of al-Giza and the secretary general of the NDP at the district level,[67] who seemed to constitute a part of one of the influential power networks at that time. As a result, Sheikh Yousef Abdel Salam Saleh, who represented the first generation of the NDP (the ASU veterans) in Kerdasa, found himself gradually excluded from the late 1980s, and in the early 1990s he died in a car accident.[68]

On the other hand, many of the personnel in the towns of the Cairo peri-urban fringe who emerged from the *da'wa* movement and its networks started to be perceived as Ikhwan grassroots. During the period of the regime's tolerance of the MB, they were able to discover the older generations of the Brotherhood and to become members of the organisation. In Kerdasa, a new generation of Islamic local leaders (Tareq Zaki Mikkawi, Abdel Salam Bashandi, Sayed Zinnari, etc.) became representatives of the MB in the town. These Brotherhood members extended and intensified their charitable activities, which, unlike in the previous period, were recognised by NDP leaders and state agencies as activities that had political ends. This led to a confrontation between the new local NDP leaders and the Brothers. Both were from the same generation and came to realise that they were rivals.

Sayed Zinnari has discussed his memories of that time, stating that:

> In the early 1980s, the *da'wa* was born. We [the Islamic activists] were young and the then NDP leaders such as Yousef Abdel Salam and Mohammad Abu Taleb were calling us *ya wād* (plu. *wlād*) (boy), and we called them *ya 'am* (uncle). In the late 1980s, the new generation of the NDP viewed us as rivals. Consequently, we started to face a new form of harassment, oppression and persecution from the security apparatuses. Many Kerdasians, though they had sympathy for us, started to view our activities as potentially harmful to the town. In the early 1990s, it increasingly became dangerous to organize activities that we had carried out previously, except on specific occasions such as Ramadan and Eid . . . Charitable work also became one of the things that many people undertook, such as businessmen and NDP members. Ever since, it has been no surprise to see a corrupt person organizing charitable events such as *Mawā'id ar-Raḥmān* (charity *Iftars* – fast-breaking meals during Ramadan), or making a donation to build or renovate a mosque.[69]

Although local MB networks had by then gained considerable experience in the domain of public work, acquiring a great knowledge of the local communities of Cairo's peri-urban fringe, from the early 1990s on their social work could be considered symbolic in comparison with the work undertaken by the second generation of the local NDP leadership. This was not only due to persecution, but also because of the easy access of the local ruling party to the state's resources and the party's ability to access networks of 'friendly' businessmen. Most importantly, it was due to the change in the definition of local politics, which became increasingly based on servicing local people (*khidmat 'ahl al-balad*). Thus, it is true that the *da'wa* movement, many of whose members joined the MB, had introduced the initial model of social work. But it was the NDP, backed by the government, that later captured it structurally.

As a consequence, beginning in the 1990s, the MB carried out social work, which in fact fulfilled the more important need for ritualised group activity, while Kerdasa's NDP, backed by the government, made serious efforts to mobilise state institutions to develop the town's infrastructure, such as building schools, paving roads, improving al-Seyahi Street and developing public services (see the previous chapter). The NDP's duties in that era were expanded to represent 'the myth of state developmentalism'.[70] The MB's engagement in social work, in contrast, was restricted to small-scale activities in mosques and during religious seasons. Khalil al-Anani called this tendency '*ikhwanism*': a sort of activism that aims to glue the Brotherhood members together, establishing shared norms and acts that could give meanings to their gatherings and embodying the identity that signifies their uniqueness and distinctiveness.[71] By the late 1990s, charitable work in Kerdasa was not associated with the MB; rather, it was attached to the 'good people' in the NDP.

In this sense, it is indeed the case that the *da'wa* movement had revolutionised 'public work' in its early period during the late 1970s and 1980s, but the evolution of local politics in the Mubarak era overran their contribution, pushing them to a sort of activism that stressed their peculiarity, which eventually distanced them from the local community. This also occurred as a result of the rise of a new generation of local NDP leaders who were assigned new roles in local governance.

From the 1990s, much has been written about the proliferation of Islamic charitable networks and private voluntary organisations, especially in Cairo's suburbs.[72] It was said that this sector, in the late 1980s and 1990s, was able to compete with the state's welfare system and in some areas replace it.[73] The earthquake that hit Egypt in 1992 was evidence of that. State institutions failed to provide immediate help to the victims while the Islamic socio-economic sector, by contrast, gave assistance right from the outset.[74]

However, other accounts underestimated the assumed competition between the state and the Islamic socio-economic sector, arguing that Islamic charitable practices had been deliberately transformed into developmental practices to fill the void left by neo-liberalism. According to Mona Atia, 'pious neoliberalism' is a policy, ideology and governmentality that 'reconfigure[s] religious practices in line with principles of economic rationality, productivity, and privatization'.[75] It 'represents the merging of a market-orientation with faith', which 'leads to new institutional forms, like private mosques, private foundations, and an Islamic lifestyle market'.[76] In this sense, the Egyptian state in the Mubarak era mobilised the Islamic socio-economic sector, directly and indirectly, to respond to increasing inequalities resulting from the state's neo-liberal policies.[77]

My research in Kerdasa also shows that the assumed relationship between the Islamic socio-economic sector and political Islam might be exaggerated.

On Cairo's peri-urban fringe in the 1990s, charitable and social work, which was considered the pillar of this sector, was a broad banner that encompassed various kinds of voluntary and semi-voluntary practices and organisations. Figures involved in this sector were from different backgrounds within the local community and most of them acted under Islamic slogans. This was not unusual since popular culture in Egypt and in the whole region, since the 1970s, has increasingly leaned towards Islamisation. Pious motivations and terminology penetrated all aspects of everyday life. For example, an anthropological survey conducted within the clinic of the Mostafa Mahmoud Mosque community, the largest mosque-based clinic in the country, showed that many doctors were unsympathetic to the MB, revealing a wide diversity of political sympathies (the NDP, the Wafd and the leftist Tajammu).[78]

My analysis is in keeping with academic studies that have argued that the Islamic socio-economic sector should not be confidently associated with political Islam, but should rather be understood as part of the expansion of informality – a process of local people setting up socio-economic institutions that parallel those in the formal sector. Informality pervades all aspects of popular communities, mobilising local people to establish their informal socio-economic institutions, which are subjected to the formal economy but at the same time complement it.[79]

In this sense, informality is a style of governance that should be recognised as subordinate to formality and as a means for a variety of dominant social actors to accommodate the needs of sections of society at a minimal cost. This modality of governance is an output of the increasing interaction between state practices and market practices,[80] by which philanthropy and charity are increasingly becoming 'modes of provision of social needs, eroding social rights of citizenship and transforming citizens into clients of notables'.[81]

In considering Cairo's peri-urban fringe, in which socio-economic life increasingly leaned towards informality, facilitated by state governance under the cover of a pious popular culture, it is understandable that the contribution of the Islamic movement would become indistinguishable from the larger currents of development. This is the reason why the MB's social and charitable activities were imperceptible in Kerdasa. In my work, most people I talked to were not aware of MB activism in the town, except on the eve of parliamentary elections. Many of my interviewees stated that they did not notice any MB activity when they were young in the 1990s.

Of course, the Mubarak regime's change in attitude towards the MB starting from 1987 also played a major role in forcing the Brotherhood to avoid being active in public. Nevertheless, another reason is that the regime in the 1990s became confident that a new generation of its local men had gained enough experience and had become sufficiently qualified to take over the role that had been played by the *da'wa* movement. However, this was at the expense of the Islamisation of local politics itself, where even those from the NDP were required to have some semblance of religiosity. The change was reflected in the amendment of local leadership titles. While the first generation of local NDP leaders on the Cairo peri-urban fringe were usually called *sheikh*s (from *sheikh al-arab*), those from the second generation were called *Hajj*s (from pilgrim). The shift from *sheikh* (e.g., Sheikh Yousef Abdel-Salam) to *Hajj* (e.g., Hajj Mohammad Abdel-Wahhab Mahjoub) reflected an aspect of the change in the definition of local politics between two generations of local leadership.

M. H., a member of the MB in Kerdasa, was in the early 2000s placed in charge of a Brotherhood group (*'usra*, lit. 'family' – the smallest unit in the MB structure). He confirmed that the MB's activities in the late 1990s and the 2000s were confined to limited religious events. When I talked to him in March 2016, he said that he had criticised the MB for its inactivity in public work. He blamed the top-down decision-making process inside the Brotherhood, which often led to the appointment of individuals who lacked the necessary skills for representing the MB. Many times, he stated, the Ikhwani grassroots had recommended individuals who were more suitable, but the Guidance Bureau (*Maktab al-'Irshād*) usually ignored their suggestions.[82]

In his opinion, Abdel Salam Bashandi was not the right person to be the MB's candidate for the parliamentary elections in Kerdasa. Bashandi, who had an Islamic bookstore in the town, lacked experience and knowledge of local needs. He was a modest public speaker and was reluctant to attend local social events.[83] For these reasons, he was barely known by most Kerdasians and no one was able to think of him as someone who might help in the town's social affairs. This was in contrast to other contemporary local NDP figures, who were always busy engaging with people, attempting to solve their problems and attending their social events. Obviously, M. H. and other MB members were evaluating Bashandi's performance compared with that of his predecessors in the 1980s such as Salah Abu Ismail (see the next section).

However, they did not observe that from the late 1990s the role of the MB's local figures had fundamentally changed. While they were previously allowed to be active in social work, under the new conditions they were barely able to represent the MB in their localities. But if the MB's activism was unseen by locals, then how could they challenge the domination of the NDP on Cairo's peri-urban fringe that had forced the regime for nearly two decades to rig the general elections? The answer is the politics of identity.

It is true that the local branches of the NDP on the Cairo peri-urban fringe, from the late 1980s, were backed by the government and given the chance to monopolise local politics, thus, having the opportunity, capacity and experience to utilise the state's resources in general elections. However, local leaders of the NDP could not reach beyond their localities, since their role was to represent their micro space, their towns. Thus, they had no means of campaigning at the district level, where every district encompasses hundreds of thousands of voters. In contrast, the local MB figures in the 1990s were barely known in their localities and had no experience in dealing with local issues. But since the MB's popular mobilisation had been articulated within a cultural framework and identity politics, they could easily campaign on a macro level without much need of patronage structures, since *symbolic capital*, as we will show in the next section, was there.

In contrast, since the NDP's socio-political mobilisation was based solely on patronage politics, it made its local branches more like a community organisation rather than local units of a political party. This meant that the local NDP in a town found itself competing for resources with the NDP in other towns. In the 1990s and 2000s, this led to fragmentation in the party as local branches constantly fought with each other. Hence, the NDP's dilemma in the 1990s and 2000s was that patronage politics, which was the core of its version of social mobilisation, could not work on the macro level. Patronage politics was indeed the regime's strongest weapon, but on the scale of the national elections, it could not overcome the politics of identity. It is no surprise, then, that for decades the Egyptian regime had been keen to adopt laws that prohibit politics with a religious character.

Spaces of Sheikhs: The Struggle over Mosques

The 1990s was a crucial juncture in the local history of Cairo's peri-urban fringe. This was the period in which the regime networks pulled the rug from under all other local networks and dominated most spheres of local politics.

The SSIS increasingly became involved in the system of local governance. Not only did it start to vet all local figures who wanted to take part in politics; it also became common for this apparatus to obstruct the organisation of *da'wa* and charitable networks, paving the way for the NDP to dominate all aspects of public social work. The locals' fear of secret informants (*mukhbirīn*) became pervasive. Islamists, therefore, were pushed back to the last remaining social space in which they could function: mosques.

However, despite all security restrictions and repressive measures taken to contain the *da'wa* movement and to deprive it of resources, the informal political field that was emerging in *'Ahlī* mosques was more competitive and a mobilising force, compared with the formal political field that was subordinated to the authoritarian system of local governance. This is because the former was rich in symbolic capital, which is unlike other forms of capital (economic, social and cultural), and calls for obedience in a disguised way that owes nothing to the logic of exploitation.[84] Thereby, from the late 1980s, mosques in Greater Cairo were subjected to an intense competition among a new generation of sheikhs over the symbolic capital that was generated in them. Nevertheless, before delving into the assessment of such a struggle it is worth providing a historical background of the development of intellectual life that was taking place there.

Until the mid-1970s, the sheikhs of the towns of the Cairo peri-urban fringe had little to do with politics. According to one of the 1980's generation of sheikhs, Khaled Sa'd, sheikhs who led mosques and were in charge of teaching local people religious affairs were 'Quranic' (*qur'aniyyūn*). Their responsibility was restricted to teaching people how to read the Quran, the correct ways to pray and fast, and explaining to them the *ahkam al-shari'ah* (*sharia* rules) of their personal life. Sa'd also referred to these figures as 'Azharis' (*'azhariyyūn*), a generation of sheikhs who studied at the University of al-Azhar or learned from Azharis, and who adopted *Ash'arism*, a flexible theology in Islam that distances its adherents from politics.[85]

From the late 1970s, however, this tendency would encounter many reasons for resentment and instability. Of those reasons was, first, the impact of Nasser's policy of marginalising al-Azhar, and undermining its relative autonomy.[86] Secondly, the proliferation of western lifestyle practices that accompanied Sadat's policies of *infitah* and the rise in middle-class income, deepened the sense of inequalities among sections of society and led to the proliferation of western life-style practices.[87] Thirdly, the Israeli–Egyptian peace agreement, the Camp David accords, were a shock for most Azharis, who believed that any political settlement with Israel should be forbidden.[88] Azhari sheikhs were consequently confronted with a new generation of populist sheikhs who rose on the eve of Mubarak's inauguration, many of whom had been released from political prison before the assassination of Sadat. Those sheikhs had been imprisoned with Salafists who were influenced by the emerging Wahhabism in the Arab Peninsula.

Across Cairo's peri-urban fringe, therefore, mosques in the 1980s and the early 1990s became an arena for debates on many issues, notably the relation between the Islamic movement and the state. Kerdasa, Nahia, Imbaba and other towns witnessed the rise of populist sheikhs who started to evoke an Islamic version of *da'wa* that blended Ikhwani thinking of the 1960s (particularly Sayed Qotb's writings) with elements from Wahhabism, and demanded that the government apply *sharia* law immediately.[89] This sort of movement was described by Khaled Sa'd as a '*da'wa* revolution'.[90] It is beyond the scope of this study to analyse the resurgence of Islamic fundamentalism, or simply Jihad, from the late twentieth century, which was subjected to a wealth of scholarship to the extent that the study of Islamic fanaticism has become an independent academic 'jihadology' industry. My aim, rather, is to focus on its implications on local governance in the examined period.

It is possible to differentiate between two intellectual currents that competed over the mosques of Cairo's peri-urban fringe. First, sheikhs who came from an Azhari background, and were left in an ideological and cultural vacuum after the Egyptian state abandoned them, therefore, became unable to relate to any cultural project sponsored by the state. These sheikhs found themselves closer to the MB, since its version of *da'wa* stresses the priority of nurturing the individual Muslim gradually and its political agenda is reformist, a version of religious practice that was not difficult to hold in a context where the public sphere was afforded a relative degree of freedom.

The second tendency comprised Salafi sheikhs, who shared much with the Azharis but adopted a more radical stance towards the government and in interpreting *sharia*. However, in many cases the line between the tendencies was blurred. If we scrutinise the rhetoric on both sides, we find that it had no coherent political agenda. Instead, it was a series of condemnations: of the current lifestyle, history, culture and politics, all of which fell under the slogan of 'Islam is the solution'. The only major difference between them was tactical rather than strategic. While the Muslim Brothers (who attracted the Azharis) called for a gradual involvement in politics, Salafists sought to challenge the authoritarian order of politics by imposing themselves immediately.

In Kerdasa, Salah Abu Ismail represented the first tendency, while Ali al-Qinawi represented the second. Abu Ismail was born in the village of Hurmos, near Imbaba. He was arrested in 1954 and 1965 for being a suspected member of the MB, but on the second occasion he was released after a declaration of repentance.[91] In 1972, he was appointed as the chief of staff of Sheikh al-Azhar, a high-profile position that allowed him to be a public figure and to be acknowledged as an Islamic scholar. Being active in the *da'wa*, as a preacher and a *khatib* in Friday prayers, made him a popular sheikh in the region, and he was therefore invited by many Islamic religious, cultural, educational and media institutions in Saudi Arabia, Kuwait, Bahrain and UAE to deliver lectures and religious talks.

By 1976, he had gained enough respect and veneration to be trusted across the whole of Cairo's peri-urban fringe, gaining the support of the local elites of Ausim, where he was elected to parliament, a position he held until his death in 1990. It is said that even the Ausim NDP (especially from the Ghurab family, the local arm of the ruling party in the town) would not think to compete with him but rather supported him as their representative. It is also said that he utilised his relations with various entities in Greater Cairo to employ hundreds from his constituency in private and public foodstuff factories.

From the early 1980s, Abu Ismail became a controversial public figure due to his stance towards the government, as well as the Islamic movement in general. His testimony before a court in 1981 for what was known as the 'al-Jihad Organisation Case',[92] which was published and reprinted several times, became one of the most important references for that decade's Islamists, even though it was no more than a legal testimony.[93] It actually provoked many other senior sheikhs from al-Azhar to respond, since it carried radical interpretations of *sharia*, explicit critiques of the government and implicit sympathy for jihadists. This was despite the fact that Abu Ismail was a member of parliament and a high-profile employee in the state itself. However, given the fact that the 1980s witnessed a degree of tolerance towards political Islam, we can understand how Mubarak's Egypt, in its first decade, stood impotently as it watched Islamisation penetrate sensitive positions that allowed it to reach the public.

From his testimony, one can get an impression of the great esteem and reverence Abu Ismail enjoyed not only from his locality, but also from jihadists behind bars and the court itself. He defended jihadi defendants,[94] promoted the MB's doctrines,[95] accused the government of not being serious in applying *sharia*,[96] and called on people with Islamic backgrounds to run in the parliamentary elections in order to force the state to change secular laws and to adopt an Islamic constitution.[97] It is not difficult, nevertheless, to notice that what provoked Abu Ismail was the proliferation of taboo items. In his testimony, he found it paradoxical that the government, at that time, imposed restrictions on the selling of subsidised meat, which is *halal*, while it did not on the selling of liquor, which is *haram*.[98] Abu Ismail, moreover, was a hard-working MP. Alone, he submitted more than seventy interpellations on various matters and he led many lobby groups inside the parliament to discuss and change several laws to be in harmony with his vision of *sharia*.

For these reasons, Abu Ismail and his followers (who were mostly from the MB) were convinced that a change within the Egyptian government was possible and a clash with the secular state could be avoided. This conclusion made him spontaneously a central figure for hundreds of MB followers who embraced him and promoted his activities, especially as his version of *da'wa* and politics was consistent with the third General Guide Umar al-Tilmisani's vision of public work.[99] Every two months in Kerdasa, Abu Ismail held a popular lecture that was attended by thousands of local people from Greater Cairo. MB followers took on the task of publicising his lectures, roaming the peri-urban fringe with their loudspeakers to invite local people to attend.[100] By the late 1980s, Abu Ismail had become a role model for dozens of Azhari and Ikhwani sheikhs who became active in the *da'wa* movement across the whole peri-urban fringe.

However, Abu Ismail had a relatively pragmatic stance towards the government. In his testimony and ongoing debates with other sheikhs in Greater Cairo's mosques, he refused to declare the infidelity of the government or rulers (*takfir*).[101] This stance was opposed by an emerging Salafi tendency within the *da'wa* movement that considered rulers not Muslims due to their reluctance to enforce *sharia* and for behaviour that, in their opinion, was in contravention of Islam. In the 1980s and 1990s, Ali al-Qinawi, who was a Kerdasian real estate contractor, was the figurehead of this tendency. At that time, al-Qinawi was one of a handful of sheikhs who were specialists in Islamic *'aqīda* (creed) in the Cairo peri-urban fringe. One of his students described him as 'the word of god walking on earth'.[102] His lessons were attended by many individuals who were later to become high-profile consultants for the state. One of these was Ahmed Hulaiel, a former consultant for the Minister of Endowments and Islamic Affairs.[103] Moreover, al-Qinawi was a respected figure in Kerdasa and its surrounding area, where he contributed to the assistance of local people, especially in reconciliation councils.[104]

Khaled Sa'd, his adherent and relative, stressed the importance of the period between 1981 and 1985 in shaping al-Qinawi's thought. In 1981, al-Qinawi was among hundreds who were arrested following the assassination of Sadat. In political prison, from 1981 to 1985, he met Hafiz Salama (one of the leaders of the popular resistance in Suez during the Israeli occupation), whose jihadi ideas had a strong influence on him. He also lived with Abdel Fattah al-Zeini, Hasan Abu al-Ashbal and Abu Ishaq al-Huweini, who had received their theological education from the leading proponents of Wahhabism, Muhammad Nasiruddin al-Albani and Abd al-Aziz ibn Baz.[105]

Unlike Abu Ismail, who was more preoccupied with seeking friends inside the state and behaving as a politician, al-Qinawi chose to work in mosques. His charisma and eloquence as well as his challenging stance towards the government made him popular with a nascent tendency of populist devout youths, who would later become the next generation of populist Salafi sheikhs and the hard-core of the al-Jihad Organisation on the Cairo peri-urban fringe. By the late 1980s, al-Qinawi was delivering five *da'wi* lectures on a weekly basis alongside the Friday *khuṭba*. Furthermore, he encouraged his adherents to install themselves in the mosques of Kerdasa and neighbouring towns. Thus, they became a nuisance to the Azhari faction and the Ikhwan.[106]

While it is said that Abu Ismail and al-Qinawi had a good personal rapport, their followers did not. This may well have been due to the Salafi attitude towards the MB, which accused it of making compromises with the state and ordinary people to attract more followers at the expense of *'aqīda*. Salafists also accused the Ikhwan and the Azharis of misinterpreting the Quran and Sunnah to avoid confronting people and forcing them to comply with *sharia* law. In other words, jihadists advocated an immediate involvement of the *da'wa* movement in politics. In contrast, Ikhwan tried their best to avoid Salafists, not only because their leaders believed that these disputes were self-consuming, but also they thought that their involvement in politics should be gradual to avoid intimidating the Mubarak regime, and, secondly, because the MB historically presented itself as a group for all factions of

Sunni Muslims in Egypt, whether they were Sufis or Salafists.[107] This is why the political knowledge of which the Ikhwan had gained an in-depth experience was merely of a practical and organisational nature. However, Salafists could not be avoided. They always sought out confrontation as they claimed that this was their duty, since they were called upon by god to enjoin good and forbid wrong (*al-amr bi-l-maʿrūf wa-n-nahy ʿan al-munkar*).

In the late 1980s, Ikhwani sheikhs in the *da'wa* movement accused Salafists of being a tool of the regime. Thus, Kerdasa mosques became an arena for serious disputes between the two movements. In many cases, Salafists and Ikhwan engaged in hand-to-hand fighting, as occurred a number of times in the al-Sheikh mosque in the middle of the town in 1990–1.[108] However, if we subject these mosque disputes to scrutiny, it appears that the Ikhwani and Azhari sheikhs had no interest in the Salafi debates themselves. In fact, they rarely engaged the Salafists in debate.[109] They were only worried about being disqualified from teaching religious affairs to lay followers. As Saʿd, who became one of the Salafi sheikhs in the early 1990s, stated: 'Ikhwan and Azharis were never keen to discuss *sharia* issues with us, or what Allah or the prophet Mohammad said, they just wanted to feel free to monopolize mosques' *manābir* (sing. *manbar*, a pulpit).'[110] In other words, the essence of the struggle was the competition over symbolic capital.

The then generation of the al-Jihad Organisation in Kerdasa was inspired by these debates. Mohammad al-Ghizlani, a prominent jihadi leader who was arrested in 1994 and released after the removal of Mubarak in 2011, was one of those for whom these debates sharpened his awareness, according to his own statements.[111] In a context in which sheikhs were competing for mosques, Salafi sheikhs developed an ideology that opposed the reformist methods that were adopted by the MB and Azhari sheikhs. Therefore, the latter were tilting towards adapting to the regime's 'red lines' and being open to the other secular parties in the political arena (i.e., the MB's alliances with the Wafd Party and the SLP). In contrast, the jihadi direction sought to invest in Islamic vanguardism to challenge the authoritarian control over politics; hence, crossing the red line. In other words, jihadists wanted to expand their influence beyond the social spaces of sheikhs and the *da'wa* movement, so would pay the consequent price.

In late 1992, this ideological mobilisation resulted in *al-Jamāʿa al-'islāmiyya* announcing the establishment of the 'Emirate of Imbaba' in the sprawling informal district of Imbaba just north of Cairo. State security forces responded harshly by besieging Imbaba and putting an end to the riot. Between 1994 and 1998, hundreds of youths were arbitrarily arrested in the towns of Cairo's peri-urban fringe.[112] In Kerdasa alone, eighty-eight youths were reportedly arrested and convicted for being members of the Islamic Jihad Organisation. From then on, the role of the Interior Ministry, led by Habib al-Adily (1997–2011), expanded greatly immense in local governance.

After crushing the Imbaba riot, the regime decided to eradicate the *da'wa* movement in Greater Cairo and elsewhere in Egypt under the pretext that *'Ahlī* mosques were a source of *takfiri* thought without distinction between its moderate and radical currents. In Kerdasa, a large security campaign began in 1994 and ended in 1997 by neutralising *'Ahlī* mosques, driving the remaining few Salafists underground, whose activities were thereafter practised on a very small-scale. When al-Adily was appointed as Minister of the Interior in 1997, he employed new tactics to extend the SSIS's domination of mosques in Greater Cairo.

In addition to filtering all *khatib*s and *imam*s and putting them under the scrutiny of the SSIS, he favoured a new strain of Wahhabism that was supportive of autocratic regimes: *Madkhalism*.[113] This version considers obedience to rulers (*waliī al-'amr*) to be a part of worshipping God, regardless of the rulers' cultural and ideological background. By the 2000s, Mohamad Said Raslan, a *Madkhali* sheikh, was backed by the SSIS to fill the vacuum that repression had left in mosques and to defame other *da'wa* tendencies. In the last decade of the Mubarak presidency, Raslan managed to deploy his adherents across the whole region. In the 2000s, the role of *'Ahlī* mosques as an arena of mobilisation waned, but with the rise of other platforms, most importantly Internet forums (and later social media), new methods of resistance and mobilisation were developing.

Conclusion

By the 2000s, Egyptian authoritarianism through its security approach definitively inhibited any alternative local politics that challenged its system of local governance. By alienating the *da'wa* movement and penetrating mosques through a new wave of loyal sheikhs who were backed by the SSIS, it became possible to say that the regime's networks had succeeded in monopolising most aspects of local politics in the towns of the Greater Cairo peri-urban fringe. Kerdasians say that the SSIS, from that time, became involved in most aspects of their lives. It intervened in NDP politics, mosques, sports clubs and schools, preventing any other local agency of suspect loyalty from emerging and forcing Political Islam to migrate to other arenas outside the town such as universities, or to virtual spheres on the Internet.

This led to the ruling party becoming the sole umbrella under which local elites could be involved in local politics. From the early 1990s, Kerdasa's local political notables became aware that there was no way to compete over positions in the political field except through drawing support from the regime's networks, which became more powerful and aggressive. However, as this chapter and the previous one elaborated, although the Egyptian regime was capable of monopolising the politics of local communities, by constantly upgrading the system of local governance, on the one hand, and hindering the development of any alternative arena of local politics, on the other, it lacked the capability to turn this into political hegemony.

The 2000 parliamentary election showed evidence of that. The eradication of *da'wa* networks and alienation of mosques as an arena for political mobilisation did not prevent the advancement of the MB in the general elections, nor did it help the NDP to win its constituencies without vote rigging and arbitrary arrests. As this chapter has explained, the lack of general trust caused a social decapitalisation of the subordinated political field, which made the NDP increasingly out of touch with local communities. Furthermore, the absence of a cultural framework meant that the NDP at the subnational level suffered from a lack of solidarity, which caused a political fragmentation and self-consumption.

From the early 2000s, and with the rise of the political profile of Mubarak's son, the authoritarian regime began a new process of upgrading the NDP to overcome its dilemma. The new reform movement aimed to decentralise the structures of the subnational levels of the party in order to make the political field more competitive, and to enhance its mobilisation functions. Nevertheless, as the next chapter will show, this process deepened the crisis among the party's grassroots and pushed the whole system of local governance deeper into the abyss.

Notes

1. Paul F. Whiteley, 'Economic Growth and Social Capital', *Political Studies* 48(3) (2000): 443–66.
2. Charles Tilly, 'Trust and Rule', *Theory and Society* 33(1) (2004): 1–30.

3. Harris Hyun-Soo Kim, 'Generalised Trust, Institutional Trust and Political Participation: A Cross-National Study of Fourteen Southeast and Central Asian Countries', *Asian Journal of Social Science* 42(6) (2014): 695–721.
4. Bernard Barber, *The Logic and Limits of Trust* (New Brunswick, NJ: Rutgers University Press, 1983), 164–5.
5. Eric M. Uslaner, *The Moral Foundations of Trust* (Cambridge: Cambridge University Press, 2002), 2.
6. Fran Tonkiss, 'Trust, Confidence and Economic Crisis', *Intereconomics* 44(4) (2009): 196–202, 199.
7. Patti Tamara Lenard and David Miller, 'Trust and National Identity', in Eric M. Uslaner (ed.), *The Oxford Handbook of Social and Political Trust* (Oxford: Oxford University Press, 2018), 57–74, 58.
8. Ibid., 58.
9. Francis Fukuyama, 'Social Capital, Civil Society and Development', *Third World Quarterly* 22(1) (2001): 7–20, 11–12.
10. Ibid., 11–12.
11. See, for example, W. Judson Dorman, 'The Politics of Neglect: The Egyptian State in Cairo, 1974–98', PhD dissertation, SOAS, University of London, 2007; Vannetzel, 'The Muslim Brotherhood's "Virtuous Society" and State Developmentalism in Egypt'.
12. David Sims, *Egypt's Desert Dreams: Development or Disaster?* (Cairo: American University in Cairo Press, 2014).
13. Bo Rothstein and Dietlind Stolle, 'The State and Social Capital: An Institutional Theory of Generalized Trust', *Comparative Politics* 40(4) (2008): 441–59.
14. Margaret Levi and Laura Stoker, 'Political Trust and Trustworthiness', *Annual Review of Political Science* 3(1) (2000): 475–507.
15. Martin Shefter, *Political Parties and the State: The American Historical Experience* (Princeton, NJ: Princeton University Press, 1993).
16. On the early history of the Egyptian modern bureaucracy, see Robert F. Hunter, *Egypt under the Khedives, 1805–1879: From Household Government to Modern Bureaucracy* (Cairo: American University in Cairo Press, 1984).
17. On the history of popular politics and Egyptian political parties prior to the July 1952 Free Officers coup, see Marius Deeb, *Party Politics in Egypt: The Wafd and its Rivals, 1919–1939* (London: Ithaca Press, 1979).
18. Asef Bayat, *Life as Politics: How Ordinary People Change the Middle East?* (Amsterdam: Amsterdam University Press, 2010), 78.
19. Which was the case of Morocco, see, for example, Saloua Zerhouni, 'Morocco: Reconciling, Continuity and Change', in Volker Perthes (ed.), *Arab Elites: Negotiating the Politics of Change* (Boulder, CO: Lynne Rienner, 2004), 61.

20. Abu Ismail, *Interview*.
21. Carrie Rosefsky Wickham, *Mobilizing Islam: Religion, Activism, and Political Change in Egypt* (New York: Columbia University Press, 2002), 97–8.
22. Michael Gilsenan, 'Popular Islam and the State in Contemporary Egypt', in Fred Halliday and Hamza Alavi (eds), *State and Ideology in the Middle East and Pakistan* (London: Macmillan Education, 1988), 167–90, 177.
23. Anwar Sadat, *al-Baḥth ʿan al-dhāt: Qiṣat Hayātī* (*In Search of Identity: An Autobiography*) (Cairo: Egyptian Office for Publishing & Distribution, 1979).
24. Gregory Starrett, *Putting Islam to Work: Education, Politics, and Religious Transformation in Egypt* (Berkeley: California University Press, 1998), 63.
25. Bassam Tibi, 'Egypt as a Model of Development for the World of Islam', in Lawrence E. Harrison and Peter L. Berger (eds), *Developing Cultures: Case Studies* (London: Routledge, 2006), 163–80, 166.
26. Saba Mahmood, *Politics of Piety: The Islamic Revival and the Feminist Subject* (Princeton, NJ: Princeton University Press, 2005), 58–9.
27. Ibid.
28. Halim Barakat, *The Arab World: Society, Culture, and State* (Berkeley: California University Press, 1993), 65–70; Ilan Pappé, *The Modern Middle East*, 2 edn (London: Routledge, 2010), 99–100; J. Gulick, 'Village and City: Cultural Continuities in the Twentieth Century', in I. Lapidus (ed.), *Middle Eastern Cities* (Berkeley: California University Press, 1986), 122–58.
29. Raymond Hinnebusch, *The International Politics of the Middle East* (Manchester: Manchester University Press, 2013), 84; Galal Amin, *Whatever Happened to the Egyptians? Changes in Egyptian Society from 1950 to the Present* (Cairo: American University in Cairo Press, 2000).
30. Nazih Ayubi, *Political Islam: Religion and Politics in the Arab World* (London: Routledge, 2003), 114–15.
31. Hinnebusch, *International Politics of the Middle East*, 84.
32. Ibid.
33. Dale Eickelman and James Piscatori, *Muslim Politics* (Princeton, NJ: Princeton University Press, 2004), ch. 2.
34. El-Sadat, *al-Baḥth ʿan al-dhāt*, 288–9.
35. Nadia Ramsis Farah, *Egypt's Political Economy: Power Relations in Development* (Cairo: American University in Cairo Press, 2009), 113.
36. Beverley Milton-Edwards, *Islamic Fundamentalism since 1945* (London: Routledge, 2014), 66.
37. *Al-Jamāʿa al-ʾislāmiyya* was a puritanical Islamic student movement in Egyptian universities that was formed spontaneously in the early 1970s, taking advantage

of Sadat's political semi-liberalisation. The movement in that time had no clear political vision, although it was, as one of its founders Egypt Abdel Moneim abou-el Fotouh stated, a response to the leftist cultural activism on university campuses. In the late 1970s, most of *al-Jamā'a al-'islāmiyya*'s leaders decided to join the MB unconditionally. A few groups in Upper Egypt abstained and formed new militias that confronted the state. Husam Tammam, *'Abd-l-Mun'im Abu-l-Futūḥ: Shāhid 'alā Tārīkh al-Ḥaraka al-'Islāmiyya fī Maṣr 1970–1984* (*Abdel-Moneim Aboul-Fotouh: A Witness of the History of the Islamic Movement in Egypt 1970–1984*) (Cairo: Dar El Shorouk, 2012).

38. Ibid., 23.
39. Ibid., 89–9.
40. Abdel Salam Zaki Bashandi, *Interview*, Khartoum (Sudan), 26 January 2017.
41. Ibid.
42. Ibid.
43. Ibid.
44. Salwa Ismail, *Political Life in Cairo's New Quarters*, xxxviii.
45. Ibid., xvii.
46. Sayed Hussain Zinnari, *Interview*, Istanbul, 4 February 2017.
47. Ibid.
48. Ibid.
49. Ibid.
50. Ibid.
51. Ibid.
52. Ibid.
53. Ahmed Mohammad Ghizlani, *Interview*, 12 April 2016; Moa'taz Mikkawi, *Interview*, Kerdasa, 16 May 2016.
54. Hinnebusch, 'The Reemergence of the Wafd Party', 114. See also Baker, *Sadat and After*, 66–7.
55. Zinnari, *Interview*; Beshendi, *Interview*.
56. Khaled Sa'd, *Interview*, Istanbul, 12 April 2016. It should be mentioned that the Muslim Brotherhood did not strictly enforce any type of organisational hierarchy during Tilmisani's leadership. Salah Abu Ismail provides a notable example here. Although not formally a member of the organisation, Abu Ismail publicly associated himself with the Brotherhood. By the 1990s, however, a structured hierarchy and membership became more important to the Brotherhood.
57. Zinnari, *Interview*; Bashandi, *Interview*.
58. Zinnari, *Interview*.
59. Ahmed Mohammad al-Ghizlani, *Interview*.

60. Annette Ranko, *The Muslim Brotherhood and Its Quest for Hegemony in Egypt: State-discourse and Islamist Counter-discourse* (Hamburg: Springer, 2012), 81.
61. Dina Shehata, *Islamists and Secularists in Egypt: Opposition, Conflict, and Cooperation* (London: Routledge, 2013), 121.
62. Ranko, *The Muslim Brotherhood and Its Quest*, 109.
63. Fahmy, *The Politics of Egypt*, 84.
64. Ranko, *The Muslim Brotherhood and Its Quest*, 109.
65. Vannetzel, 'The Muslim Brotherhood's "Virtuous Society" and State Developmentalism in Egypt'.
66. Mikkawi attitudes towards politics will be discussed in the next chapter.
67. Names are withheld at the request of the interviewees.
68. Chapter 4 will discuss the struggle between two generations of the local NDP (the ASU veterans and the NDP veterans in detail).
69. Zinnari, *Interview*.
70. Vannetzel, 'The Muslim Brotherhood's "Virtuous Society" and State Developmentalism in Egypt', 225.
71. Khalil Al-Anani, *Inside the Muslim Brotherhood: Religion, Identity, and Politics* (Oxford: Oxford University Press, 2016), 119.
72. See, for example, Springborg, *Mubarak's Egypt*, 225; Ayubi, *Political Islam*, 148–50; Alain Roussillon, 'Republican Egypt Interpreted: Revolution and Beyond', in Martin Daly and Carl F. Petry (eds), *The Cambridge History of Egypt* (Cambridge: Cambridge University Press, 1998), 334–93, 375–6.
73. Denis J. Sullivan, 'Extra-State Actors and Privatization in Egypt', in Iliya Harik and Denis J. Sullivan (eds), *Privatization and Liberalization in the Middle East* (Bloomington: Indiana University Press, 1992), 33–42, and *passim*; Denis J. Sullivan, *Private Voluntary Organizations in Egypt: Islamic Development, Private Initiative, and State Control* (Gainesville: University Press of Florida, 1994), 57–98.
74. Ranko, *The Muslim Brotherhood and Its Quest*, 118.
75. Mona Atia, *Building a House in Heaven: Pious Neoliberalism and Islamic Charity in Egypt* (Minneapolis: University of Minnesota Press, 2013), xvii.
76. Ibid.
77. Ibid., 159.
78. Janine A. Clark, *Islam, Charity, and Activism: Middle-Class Networks and Social Welfare in Egypt, Jordan, and Yemen* (Bloomington: Indiana University Press, 2004), 66.
79. Diane Singerman, *Avenues of Participation: Family, Politics, and Networks in Urban Quarters of Cairo* (Princeton, NJ: Princeton University Press, 1995).

80. Manuel Castells and Alejandro Portes, 'World Underneath: The Origins, Dynamics, and Effects of the Informal Economy', in Alejandro Portes, Manuel Castells and Lauren A. Benton (eds), *The Informal Economy: Studies in Advanced and Less Developed Countries* Baltimore, MD: Johns Hopkins University Press, 1989), 12.
81. Salwa Ismail, 'Authoritarian Government, Neoliberalism and Everyday Civilities in Egypt', *Third World Quarterly* 32(5) (2011): 845–62, 858
82. M. H., *Interview*, Kerdasa, 12 May 2016.
83. Ibid.
84. Swartz, *Culture and Power*, 43.
85. Khaled Sa'd, *Interview*.
86. Zouheir Ghazzal, 'The "Ulama": Status and Function', in Youssef Choueiri (ed.), *A Companion to the History of the Middle East* (Oxford: Blackwell, 2005), 71–86, 78–80.
87. Gilsenan, 'Popular Islam', 179.
88. 'Mosque and State in Egypt', *Third World Quarterly* 7(4) (1985): 11–16.
89. On the evolution of Salafi thoughts in Egypt, see Richard Gauvain, *Salafi Ritual Purity: In the Presence of God* (London: Routledge, 2013), 22–51.
90. Khaled Sa'd, *Interview*.
91. *al-Raya Newspaper*, 8 August 2012, available at: http://www.raya.com/home/print/f6451603-4dff-4ca1-9c10-122741d17432/5c3b0966-fad8-484d-9218-fda915c9d023.
92. 'The Case of al-Jihad Organization' was a series of trials that were held after the assassination of Sadat. Over two years, hundreds of people from different locations were called to the court to testify. The State Security Court ruled in 1984 that the confessions of many defendants were obtained through torture, describing the use of torture during interrogation as 'medieval, inappropriate for the modern age, and a violation of human rights and the constitution'. Nathan Brown, *The Rule of Law in the Arab World: Courts in Egypt and the Gulf* (Cambridge: Cambridge University Press, 1997), 98.
93. Salah Abu Ismail, *ash-Shahāda: Shahādat ash-Shaykh Ṣalāh 'Abu 'Ismā'īl fī Qaḍiyyat Tanẓīm al-Jihād* (*The Testimony: The Testimony of Sheikh Salah Abu Ismail on the Case of the Jihad Organization*) (Cairo: Dar al-I'tiṣām, 1984).
94. Ibid., 93–4.
95. Ibid., 43–4.
96. Ibid., 29.
97. Ibid., 66.
98. Ibid., 73.
99. For further details on Tilmisani's role in the MB's political activities in the

1980s, see Alison Pargeter, *The Muslim Brotherhood: From Opposition to Power* (London: Saqi, 2013), 100–1.
100. Sa'd, *Interview.*
101. Abu Ismail, *ash-Shahāda*, 60–1.
102. Sa'd, *Interview.*
103. Ahmed Hulaiel, *Interview.*
104. Hussain Saleh Omar, *Interview*, Istanbul, 11 May 2016.
105. Sa'd, *Interview.*
106. Ibid.
107. Ashraf Rajab, *Interview.* Rajab said that at that time Salafi sheikhs were criticising Azharis and Ikhwan for saying '*ṣadaqa allahu al-'aẓīm*' ('Allah Almighty has spoken the truth') after reading the Quran, claiming that it is *bid'ah* (innovation).
108. Sa'd, *Interview.*
109. Rajab, *Interview.*
110. Sa'd, *Interview.*
111. Mohammad Ghizlani, *Interview*, Istanbul, 21 March 2016 (not to be confused with Mohammad Sayed al-Ghizlani).
112. Kienle, *A Grand Delusion*, 134.
113. *Madkhalism* is a direction within the larger Wahhabi movement based on the writings of Rabee al-Madkhali, a Saudi sheikh who became influential in the 1990s, backed by the Saudis. For further information on the emergence of Madkhalism in Cairo, see Gauvain, *Salafi Ritual Purity*, 43–4.

4

CLANNISM WITHOUT CLANS: LOCAL GOVERNANCE AND THE ASCENDANCE OF KIN-BASED POLITICAL MOBILISATION

One day in 1990, Sheikh Yousef Abdel-Salam Saleh, one of the most respected figures in the Omar family, went to a light-vehicle factory on the edge of Kerdasa. Abdel-Salam Saleh gave a speech to the workers there, in which he claimed that the owner of their small factory was intending to expand one of his construction projects at the expense of the village's cemetery. He warned them that such an act is forbidden in Islam, reminding them that everyone would eventually die and might not find a burial place if they did not prevent this. Abdel-Salam Saleh also went with a delegation to the police station in Imbaba (Kerdasa at this time did not have a station, but rather a police post) and filed a complaint against Ahmad Abdel-Wahhab Mahjoub, the head of the sheikh family and the then head of the local council. He accused him of facilitating the exploitation of a plot of land by a Cairene entrepreneur that was in fact state property.

In the towns of the Greater Cairo peri-urban fringe (and perhaps throughout the whole country), people owe their sense of 'communityness' more to cemeteries than to any other place. In Kerdasa, as with any other community in Egypt, local people are as afraid of being buried alone as they are of living alone. But as Abdel-Wahhab Mahjoub denied the accusation and claimed that he, as the head of the local council, was using a voluntary donation from the businessman to build a wall for the village cemetery,[1] this story may reveal a different side of local politics. As this chapter suggests, this may also reflect the contestation of two generations of local NDP leadership who had different understandings of public work.

The previous chapters addressed the process of upgrading the system of local governance. It has been argued that although the structure of *authority*, represented by the system of local administration, was immune to reform during the era of Mubarak, the upgrading process was accorded to the structure of *power* represented by the regime networks, which led to intergenerational conflict among the NDP grassroots. The previous chapters also elaborated on the dilemma of the NDP, which despite its over-dominance of community politics, especially after crushing the *da'wa* movement in the 1990s, failed to translate it into political hegemony. This chapter will shed a light on the evolution of the strategies that were employed by the local NDP leaders to compete over positions in the formal subordinated political field. While the NDP grassroots generally employed various strategies to consolidate themselves in the power networks, the most prominent strategy local notables used in the towns of the Cairo peri-urban fringe was political clannism and kin-based mobilisation.

The advancement of political clannism from the late-1980s to the early 2000s was an outcome of two interrelated political and socio-economic dynamics. The first is related to the social mobility[2] that took place on Cairo's peri-urban fringe in the 1980s and 1990s, which was reflected in the increasing number of lesser notables who competed for positions in the political field, pushing them to politicise social capital in the battle for recognition. The second dynamic was due to the process of upgrading the system of local governance, which involved strategies of decentralisation to manage patronage networks. The emergence of elections as a market system of managing and decentralising the power networks at the subnational level, pushed local agents to stir up political clannism as an instrument for political mobilisation.

Accordingly, the first part of this chapter will address the dynamics that accelerated social mobility, leading to the emergence of new empowered local elites. The transformation of the local economy in the 1980s on Cairo's peri-urban fringe led to the rise of two waves of empowered lesser notables, which led to a 'glut' in their numbers (many of them came with the flourishing of the real-estate business) and, consequently, a fierce political competition among them over the subordinated formal political field. The second part will examine how clannism was employed and deployed in this struggle.

As will be shown, clannism was often created *ex nihilo*, as many local agents invented an imaginary family history of political involvement to prove their rootedness in their towns, in order to establish an 'authentic' claim to represent the local community. This practice often took recourse in a form of symbolic violence aimed at other families, in an attempt to exclude their agents from the political field. However, with the new decentralisation movement led by Mubarak's son in the early 2000s, the role of political clannism declined, and the road was opened for a new generation of local NDP leaders who lacked the rootedness in their home towns but brought money with them instead.

The Age of Real-estate Contractors

The period from the late 1980s to 2000 marks a watershed in the socio-economic history of Kerdasa. In the early 1980s, Kerdasa was a medium-sized town accommodating a growing society that consisted of a few large families, along with a larger number of medium and small families. According to government statistics, the population of Kerdasa was 32,972.[3] A study of Kerdasa conducted in the early 1980s estimated that agrarian activities constituted approximately 3 per cent of the town's total production and were exclusively dedicated to the production of dates and vegetables to be consumed in Cairo. Land ownership was fragmented, with the vast majority of landowners possessing less than three feddans.[4] The main economic sector in the town was the production of handcrafted items, in connection with which 2,497 families had household looms. Furthermore, there were thirteen medium-scale textile workshops in Kerdasa, whose owners had previously worked in agricultural activities, and who had mostly categorised themselves among low income families before working in this sector.[5] The study also indicated that in the early 1980s, the vast majority of the Kerdasians were born in their town with an annual increase explained by natural growth and with no tendency to emigrate from the town.[6]

From the early 1980s to the early 2000s, two interrelated 'waves' of lesser notables emerged and dominated local economies on Cairo's peri-urban fringe. First, the *infitah* beneficiaries, a broad category that arose as a result of Sadat's open-door policy in the 1970s. This category encompassed small merchants and importers, artisans and tourism operators. The second wave emerged in the late 1980s as a result of the process of urbanisation and the Cairene real-estate boom. It consisted mainly of real-estate contractors and speculators, for whom the *infitah* had also provided an initial impetus.

The first wave had benefited from the oil boom of the 1970s. The rise of external rents (i.e., oil exports, Suez Canal revenues and tourism), as well as emigrant worker remittances, had increased the real income of wide sections of Egyptian society. According to Galal Amin, this boom pushed 'large numbers of the population up the social ladder, who traditionally had belonged to the lowest levels of society and allowed them to compete successfully with sections of the middle class who found their social status rapidly declining'.[7] In Kerdasa, those who invested in tourism-related industries constituted the majority of this segment. It has been stated that the town was receiving around 300–500 tourists on a daily basis at this time, and that 1,000–3,000 tourists were present during the holiday and 'Eid seasons.[8]

The rise of the second wave, as stated, was an effect of the process of urbanisation, especially the Cairene real-estate boom in the late 1980s and above all the early 1990s. Cairo's peri-urban fringe witnessed a rapid phase of urbanisation. This was mainly because it offered a solution to the housing problem in the capital and its suburbs. According to David Sims:

> The main reason for the growing attraction of peri-urban areas can be said to relate to the array of affordable housing solutions that the mainly informal housing markets generate in these areas. Land accessibility and price are conducive to informal settlement creep and infill. Also, since development is largely out of sight, there is less prohibition on building on agricultural land than along the informal fringes of the core agglomeration of Greater Cairo . . . In all of peri-urban Greater Cairo, eighteen village administrative units recorded annual growth rates in excess of 4.2 percent per year in the 1996–2006 decade, and together these units contained a population of 722,000 in 2006.[9]

This led to the social rise of a new real-estate sector within local communities residing on the capital's outskirts, which acquired a new means of accumulating wealth. This second wave can be divided into three interrelated subcategories. The first group was those who had previously been agrarian workers and had retained plots of land (originally designated for agricultural activities), and who suddenly found themselves in possession of valuable assets due to the process of metropolitanisation, having previously been threatened economically due to the decline of the local agricultural sector. The second group was those who had worked in the oil-based states and used their remittances from the late 1970s to invest in the real-estate sector, as a way to secure their savings from inflation. Thirdly, some individuals from the first wave (*infitah* beneficiaries) sought to invest in the emerging sector (in Kerdasa they were a minority).

In Kerdasa, the real-estate business enabled many families to climb the social ladder, such as the Ghizlani, al-A'fifi and al-Sa'idi families.[10] The growth of tourism from the late 1980s also improved the socio-economic situation of a number of medium- and small-sized families, such as Abu Rkissa and Abu Issa, who owned textile workshops on al-Seyahi Street ('Tourist Street', previously named 'Market Street') in the town centre.[11] From the 1990s, however, those who worked in the real-estate business, or in any other sphere related to the construction sector, enjoyed much more prosperity and leeway for development than any other local economic sector.

To explain this further, it is useful to draw a comparison between those who worked in textile manufacturing, on the one hand, and real-estate contractors, on the other. The owners of textile workshops had reasons to fear the regime's networks. They usually earned their living under constant pressure and threats.[12] Since most workshops in Kerdasa, and their labour power, were considered informal and of ambiguous legal status, they usually tended to avoid making trouble with the regime's networks of power. This led them to behave submissively towards many actors in local government, who were often involved in corrupt practices, in return for their silence with regard to any suspicious economic transactions.[13] A large proportion of materials and supplies for this sector were frequently obtained on the black market. Nearly all workshops were illegally based in residential buildings (namely, apartments or stores in residential buildings).[14] Labourers also worked in shifts without any kind of contract and almost without any legal protection.[15] Thus, those who invested in this sector had to avoid the state as much as possible and to safeguard themselves by seeking protection from informal networks inside the state itself.

Furthermore, because textile manufacturing has mainly been based on tourism, as well as the export of textile products to other countries such as the Gulf States, Sudan and southern Europe, investors in this sector often found themselves dependent on the state institutions that control trading and levy taxes.[16] These institutions could easily jeopardise a whole year's production within a workshop if they decided to delay or freeze a certain shipment of products during the tourist season. Finally, and like any economic activity that depends on tourism, textile artisans were largely dependent on the country's stability and security, which required political stability and economic growth in general. For example, Mohammad Azayzeh, who had been the owner of a textile workshop since the late 1970s, stated that sales of textile products fell considerably after the wave of terrorist acts in the 1990s.[17] For these reasons, textile manufacturers rarely participated in any kind of politics, preferring to maintain 'good relations' with actors on all sides of the political spectrum, who are all potential customers.

Real-estate contractors were another important category in the class of lesser notables on Cairo's peri-urban fringe. They had their first impetus from the *infitah,* but flourished from the early 1990s due to the increasing price of land in the Cairene property boom. This boom is said to have doubled the city's size, or at least added land 'equivalent to more than a third of the existing city and suburbs'.[18] Many of the upper classes subsequently abandoned the city to live in gated communities on the outskirts. A large number of residential projects, therefore, have been undertaken. Yet Egypt's observers have been oblivious to the 'collateral impacts' of this phenomenon, not least the fact that these projects actually recruited hundreds of thousands of workers in the construction sector, such as contractors, workers and others from the mining and quarrying sector. Although these jobs were short term, unskilled and an economic cul-de-sac, one should not overlook the consequences of the rise of a new sector in the economy, and the socio-political networks that emerged at both the national and local levels.

Unlike merchants and tourism-dependent craftspeople, who were more vulnerable, real-estate entrepreneurs had a greater leeway for action, making their situation a more comfortable one. However, it should be noted that this 'leeway' was a result of contradictory state regulations and laws that implicitly allowed real-estate contractors not only to pursue informal economic activities, but also to enjoy the protection of the state itself. Since the late 1980s, the vast majority of urban construction has been developed on what had been privately-held agricultural land, and must therefore be considered informal.[19] However, in Cairo's informal areas 'the security of building owners, apartment owners, and apartment renters is remarkably good'.[20] Residents have no reason to fear eviction, 'mainly because the state maintains a policy of providing compensation or alternative accommodation for affected families, regardless of their documented property claims or lack of them'.[21] Therefore, any attempt to clear an informal development would prove practically impossible.

Furthermore, although property owners in informal areas have no 'clear, registered title to their plots of land, this does not at all limit their ability to sell properties at full market values through a number of quasi-legal and informal means',[22] thus prompting their occupants to invest continuously in the development of their properties. Moreover, security of tenure has also been beneficial for the rental of housing units. Both the old and new rent-control systems favour tenants over landlords, even if there is no written rental contract. This has meant that informal urban construction has had to be continuously active, since owners have become increasingly unwilling to lease, preferring to keep their properties empty for the sake of the future (i.e., their offspring), a tendency that also encouraged more development to meet the local need.[23] Hence, 'long live informal real-estate contractors!'

Ironically, the state's tolerance of (or powerlessness towards) informal urbanisation worked to empower sections of the local populace, which later produced emboldened opponents who challenged the regime. As we will see, those who worked in the real-estate business had different attitudes not only towards their local communities, but also towards the state. First, their work allowed them to cultivate connections with various entities and groups at the local and regional levels, including figures in the bureaucracy, as well as to access both formal and informal markets. Secondly, because they were less subordinated to the state agencies, they were more likely to challenge them. Not surprisingly, many Islamists worked in this sector, or at least did so at one stage of their lives.

On Cairo's peri-urban fringe, the construction sector has attracted hundreds of thousands of labourers since the late 1980s. The rapid real-estate expansion in Egypt's desert cities drew in a large number of national and international corporations. The expansion in informal areas and the peri-urban frontier, on the other hand, attracted mainly local small-scale contractors, who managed through their savings, as well as their social relations with local communities, to establish small firms to meet the needs of local expansion. In Kerdasa, many people from different families established construction firms and recruited Kerdasians to work on their projects. The following paragraphs will examine figures from the Omar family, who were involved from the 1980s in the real-estate sector.

The first figure we will consider is Sheikh Mohammad Mahdi Ghizlani of the Omar family, who returned from Kuwait in the late 1980s. Through his personal savings and the support of his family, he established a construction firm, which aimed to accommodate the local expansion of the town. In the 1990s, Kerdasa witnessed an unprecedented expansion in which people started to leave the old town and build on the agricultural land that surrounded it. New neighbourhoods were built to accommodate the population growth and the waves of immigrants, who came mainly from other suburbs in Greater Cairo. Mahdi Ghizlani's firm constructed large parts of the new buildings in the 1990s. As a member of the Omar family, one of the largest *'ā'ilāt* in Kerdasa that has had kinship and marriage relations with other large- and medium-sized families in the town, he was easily able to implement many small-scale projects by utilising his kinship network. Furthermore, because he was involved in the *da'wa* movement, many people considered this to be a sign of honesty (*amana*) and perfect morality. Later, in the late 1990s, he was able to expand his business outside the town to develop other residential projects in the 6th of October City, al-Muqattam and New Cairo City.

As we have seen, working as a contractor in the real-estate sector in the 1990s and 2000s had many advantages. Besides the quick profits and low risks entailed once the initial investment was secured, contractors were able to have access to a wide range of networks from different sectors of society at both local and regional levels. They would usually be open to other entrepreneurs they worked with, as well as hundreds of workers and artisans of different backgrounds. Most importantly, they would have connections to figures from the upper middle class, who often sought small-scale contractors as they were more affordable than the large formal companies. These upper middle-class personages usually came from varying social sectors, such as high-ranking public employees, professionals and employees of international corporations, among others. Such connections were useful as they attracted more customers.

Many small-scale contractors hope to be referred by their upper middle-class customers to other customers by word of mouth. By building a good reputation, they would thereby be able to expand their business. A few of them would parlay their 'important connections' into long-term futures, like Mahdi Ghizlani, who helped his relatives especially, along with friends and Kerdasa's inhabitants (*'ahl al-balad*) generally. In the early 2000s, for example, Mahdi Ghizlani undertook a project to develop a gated neighbourhood in Cairo owned by a Cairene entrepreneur. This entrepreneur was known to have kinship ties with persons high up in the judiciary. Due to these kin relations, he was able to arrange for one of his young relatives in the office of the district attorney to be appointed as a judge. Likewise, he offered his 'free services' to many Kerdasians, most of whom had bureaucratic problems regarding licences of various kinds, and some of whom wanted to be hired by the public sector.[24]

By the mid-1990s, Mahdi Ghizlani had gained the title of *shaykh al-ʿarab*. This informal title refers to any trusted person who is active in solving local problems. It is said that he was called on by families from other towns in the region to settle disputes and hostilities between local people. Thus, he was a 'mediator'. As mentioned in the previous chapters, mediating as a social practice had been the main 'political' role for local figureheads prior to the late 1980s including the first generation of the NDP local leadership (the ASU veterans). However, as previous chapters have shown, local politics changed fundamentally from the late 1980s, and social mediating became less important as a political practice. Sheikh Mahdi would later become, during the January 25 Revolution and afterwards, the head of the Popular Committee in Kerdasa, which administered the town for more than a year (as will be discussed in Chapter 5).

Hajj Hasan Sayed Ghizlani, also from the Omar family, is another figure who exemplified the role of real-estate contractors in Kerdasa, albeit in an indirect way. From the second half of the 1980s, Hajj Hasan became one of the most prominent real-estate entrepreneurs in Kerdasa. He inherited many plots of land in the town and its surrounding areas, and when real-estate prices rose, he started up his business, buying large plots of agricultural land and subdividing them.[25] Hasan Ghizlani's activities were facilitated by legislation passed by the Egyptian parliament in 1981, which excluded agricultural land around cities (adjacent to the urban fabric) from the Protection of Agricultural Land Law (Law 116 of 1983.). Other legislation also revised the law concerning the relations between owners and tenants in these areas. These laws allowed landowners in Kerdasa, and in many towns on Cairo's peri-urban frontier, finally to build on their lands legally. Such areas were desirable to many of the middle class who wanted to settle near their jobs, did not want to live in informal areas, and could not afford to move to the new desert cities.

Hence, those locals fortunate to retain their agricultural land were able to benefit from the new situation. Hajj Hasan was one of them. He was also shrewd enough to realise that the purchase of large parcels of land in order to subdivide and develop them, essentially by providing basic infrastructure and connecting them with the town by proper roads, would attract many of Kerdasa's new families, as well as newcomers from other suburbs in the capital.[26] This practice eventually flourished throughout the whole region and quickly raised the socio-economic level of those who pursued it. As with many real-estate entrepreneurs in the towns of the Greater Cairo peri-urban fringe, Hajj Hasan, who was uneducated and the eldest of his brothers, began to diversify his business. But most importantly, he took on the responsibility of raising, educating and supporting his family.[27]

Hajj Hasan and his doctor brother, Mohammad Sayed Ghizlani, opened a clinic in Kerdasa in the late 1980s. As we saw in Chapter 3, Mohammad Sayed was active in the *da'wa* movement in the late 1970s and early 1980s, and tried to run in the parliamentary elections on the Wafd list. The authoritarian regime, however, by using its local proxies, was able to obstruct the rise of any independent leader (see the previous chapter). Later, in the early 1990s, Mohammad Sayed Ghizlani expanded his clinic into a small hospital with a medical lab, which still serves thousands of townspeople monthly at reasonable prices. His hospital employed more than fifty doctors, nurses and workers. From the mid-1990s, the hospital started to perform complex surgery on a par with any public hospital in Cairo. Although some people interviewed by the author considered Ghizlani's project to be a business investment primarily, many others have promoted it as a semi-charitable institution that serves poor and low-income families (*al-ghalāba*). Ahmad Mohammad, al-Ghizlani's son, told the author that his father was a 'full-time community service worker'.[28]

However, it is not difficult to observe that such projects exist because they target low-income families. A private hospital in a town on Cairo's peri-urban fringe could not have functioned without offering an alternative to the existing public hospital there. While government health institutions are notorious for their poor services, a private hospital would have a very good chance of succeeding if it provided better treatment without charging high prices. These businesses work by seeking to attract those who are not satisfied with public health institutions and cannot afford luxurious hospitals in the capital. Dr Sayed Ghizlani, through his very successful hospital and its services, was able to consolidate his social status to become one of the most respected figures in Kerdasa. Before the January 25 Revolution, he had refused to play any role in politics, despite continuous approaches from the MB, who encouraged him to run as a candidate in general elections.[29]

Dr Mohammad would become one of the prominent figures supporting the Popular Committee in Kerdasa in the post-revolutionary period. On 19 September 2013, the Egyptian Security Forces arrested him along with hundreds of other Kerdasians, as will be discussed in Chapter 5. He died in prison as a result of the terrible conditions there. In February 2014, his funeral was attended by thousands of his townspeople and others from nearby towns and villages. Posters of him were circulated and hung on town walls, leading him to be called the 'martyr of Kerdasa' (*shahid* Kerdasa) by many Kerdasians.

Both of the figures examined in this section indicate that there was an association between the rise of a new local elite in Cairo's peri-urban frontier and the prosperity of real-estate businesses in Greater Cairo. In her 2006 study of Bulaq Dakrur, Salwa Ismail suggested that 'merchants and contractors, as a class of lesser notables, are emerging as political actors'.[30] Ismail also predicted that these actors, by virtue of their influence within their communities, would either be co-opted by one of the regime's institutions or that their increasing influence would lead to 'confrontation and clash with state authorities'.[31] Ismail examined the rise of local compacts in one of the largest informal communities in Cairo. As this section will show, my research on Kerdasa, which is one of the largest communities on Cairo's peri-urban frontier, supports Ismail's conclusions.

Nevertheless, Ismail placed both real-estate contractors and merchants in charge of wholesale retailing firms within the same category. My analysis differentiates between these two sectors. The rise of local real-estate contractors in Kerdasa in the late 1980s and 1990s cannot be comprehended without its being placed in a wider socio-economic context. It is the Cairene property boom that has had the greatest impact on shaping the social conditions of rising local elites, and which has most provided a new sector of local communities with the means to acquire wealth and power. The Egyptian capital's natural expansion and the construction of new desert cities not only raised the social level of small landowners on the outskirts, but also elevated small-scale contractors who recruited labourers for construction projects.

The state's amendments to building legislation also played a vital role, since this allowed local contractors to establish their firms legally, facilitating the transfer of capital from the old socio-economic strata to a new segment that was lucky enough to keep its agricultural land or to invest in the purchase of new land. Finally, the real-estate sector generated its own 'political economy', in which contractors found themselves inevitably mediating between various segments of society, which enabled them to penetrate different networks: formal and informal, inside and outside the state, on both local and national levels.

This is not to say, however, that social conditions and social statuses were enough per se to drive social agents into politics. It only enhances social actors' opportunities in the political process once the structure of opportunity changes to allow new political actors to emerge. Chapter 5 will show how this segment came to play a critical role after the revolution, but for now, we will trace how intensification of social mobility led by the early 1990s to a 'glut' of lesser notables, who considered themselves eligible to compete in the political field. The increase in the number of empowered lesser notables who competed over few positions in the political field pushed them to employ strategies in the battle for recognition. One of the most prominent strategies was political clannism.

Many Lesser Notables, Few Positions and Blurred Clans

It is widely agreed that kin-based networks have played an important role in Egyptian local politics, particularly in local mobilisation and electoral politics. On the eve of every parliamentary election, dozens of reports and analyses appear that discuss the way in which the regime induces its local proxies, in rural and peri-urban settings, to mobilise their *'ā'ilāt* to vote on its behalf. It has usually been stressed that 'moving to a candidate-centric system and eliminating the requirement of party nomination meant that many of the largest kin networks suddenly found the costs of participating in electoral politics dramatically lowered'.[32] Many of these analyses have been based on the long-standing presumption that social identity in Egypt has been closely linked to 'status in the network of kin relations' and that the 'socialization of children [has] emphasized integration among their kin group'.[33]

Research on informality has also been based heavily on the political potential of family networks, whereby familial ethos has been viewed as a 'subaltern counterpublic' alternative to the western 'civil society'. Familial structures in the *sha'bi* (popular) quarters, according to Diane Singerman, have been used by people to set up informal socio-economic institutions that parallel those in the formal sector. Not only do these structures aim to maintain service distribution channels, they are also a tool of political participation that *sha'bi* people use to temporise, evade and curb bureaucracy.[34]

A consideration of the politics of kinship networks is essential to understanding the contemporary forms of local socio-political mobilisation in many areas in Egypt, especially in rural and peri-urban settings. However, in the Egyptian context (and perhaps in many areas in the Arab World), scholarship has usually referred to the role of clans and tribes in an ambiguous way. This is because the concept of 'clan' is itself ambiguous and fluid, and theoretically cannot be isolated and extrapolated from its settings, to the extent that made Rodney Needham bluntly state that 'there is no such thing as kinship, and it follows that there can be no such thing as kinship theory'.[35]

Marshall Sahlins defines kinship as 'mutuality of being',[36] whether it is 'construed genealogically or may also be constructed socially',[37] and long ago, Maurice Godelier came to the conclusion that the tribe/clan *is* the political and ritual relation that is constructed when a group(s) decides to exercise a 'sort of sovereignty over a territory . . . because the social units sharing the territory are kin groups'.[38] In this sense, the key to understanding tribalism/clannism is not to search for the tribe/clan in itself, but rather to look for the power relations it represents. Godelier's research was focused on what can be described as a tribal society. Nevertheless, he asserted that no society can be kin-based. On the other hand, the societies of the Cairo peri-urban fringe have had differing structures. They are far from being exclusively clan-based. In fact, as this analysis will show, clans were not politically important in Kerdasa, at least from the early nineteenth century.

Political clannism on Cairo's peri-urban fringe should be viewed as an outcome of two processes. The first is related to the development of the system of local governance, one aspect of which was the emergence and the consolidation of elections as a market system of managing and decentralising the NDP grassroots and the regime's networks at the subnational level. The second process was the increase in number of empowered lesser notables as a result of the transformation of local economies, as was described in the previous section. The interaction of both processes led to the ascendance of political clannism among the NDP grassroots as a *strategy* in the struggle over the political field.

Bourdieu considers strategies to be an expression of 'practical sense, of a particular social game',[39] by which social agents, individually or collectively, defend their positions, 'imposing principles of hierarchization' that favour them.[40] In the towns of the Cairo peri-urban fringe, clannism was the most prominent strategy to be used by local agents in the political field.

The phenomenon of clannism, however, should be disassociated from that of clans. Clannism is a strategy that involves, first, the claiming of a history of an 'imaginary clan' that could be interpreted as a history of the local community. Secondly, it involves a symbolic violence that aims to exclude 'others' from being recognised as representatives of the local community. Thus, while clans on Cairo's peri-urban fringe had blurred structures, clannism, as will be shown in this section, has been very much a concrete reality. Succinctly, what we find is clannism without clans.

Clannism without Clans

As mentioned in Chapter 1, Kerdasa had been a merchant community from – at least – the late eighteenth century, taking advantage of its location as a station for serving the trade routes between the Maghreb, Siwa Oasis, and the rest of Egypt to the east and south, marking 'the limit of Egypt on the west and the beginning of Barbary'.[41] Kerdasa was just one in a network of centres that controlled the trade route, based on a complex form of local agreements that involved nomadic tribes and backed by the Mamluks. The German explorer, Frederick Hornemann, was one of the first Europeans to accompany the caravan trade journey from Kerdasa to Siwa in 1797. He stated that the merchants owned a home at each of the trading centres within this network, with many of them having 'a wife and family establishment at each of these houses; and others take a wife for the time, if the stay of the caravan is longer than usual'.[42]

In observing 'the general character' of these communities, Hornemann said, he could not but express a sense of 'degradation, self-interestedness, and mean and shuffling disposition, derived from early habits of petty trade, and the manner in which it was conducted, as contradistinguishing those engaged in this traffic, and those who remained at home'.[43] Such a description is quite consistent with his vision of Egypt as 'the land of infidels'.[44] Nevertheless, to have more than one commercial base in the region suggests that the merchants depended on a socio-political structure that crossed kinship boundaries. Wider compacts and alliances among various groups and territories were needed and might have undermined clan-based mobilisation.

Until 1812, Kerdasa, among other villages in the rural hinterland, was ruled by Mohammad Ali Mikkawi, whose offspring, as Ali Pasha Mubārak informs us, were given luxurious houses and palm orchards. However, Mikkawi's rule was too complex to be considered clan-based. His power was that of a merchant-ruler in the age of merchants. He was one part of a regional network and his power can be explained by what we would now call 'geopolitics'. Nevertheless, the Mikkawis' so-called glorious history was apparently a rather short story. With the fall of the Mamluks, they were subjected to the Pasha's revenge and were crushed in 1811–12. According to contemporary Mikkawis, many of their forefathers escaped to Upper Egypt, with the ruling members probably finding refuge with their commercial partners in Tripoli.[45] As mentioned in Chapter 1, some of the Mikkawis managed gradually to return to Kerdasa, but they were now almost powerless.

We do not know much regarding the Mikkawis' status from this point until the later part of the century, for written history rarely records the subsequent narrative of the defeated. We do know, however, a great deal about the social history of Egypt, and some very general knowledge about Kerdasa, in this era. In Egypt, we certainly know that local positions, and the role of middlemen generally, were declining in tandem with the consolidation of a modern bureaucratised state. The state was in the process of replacing rural middlemen with a new class of urban-based landowners, who lacked any rootedness in local societies. Local positions, therefore, shrank in size and became restricted to small administrative posts, as represented by the *umda* and more than one *sheikh al-balad*. These appointments were distributed to more than one family as a way of establishing a domestic balance. From 1866, the Mikkawis seized the *umda* position in Kerdasa, while the *sheikh al-balad* positions were distributed among the other families, mainly the Omars. Nevertheless, these posts were also declining to the extent that in royal Egypt it was not uncommon to find impoverished *umdas* in many Egyptian villages.

Based on written records, we can conclude that political clannism had barely any history in Kerdasa until the early twentieth century. In fact, there is also no evidence that kin-based mobilisation played a significant political role afterwards. From the early nineteenth century, the town was not isolated from the external world. Many travellers and missionaries visited Kerdasa, especially from the mid-nineteenth century. One of those travellers, G. W. Murray, wrote a book on nomadic tribes in Egypt and Libya. He indicated that the Mujabra tribes, who had been based in Cyrenaica (the eastern coastal region of Libya and later in Siwa), had been 'active slave-traders, and a small colony of them exist[ed] at Kerdasa'.[46] The Mujabra, who had been 'the merchant princes of the Libyan Desert',[47] had disappeared from the hinterlands probably in tandem with the rise of Mohammad Ali Pasha.[48]

Thus, no one in early twentieth-century Kerdasa could assume any connection with them. This is supported by the observations of another European traveller in the early 1880s, who saw that many of Kerdasa's inhabitants were preoccupied with 'cutting flints for the primitive guns'.[49] This practice could be explained as belonging to the new occupations that accompanied the emergence of modern warfare. The age of the modern state had taken control.

Perhaps the richest description of Kerdasa on the eve of the twentieth century came from the German missionary, Karl Kumm, the founder of the Sudan United Mission, who lived in the town for two years from 1898, during which he learned Arabic.[50] Kumm lived with the Kerdasians, dressed and ate like them, and even wore a *tarbush* (the felt cap that became emblematic of Egyptian *effendis*) and *gallabiyya* (the traditional long robe worn by men, particularly in rural areas). He was hosted by many of them, notably the *umda* and his family (the Mikkawis). In one of his reports to the Mission in Sudan, Kumm gave a detailed account of local habits, food and economics, among other features. He stated that the town contained 1,500 inhabitants, most of whom were Muslims except for a few Coptic families. Kumm accompanied a caravan to the desert, where he met many Bedouin and learned the desert culture. Finally, he claimed in one of his reports that he had managed in the last two weeks of his stay to treat twenty *fellahin* on a daily basis. However, Kumm's reports do not contain a single word to suggest that clans played a political role in Kerdasa.[51]

Although Kerdasa had lost the political status that it once had in the era prior to the modern state, its local economy continued to adapt and evolve, mainly due to its location near Cairo. The development of a service market increasingly undermined landowners and allowed other groups to rise up socially. For instance, a government survey in 1925 indicated that Kerdasa was 'quite a centre for weaving, apparently having 920 looms at work'.[52] It was also reported by an American botanist, who visited Kerdasa in 1921, that the town had nearly 20,000 date palms, taking advantage of the Nile flood basin.[53] In consequence, unlike most villages in rural Egypt, Kerdasa witnessed a relatively plural degree of prosperity, in which many of its local inhabitants had better educational prospects. In the second half of the nineteenth century, many families were able to send their children to the *kuttāb* (pl. *katātīb*), where they were taught a basic level of reading and writing, and adults were instructed in religious affairs.[54] However, this was not unusual since most Egyptian villages had this kind of traditional institution. What was peculiar was that many locals from various families became sheikhs, who were regarded by local people as scholars.[55] This is one of the reasons that might explain why many families in Kerdasa today have Sheikh as their surname (keep this in mind, we will need it later).

The title of sheikh was not restricted to those of religious status, but was also a social honorific.[56] This suggests that in villages like Kerdasa, the acquisition of social and cultural capital was possible for a much wider range of people than in the typical village in the remote countryside. Obtaining social and cultural capital later on in royal Egypt was also possible, since many were able to receive an Azhari education or a modern one, and were able to work in the public sector in the city, which was also considered prestigious. However, because 'local politics', in a developed form, was not yet possible, such cultural, social and economic capital could not yet be converted into political capital. This conversion would become possible with the development of the system of local governance which entailed a market-style management of local elites.

Clan-based political mobilisation was also not apparent in late royal Egypt, or in the Nasser and Sadat eras. As we saw in Chapter 1, Mahmoud Fahmi Mikkawi was not elected to parliament because of his family, but due to his relations with the palace and his title as a pasha. However, he was also European-educated and was able to draw on his personal resources to develop his home town and create interest-based alliances. In fact, we know from contemporary Mikkawis that Mahmoud Fahmi was often criticised by his extended family for wasting his resources on building a symbolic legacy. Mahmoud Fahmi was behaving as a pasha by the standards of his time. He was a man driven by concern for his 'nobility',[57] which meant in part by the cultural values of the old upper class that focused on legacy at the expense of wealth.[58] The pasha was expected to have generous manners and to be remembered for his endowments to *waqf* and local communities. The pasha should behave as a pasha and he should pay for this. In Bourdieu's terms, Mahmood Pasha was buying social capital with economic capital.

In the Nasser period, there is also no evidence that clan-based political mobilisation was significant in Kerdasa. In fact, due to the regime's socialist policies, which aimed to neutralise traditional power in the countryside, bureaucratic sprawl impinged on local communities in such a way as to reduce the need for primordial associations.[59] In 1964, the government issued Law 59 of 1964, which prohibited the occupying of administrative posts by more than one family member and relatives of *umdas* were also prohibited from taking up the office of sheikh.[60] By the late 1960s, the new political system, including local administrative units and the local ASU branches, largely undermined any assumed political role for kinship-based structures.

As for the late Sadat and early Mubarak period, we have a survey conducted between late 1978 and 1980 that indicates how positions in the local council were distributed. Those elected (namely, Kerdasians) were twelve members from eleven families.[61] The head of the local council was Mahmood Fahmi Mikkawi,[62] who, in addition to his impressive legacy in the town, was also a figurehead in the ASU at the national level. Hence, there is no reason to assume that the then local council was based on clan-based distribution. Nevertheless, as was mentioned in Chapter 2, a few elected members seemed to be taking the new local council seriously in the late 1970s and early 1980s.

Political clannism in the modern political sphere, however, began to become evident from the late-1980s following the upgrading of the system of local governance, which entailed decentralisation strategies such as liberalising elections by the introduction of a candidate-centric electoral system and the gradual shifting of Egypt's political economic agenda that required the mobilisation of local communities to minimise the costs of urban development and public service. These developments led to a competition for positions among newly empowered lesser notables who rose in number due to the transformation of local economies. Therefore, people in the towns of the Cairo peri-urban fringe became familiar with kin-based political mobilisation, in which local notables made efforts to politicise social capital in order to cultivate the grassroots through their kinship networks.

Political clannism was also accompanied by a tendency to politicise social spaces as a strategy to claim a 'genuine' history in the town. In Kerdasa, people experienced a new division that had never before existed in political practice, one that articulated lived spaces with clannism. Many members of the Omar family started to emphasise a division between *baḥrī* (lit. 'sea', but here meaning 'towards the sea') and *qiblī* ('towards the desert'). *Baḥrī* is the western side of the old town, where the Omars have historically lived, while the eastern side (*qiblī*) has been historically the home of the Mikkawis. However, this division has become anachronistic due to the town's expansion, in which the movement of people has blurred any imagined borders.[63]

The Mikkawis, however, were not interested in playing this game. First, because they were a minority. Many of them had moved to other parts of the country for their own reasons, one of which was that they were losing their attachment to the town, especially after the selling of their land by Mahmood Fahmi Mikkawi (it is no wonder that Mahmood Fahmi was retrospectively criticised by his relatives). The logic of the landownership economy in the monarchical era was not to think of investing in another sector of Kerdasa, as many families had done.[64] Secondly, they did not feel that clannism would be useful to them. Despite the legacy earned by Mahmood Fahmi, the history of the Mikkawi family was not perceived by many locals as a glorious one, but rather as a history of exploitation and repression, especially after the July 1952 Revolution, which built its legitimacy on the stigmatisation of the old rural elites.

In fact, many Kerdasians to this day circulate stories of the cruel way that Mikkawis in the monarchical era treated many *fellahin* (it might be why many Mikkawis had left their home town). These stories were frequently invoked, but were extensively recounted during two main periods. The first was the early twentieth century, when new families who had been socio-economically impoverished and exploited in the previous century were able to climb the social ladder to become peers to many of the Mikkawis, leading to small disputes in which the history of the Mikkawis' exploitation of the people when in power was often stated publicly (see Chapter 1). The second period was the 1980s, when many of the Omars sought to draw on clannism, claiming a brave history of confronting the Mikkawis, as will be discussed in the following section.

Ironically, the Mikkawis, the only family with an actual history of a connected and settled lineage in Kerdasa, at least from the early nineteenth century, had no interest in claiming their 'originality' to the town in the 1980s. Their past was not helpful. In the 1980s, none of the Mikkawis thought to use clannism as a strategy to compete over the political field, while figures from other families, who *ex nihilo* created 'imagined' lineages, extensively utilised it in the battle for representation. This suggests that, within Kerdasa, clannism has only ever functioned successfully in ideological terms, often by reference to an imaginary, fictional past. A 'real' history of clannism would function the same way. Clannism is here contingent on a past that predates the clans; 'clans' and 'clannism' serve to contradict each other historically. This is, however, an abstract argument. What is less abstract is that clannism should be dissociated from the idea of actual clans to be understood. Clannism is a modern strategy that emerges in a specific period when social agents (individuals or groups), in the context of their struggle over the political field, recall imagined clans or an imagined history of kin-based solidarities. The following section will demonstrate this idea, with a focus on two examples in Kerdasa: the Omars and the Sheikhs.

The Omars

Yousef Abdel-Salam Saleh, the central figure among the Omars in the 1980s, has appeared twice before in this book. In Chapter 2, we saw how he represented the first generation of the NDP local leadership, who were faced from the late 1980s by a new generation who stood for a new trend in local politics, one that was influenced by expanding the boundaries of the political field as a result of upgrading the system of local governance. He also appeared in Chapter 3, offering protection for Islamic activists from the *da'wa* movement, and enabling to them hold activities in Kerdasa. In this section we will examine how he became the most respected figure in the Omar *a'aila*. He has become regarded retrospectively by many Omars as the person who has most represented their claims, in an established political role, in the whole history of Kerdasa.

The rise of the 'actual' Yousef Abdel-Salam, however, could be attributed to a broader historical process that took place in the towns of the Cairo peri-urban fringe. This was due to the social rise in Egypt of a class of lesser notables in the post-1952 era generally.[65] Nevertheless, on Cairo's outskirts it was also due to the relative prosperity that had emerged prior to that, as we have seen, which increased the opportunity for many locals to be educated and to work in the public sector, thus obtaining social and economic capital. In Kerdasa, many families were able from the early twentieth century to buy plots of land from the Mikkawis. These were, as we have noted, mainly used for growing date palms and vegetables to accommodate the needs of Cairo.

Abdel-Salam, Yousef's father, was at the head of one of those families. Yousef Abdel-Salam was born in 1929. According to his son, in the 1950s he was able to diversify his business, at a time when he worked in the construction sector, and in the 1960s held a position within the local unit in Kerdasa.[66] Yousef was also a local leader in the ASU in the 1950s and 1960s.[67] He was one of the village youths who was selected on behalf of the *fellahin* when Nasserist policies were oriented towards benefitting and mobilising small landowners.

By the 1970s, Yousef had become one of the most respected figures in the town. By the early 1980s, he had become the local secretary general of the NDP, the head of the town's sports club, and the second person to be elected as the head of the local council after Mahmoud Fahmi Mikkawi. However, the role played by Yousef in his locality might be categorised as that which any 'mediator' might be expected to perform. The definition of local politics in this time was not yet developed enough to allow him to progress beyond that role. Hence, from the 1970s, Yousef became known as Sheikh Yousef. The title of 'sheikh', in this context, did not refer to a religious status, but rather to *Sheikh al-Arab*, a person who was trusted in his locality to act as a mediator. Such a person was eligible to set up reconciliation councils (*majalis al-sulh* or *majalis al-arab*), and to resolve disputes and hostilities between townspeople and sometimes members of the same family. Most disputes were over money, such as the distribution of inheritance (especially land), or settlements between partners in a workshop. Sheikh Yousef also at times solved problems relating to crimes such as fights between families, robberies and even homicide.[68]

Traditional courts and customary law (*'urf*) are still widespread in both Upper and Lower Egypt, and in most cases informally acknowledged by the formal authorities. Many accounts have considered this to be an indicator of the communal tendency to keep the state out of local affairs.[69] In this matter, the state is considered an 'outsider', which does not have the necessary experience to solve local problems.[70] In his ethnographic account of the district of Idfu in Upper Egypt, Nielsen has argued that customary law reflects 'the predominance of the oral over the written in legal matters under Islamic jurisprudence'.[71] This is despite the fact that the Quran and Islamic jurisprudence (*Fiqh*) explicitly stipulate the necessity of writing down debts and contracts. Nevertheless, Nielsen also points to other reasons that lie behind customary law, such as the local tendency to emulate official administrative procedures. This was facilitated by the slow procedures that mar the Egyptian legal system, which delay work on cases that need to be settled urgently before they escalate into large-scale feuds between two or more families. However, Nielsen observed that many people who might choose to go to the *majlis al-sulh* to handle some cases might also prefer to stand before an official court in other cases.[72]

In this sense, local notables such as Sheikh Yousef were expected by their communities to apply customary law. Also as Sheikh Yousef, in the 1970s, was a figurehead in the local ASU, it can also be suggested that this is what the state expected him to do. However, after upgrading the system of local governance, the application of *'urf* has become just one role among several played by local figureheads. From the late 1980s, their role was fundamentally transformed as Chapter 2 showed, and they assumed functions that had previously been considered above their predecessors' station. This did not mean that customary law disappeared, but rather that many 'respected people' became eligible for the role especially after the rise of *da'wa* movement, which also produced locally renowned personalities, as we saw in Chapter 3. In 1991, Sheikh Yousef died in a car accident while travelling from Egypt to Libya, after he had lost the presidency of the local council to Mohammad Abdel Wahhab. The death was a shock for the people of Kerdasa. As a result, members of the Kerdasa Sports Club decided to name a new football stadium in the town after him.

As can be observed, Sheikh Yousef did not obtain his status from his family. Neither did he need a kin-based mobilisation to gain his townspeople's respect. We know, furthermore, that his relations with Mahmood Fahmi Mikkawi were very good. They not only worked together in the local council, but Sheikh Yousef was also elected chairman of the local sports club that had been established by Mahmood Fahmi. Yousef achieved his legacy perhaps because he was a self-made man, perhaps due to his history in the ASU, or his charisma or perhaps all of these together – but his social status could not be attributed to his family, which he did not need. However, Sheikh Yousef would be portrayed after his death by many of his siblings as Yousef Abdel-Salam Saleh-Omar.

Prior to this time, Kerdasians did not use the name *'ā'ilā* (clan) to identify a person, but rather just the branch name. This is probably because most people who belonged to small-and medium-size families did not know their clans' names or did not care to know. On the other hand, those who came from relatively old and established kinships and knew their clan names were not in the habit of using them. This is because it was quite odd for people to identify themselves with three middle names instead of two. Furthermore, the government system for identity cards requires just four names and the vast majority of formal transactions that require forms do not have room for a fifth.

It is worth mentioning, nevertheless, that there had been an earlier tendency that led people, from the early twentieth century at least, to avoid using their clan names. In communities that were trade-based, many people were keen to be identified by names deriving from their occupation or social status, rather than to be affiliated with a group of hundreds who shared nothing beyond kinship relations.[73] For example, Ghizlani is a family name in Kerdasa, which is a branch of the Omar *'ā'ilā*.[74] Ghizlani literally means 'weaver', therefore, it is probable that it referred to a famous weaver from the Omar family who later became known by his occupation. The Ghizlani family today consists of hundreds of members, many of whom do stress their descent from the Omars.

The tendency to emphasise clan affiliation began in the late 1980s. This was again due to the intense competition in the local political field after the region witnessed a 'glut' of empowered lesser notables. Politicising social capital, therefore, emerged as a strategy that could be used by local social agents to utilise the potential grassroots that might be mobilised. In Kerdasa, one of its most important impacts was on local terminology, as many townspeople started to use the name of their *'ā'ilā* as a surname (*'ā'ilā* literally means family but actually refers to a clan that compromises many families). Prior to that, the common term used locally had been *dār* (pl. *dūr*), which literally means household but locally refers to the branch. For instance, as we have seen, both the Saleh and Ghizlani families are branches of the Omar clan. While, prior to the late 1980s, local people had referred to themselves separately as *dār* Saleh and *dār* Ghizlani, from the late 1980s it became not uncommon to attribute members of both families to *'ā'ilāt* Omar.

Thus, in the 1990s, Sheikh Yousef's legacy was represented by many of the Omars as belonging to their legacy as a whole clan. Stories of the Omars' history in confronting the Mikkawis' repressive measures in the monarchical era were extensively circulated among the new generation of Omars. Not only did this strategy aim to conjure up an overall historical narrative of the clan that integrated the stories of small disputes from the royal era,[75] but it also involved a form of symbolic violence against potential competitors in the Mikkawi family. The latter could not in turn use clannism as a strategy, for the reasons discussed in the previous section.

For example, it was claimed that al-Haswaya, a neighbourhood on the *baḥarī* side of the old town, was the original centre of Kerdasa. This was the neighbourhood in which the Omars had historically lived and worked. It possessed a mosque and a *kuttāb*, both bearing the name 'Qasim'. In the royal era the *kuttāb* became a guest house of the same name (*maḍāfa* Qasim), probably as the role of *kuttāb* had declined with the spread of modern education. Next to al-Haswaya is al-Tahuna, which used to be a house that hosted the Omars' social gatherings. Tahuna literally means 'mill', and therefore one can assume that it was originally a building in which grains were milled, before the government subsidised the selling and distribution of bread. However, in the 1990s, al-Tahuna was portrayed as though it had been among the socio-political headquarters of the Omars, in contrast to Duwwār al-Mikkawi, where the *umda*s lived and carried out their work.[76] Lastly, it was also claimed that Sheikh Yousef-Abdel Salam Saleh-Omar was the founder of Kerdasa's sports club. This claim was made despite the fact that inside one of the halls of the club there is a marble plaque commemorating of the club's establishment by Mahmoud Fahmi Mikkawi in 1967.

Was it worth it? After more than two decades, there is no way to determine this precisely. Nevertheless, we know that in 1994, Ibrahim Hussain Saleh-Omar was elected as head of the local council and Abdel-Aziz Saleh-Omar was elected as chairman of the sports club of Kerdasa. Both men had played no role in the political field prior to that.[77] Was the claim driven solely by politics? This, however, was only one of its motivations. The process of self-identification is too complex just to be explained by political motivation, as will be discussed in the next section. However, although political clannism might bring benefits for social agents, it might also cause them problems, especially when one or more members of the family is involved in activities that are considered by the security agencies to be a threat. In this case, the typical response from the SSIS is to consider most of those who belong to the family or its friends as suspicious persons who should be denied any access to most representative positions.

This occasionally happened from the mid-1990s, when members of the Ghizlani family were arrested for being members of the Jihad Organization. Therefore, the SSIS started to become suspicious of the Omars. In 2000, the Egyptian security agencies excluded Ibrahim Hussain Saleh from running in the mid-term election for the local council, most likely because a competitor had informed the SSIS about possible relations between him and the MB. A few years later, Abdel Aziz Saleh was prevented from participating in the Kerdasa Sports Club elections because his son was suspected of being a supporter of the MB. However, this could also be attributed to the growing decision-making role played by the Egyptian security agencies in the 2000s, with the aim of creating a new political atmosphere that might help to groom

Gamal Mubarak as his father's successor as president of Egypt, as will be discussed in the next chapter.

As can be seen in the case of the Omars, clannism in the towns of the Cairo peri-urban fringe may not be understood without an awareness of its relationship to the development of the system of local governance. In essence, it is an attempt to merge the history of the local community with the imagined history of the imagined clan. This is what sometimes made it effective, as it allows local agents to expand their support beyond consanguineous and affinal relations, thus expanding their influence and political-economic scope. It allows them to claim that they are not only representing their 'clans', but also the whole town, its amenities and its cultural and economic institutions.

The Sheikhs

The story of the al-Sheikh *'ā'ilā* can be attributed entirely to one person in Kerdasa: Mohammad Abdel-Wahhab Mahjoub. Mahjoub appeared in Chapter 2 as the representative of a new generation of NDP local leaders, who arrived with a new model of local politics that was influenced by its changing definition. In Chapter 3, we saw how he was considered by many Islamists to be a monitor of their activities for the police, representing a fundamental transformation in the attitude of NDP men towards them. In this section, we will consider him in his role as head of the al-Sheikh *'ā'ilā* and its sole public representative, according to many of the Sheikhs. This is because he was the only person to narrate their story.

We do not know much about the history of the Sheikh family prior to the 1980s. In fact, all my interviewees from this family referred me to Abdel-Wahhab Mahjoub for information concerning their history. We know from different sources, however, that the *dār* of Mahjoub shared extensive affinal relations with the Mikkawis, at least from the royal era. Mahjoub himself, said that he was an assistant to Mahmoud Fahmi Mikkawi and was almost 'adopted' by Nazmi Rashid Mikkawi (the last *umda* in Kerdasa), who supported him when he ran for, and subsequently won, the nomination for presidency of the local council in 1984.[78] As we saw in Chapter 2, Mahjoub's work was impressive. He introduced a new model of public service that went far beyond the traditional role of mediation, as exemplified by his predecessor (Sheikh Yousef). His office in the local council was said to resemble a beehive in its whirl of activity.[79]

Mahjoub was also a steely-eyed man but somewhat rash. He was aware, from the late 1980s, of the advantages of clannism. Therefore, he drew on his relations to issue an identity card that bore 'Mikkawi' as his fifth name (*laqab*), which he also believed genuinely to be the case. Thus, he became for a while, Ahmed Mohammad Abdel-Wahhab Mahjoub al-Mikkawi. He probably thought that being a Mikkawi would improve his chances in the competition for success in the political field. However, the new generation of Mikkawis did not recognise him. They were not interested in playing this game since the Mikkawi clan had acquired a bad reputation, as we have seen. In fact, most Mikkawis were unwilling to revive their family status as they knew this would not be in their interest. Clannism for the Mikkawis, therefore, was anachronistic. But for Mahjoub, the rejection provoked an existential crisis. He called it a *fitna* (sedition).

In my interview with Mahjoub, he insisted that until the mid-1980s, both the Mikkawis and the Sheikhs were one *'ā'ilā*. The person who first established Kerdasa, he said, was Abdel-Rahman al-Sheikh, who belonged to the dynasty of Oqba Ben Nafea' (one of the Prophet Mohammad's companions). Abdel-Rahman al-Sheikh, according to Mahjoub, was the father of thirty-three branches, which became the first community in Kerdasa. As a result, he said, even the Mikkawis themselves are a branch of al-Sheikh, and he called both Mahmoud Fahmi Mikkawi and Nazmi Rashid Mikkawi his uncles.[80] Nevertheless, anyone in Mahjoub's position can theoretically be correct in such claims. Due to the fact that a great number of Kerdasa's families are intertwined and interrelated by marriage over decades, it is not difficult to find a mutual origin that connects several families together as a new reference point.[81]

After what was described by him as *fitna*, Mahjoub had to find his own path to construct a new version of clannism. He managed to form a new 'coalition' of families under the name of the Sheikhs, or as one of the Mikkawis has described it, 'the confederation of al-Sheikh'.[82] By combining five medium-sized families (the Mahjoub, Babah, al-Saber, Haidar and Abu-Taleb), along with other smaller families that have had extensive mutual marriages and affinal relations, he has become the head of one of the largest (and newest) *'ā'ilāt* in Kerdasa. This was possible because many families in Kerdasa could add 'al-Sheikh' after their surnames to become the fifth element.

As we saw previously in this chapter, since many families from the late nineteenth century were able to send their children to the *kuttāb*, the town needed many sheikhs to meet the local demand. The title of sheikh in the Ottoman period, and in the early Mohammad Ali Pasha's state, was also given to 'Chiefs of Crafts' (*ḥiraf*, sing. *ḥirfa*). The Chief of Craft was the man who carried out the registrar's orders and 'summoned the guild notables to set prices of purchase and of sale to the public'.[83] Therefore, many families through the nineteenth and the early twentieth century might have temporarily held 'Sheikh' as a surname before they settled on a new one when their lineage was extended, and at a time when people tended to be more specific in identifying themselves.[84]

It is also worth mentioning that once clannism became pervasive, it tended to create the feeling that everyone should affiliate themselves with a clan. This is one of the hallmarks of the modern age, which has seen a tendency for people to overthink their origins.[85] Hence, in this period, Mahjoub was perhaps proposing a satisfying answer not only for many people, but also for himself. One can also conclude that Mahjoub was not only driven by politics, but also by the need to locate himself and his lineage within a narrative. Hence, Mahjoub was to become Ahmed Mohammad Abdel-Wahhab Mahjoub al-Sheikh.

Even so, it was not so easy to build up a new 'clan' in this relatively contemporary period. Though many people accepted the new clan, many did not, while the vast majority did not care enough to investigate its factual veracity, and therefore let it go.[86] Nevertheless, Mahjoub persisted in his strategy of constructing a legacy for the Sheikhs, and articulated this with the social history of the local community. From his position as the head of the local council, he is said to have utilised his connections with the governorate in order to change the name of a street in the town centre to 'al-Sheikh Street'. He also named a mosque in the street after his 'clan', claiming that these had been their original names for hundreds of years. Mahjoub also claimed that even the Mikkawi *duwwār*, which was the location of the *umda*'s headquarters, had been known in the past as the '*duwwār* of Sheikh', before the Mikkawis changed its name.[87]

As discussed in Chapter 2, Mahjoub contributed to the development of his locality during his term of office. By manoeuvring among various local state institutions in the system of local administration, through his connections with the NDP's business circles and by his employment of clannism to mobilise the grassroots, Mahjoub led many initiatives that were real achievements (*'injāzāt*) for Kerdasa. Furthermore, Mahjoub belonged to a new generation of the NDP, who alienated their predecessors (the ASU veterans) by introducing a new model of public service influenced by the conditions of their era. This was demonstrated by Sheikh Yousef Abdel-Salam Saleh, who in 1989 resigned from his position as the NDP's local secretary general, after Mahjoub had bypassed him by submitting an informal electoral list for the local council, in the name of the ruling party, through back channels. Hajj Mahjoub won the battle, but not without resistance from Sheikh Yousef. Before reaching the end of his life, Sheikh Yousef had been able metaphorically to slap his rival in the face.

The dispute between Abdel-Salam Saleh and Abdel-Wahhab Mahjoub, as described in this chapter's introduction, reveals one aspect of this struggle. Sheikh Yousef was able to force the Giza Governorate to issue an order to remove any construction that had been built on the land of Kerdasa's cemeteries. The havoc that accompanied this case was a source of mental pain for Mahjoub, especially after the death of Sheikh Yousef and the eulogising of him that followed. He was on the verge of quitting politics when he was placated by the governor, who selected him to work in the Governorate of al-Giza's administration, which led him to leave the local council and later return to the town as the local secretary general of the NDP.[88] From then on, he became one of the most important pillars of the NDP in Kerdasa, consequently learning a great deal about electoral politics, especially after the 1995 parliamentary election, when he worked extensively to mobilise backing for the NDP's candidates.[89]

Eventually, Mahjoub sought to take a further step, drawing on years of hard work by running for Kerdasa in the 2000 parliamentary election. However, the Egyptian regime sought to block access to all voting stations in which the MB might do well. Kerdasa's station was one of these, in which Tariq Zaki Mikkawi was running for election on behalf of the Brotherhood. On the day of the election, Mahjoub went to the voting station to protest against the police, where he was physically assaulted by a security officer. As a result, both Mahjoub and Tariq lost the election, leaving the seat to Farida al-Zomor, an NDP figurehead from the town of Nahia. Although the police had illegally closed Kerdasa's voting station, Mahjoub claimed that he had managed to win more than 2,000 votes.[90]

This is a case of the regime's proxies suppressing not just its ideological opponents, but also someone who was supposedly a client of the regime. The instance of Abdel-Wahhab Mahjoub should be situated in a context in which the Egyptian regime from the late 1990s had started to lose control over the continuous rise of empowered lesser notables. It reflects one aspect of the dilemma of the system of local governance on the eve of its second major upgrading movement, in which the NDP subnational level was consumed by the struggle among its networks to the extent that the regime in general elections was employing a security approach against its men. By the early 2000s, the authoritarian regime started a new reform movement on the NDP platform and electoral protocols for nominations of local, district and governorate positions. The new decentralisation strategy weakened the intermediate leadership of the NDP by eliminating the formal nomination and obliging NDP men to compete among themselves in electoral primaries, which allowed the strongest candidates, who were more likely to represent their localities, to win local positions. While the reform movement in some cases enhanced the role of political clannism,[91] in the towns of the Cairo peri-urban fringe, this development undermined it since it allowed newcomers to employ new strategies to compete over the political field through direct connections with the SSIS.

For Abdel-Wahhab Mahjoub, his failure to win a seat in the 2000 election was not, however, the end of his political career. In 2003, when the NDP was about to exclude him from the post of local secretary general, he used what remained of his influence to compel the NDP to divide the position of party secretary of Kerdasa into two secretaries. Henceforth, he had his 'own' secretary. His political career, however, would be ended a year later when the rules of the game were changed and new 'players' imposed by a political decision came to dominate the political field. He was confronted with new 'arrivals' who lacked any rootedness in their communities, but brought money with them instead and the support of the SSIS. In 2004, Ahmad Mohammad Abdel-Wahhab Mahjoub al-Sheikh went into social isolation under the pretext of being unwell and after recovering, he quit politics.

Conclusion

From the late 1980s to the early 2000s, clannism on Cairo's peri-urban fringe was widely employed by the NDP's men as a strategy to defend and improve their positions inside the political field. This chapter has examined the historical context that led local social agents to pursue kin-based mobilisation in their competition for local positions. The first part of this chapter traced back to the rise of two waves of empowered lesser notables from the 1980s, leading to an intense competition for power in local politics. This development prompted social agents to politicise social capital in their competition over the political field. However, as the second part of the chapter showed that clannism cannot be understood without seeing how it has been shaped and influenced by the development of the system of local governance. In Kerdasa, social agents used clannism to claim their rootedness in the town and therefore their entitlement to represent their localities. This is why clannism was not, in essence, trying to claim the history of a lineage, but rather to claim the history of the local community.

What made local agents in Kerdasa employ clannism as a strategy of mobilisation in the first place? They did so because they had tried to participate in politics in other formal and informal ways, but had failed. As we discussed in Chapter 3, the towns of the Cairo peri-urban fringe in the 1980s witnessed different forms of political mobilisation that were eventually suppressed by the regime from the late 1980s. Mohammad Sayed Ghizlani in 1979 was assaulted when he decided to run in the parliamentary elections on the Wafd list. The *da'wa* movement was also subjected to repressive measures and eventually alienated in the late 1990s. The 1990s also witnessed a large security campaign that targeted most Islamists under the pretext of uprooting Jihadists. Kerdasians say that since that time, the SSIS has become involved in almost all aspects of their lives.

Political clannism is a manoeuvring strategy that helped local agents to appear 'neutral' and 'natural' in an authoritarian setting. Since clannism claims to be based on blood relations, it helped social agents and advancing elites to practise politics and to cultivate connections with power centres without coming under suspicion of being affiliated with opposition movements. Clannism was also an efficient way to convince the authoritarian rulers that local agents genuinely represented their local communities. But at the same time, it was also a real strategy of social mobilisation, involving narratives that engaged with people's questions of identity, and, thus, belonged to the larger process of self-identification that has been a characteristic of the modern age.

The role of political clannism on the Cairo peri-urban fringe was to become less important from the early 2000s but was largely undermined by the late 2000s. This was because the regime changed the rules of the game after the rise of Gamal Mubarak. The NDP informally abandoned its semi-democratic procedures, turning its back on Mahjoub's generation. From the mid-2000s, a new wave of NDP rivals came to replace the NDP veterans, who had been more rooted and established in their localities. The new NDP men, by contrast, had little knowledge of their localities; they came only with money. It was a reckless mistake strategically – for which the Egyptian regime would pay dearly in January 2011.

Notes

1. Mahjoub, *Interview*.
2. Galal Amin defines social mobility as 'the degree to which different classes or sections of the population move upward or downward in relation to each other over time, [which is] intimately connected with the most powerful of the social forces that drive us, such as the desire to acquire the esteem and respect of others, the urge to prove oneself superior or to dominate, and the fear of losing any of these'. Amin, *Whatever Happened to Egyptians?*, 4.
3. Hefny, 'Content Analysis for Counselling Meetings Committee', 41.
4. Habashi, 'Social Values', 303–4.
5. Ibid.
6. Ibid., 306.
7. Amin, *Whatever Happened to Egyptians?*, 18. Social status, according to Max Weber, is 'every typical component of the life-fate of men that is determined by a specific, positive or negative, social estimation of honor'. Max Weber, 'Class, Status, Party', in *From Max Weber: Essays in Sociology* (Oxford: Oxford University Press, 1946), 180–95, 186–7.
8. Habashi, 'Social Values', 304–5.
9. Sims, *Understanding Cairo*, 72.
10. Mohammad Azayzeh (textile workshop owner), *Interview*, Kerdasa, 28 May 2016.
11. No data is available for either the real-estate business or the textile industry's activities in Kerdasa since most of these activities are considered informal.
12. Ibid.
13. Ibid.
14. Mohammad Khamis Abu Issa (textile workshop owner), *Interview*, Kerdasa, 12 April 2016.
15. Azayzeh, *Interview*; Abu Issa, *Interview*.
16. Ibid.
17. Ibid.
18. W. J. Dorman, 'Exclusion and Informality: The Praetorian Politics of Land Management in Cairo, Egypt', *International Journal of Urban and Regional Research* 37(5) (2013): 1584–610, 1601.

19. Sims, *Understanding Cairo*, 97.
20. Ibid., 110.
21. Ibid., 110.
22. Ibid., 110.
23. Ibid., 110.
24. Husain Saleh, *Interview*.
25. Ahmad Ghizlani, *Interview*.
26. Ibid.
27. Ibid.
28. Ibid.
29. Ibid.
30. Ismail, *Political Life in Cairo's New Quarters*, 54.
31. Ibid., 52.
32. Tarek Masoud, *Counting Islam: Religion, Class, and Elections in Egypt* (Cambridge: Cambridge University Press, 2014), 69.
33. Hooglund, 'The Society and its Environment', 124.
34. Singerman, *Avenues of Participation*.
35. Rodney Needham, *Remarks and Inventions: Skeptical Essays about Kinship* (Abingdon: Routledge, 2004), 42.
36. Marshall Sahlins, 'What Kinship Is (Part One)', *Journal of the Royal Anthropological Institute* 17(1) (2011): 2–19.
37. Ibid., 3.
38. Maurice Godelier, *The Metamorphoses of Kinship*, trans. Nora Scott (London: Verso, 2011), 39.
39. Pierre Lamaison, 'From Rules to Strategies: An Interview with Pierre Bourdieu', *Cultural Anthropology* 1(1) (1986): 110–20, 112.
40. Bourdieu and Wacquant, *An Invitation to Reflexive Sociology*, 101.
41. Thomas Walker Arnold et al., *The Encyclopaedia of Islam: A Dictionary of the Geography, Ethnography and Biography of the Muhammadan Peoples*, vol. VI (Leiden: E. J. Brill, 1908), 464.
42. Friedrich Conrad Hornemann, *The Journal of Frederick Horneman's Travels, from Cairo to Mourzouk, the Capital of the Kingdom of Fezzan, in Africa, in the Years 1797–8* (London: G. & W. Nicol, 1802), 38–9.
43. Ibid.
44. Ibid., 2.
45. Mo'ataz Mikkawi, *Interview*.
46. G. W. Murray, *Sons of Ishmael: A Study of the Egyptian Bedouin* (London: George Routledge, 1935), 299.
47. Ibid.

48. But even when the Grand Sanusi came to preach in Cyrenaica in the 1840s he found the kind of society where tribes could hardly be political units. According to Evans-Pritchard's *The Sanusi of Cyrenaica*, he found 'a congeries of tribes without law or effective government, for the Turks had little control over the interior, but with like values and habits and a community of life which crossed tribal boundaries'. E. Evans-Pritchard, *The Sanusi of Cyrenaica* (Oxford: Clarendon Press, 1954), 62.
49. K. Baedeker, *Egypt: Handbook for Travelers*, 2nd edn (London: Karl Baedeker Publisher, 1885), 370.
50. Christof Sauer, 'Reaching the Unreached Sudan Belt: Guinness, Kumm and the Sudan-Pionier-Mission', PhD dissertation, University of South Africa, 2001, 98.
51. Ibid., 97–8.
52. '*Nubdha Sinâ'iyya*', in *Sahīfa al-Tijāra*, 4, July 1925, 2. Cited by John Charlcraft, 'The End of Guilds in Egypt: Restructuring Textiles in the Long Nineteenth Century', in Suraiya Faroqhi and Randi Deguilhem (eds), *Crafts and Craftsmen of the Middle East: Fashioning the Individual in the Muslim Mediterranean* (London: I. B. Tauris, 2005), 338–76, 362.
53. S. C. Mason, *Saidy Date of Egypt: A Variety of the First Rank Adapted to Commercial Culture in the United States* (Washington, DC: US Department of Agriculture, 1924), 23.
54. As Lucie Ryzova puts it: 'Religious knowledge taught in the *kuttāb* ought to be understood within the context of relative prosperity, as a form of social capital defined by piety. Sending a child to a *kuttāb* defined a middling ("respectable") social position marking the family as one that has the means to invest into religiously defined culture.' Ryzova, *Age of the Efendiyya*, 107.
55. This also explains why the Grand Sennusi chose to reside in Kerdasa for an unknown period, according to a British intelligence report in 1853. Intelligence Report [January 1853]: Egypt, Volume 1 (Great Britain: War Division, n.d.), 46. The Sennusi also established a *zawya* (monastery) in the town. F. Jong, *Turuq and Turuq-linked Institutions in Nineteenth-Century Egypt: A Historical Study in the Organization Dimensions of Islamic Mysticism* (Leiden: E. J. Brill, 1978), 151.
56. Hamed Ammar, *Growing up in an Egyptian Village: Silwa, Province of Aswan* (London: Routledge, [1954] 2013), 208–9.
57. The pashas' code of morality was observed by Cromer, who compared them with the European nobility, see Earl of Cromer, *Modern Egypt*, 6:222–5.
58. Galal Amin argues that prior to the July 1952 Revolution the old upper class (which mainly consisted of landowners) did not hate the classes beneath them

because they were not afraid of them. The principles of hierarchisation in royal Egypt were established and inherited in such a way that it was unimaginable by both rich and poor that they might exchange positions under any circumstances. In Amin's words, social mobility was highly limited. This social structure over time created a system of values and a form of morality among the old upper class that downplayed economic status and extolled personal legacy. After the revolution, and with the fragmentation of landownership, social mobility was unleashed, and it became imaginable for the classes to exchange positions. Hence, a new system of values emerged whereby hatred did become evident between the new classes. Amin, *Whatever Happened to Egyptians?*

59. On this point, see Harik, 'The Political Mobilization of Peasants', 213–14.
60. Ansari Hamied, *Egypt: The Stalled Society* (New York: SUNY Press, 1986), 90.
61. Hefny, 'Content Analysis for Counselling Meetings Committee', 55.
62. Ibid.
63. It may be confusing, but in many other towns in Egypt, *barī* refers to the north, to the Mediterranean Sea, while *qiblī* refers to the south (Upper Egypt). This could also be applicable to Kerdasa, but after the construction of the Aswan High Dam, Kerdasians started to use *baḥrī* to refer to the new land along the Nile that had become inhabitable. This allowed the expansion of the town to the east, which also increased the opportunity for many families to own plots of land.
64. Mo'ataz Mikkawi, *Interview*.
65. Mohamed Fahmy Menza, 'Neoliberal Reform and Socio-Structural Reconfiguration in Cairo's Popular Quarters: The Rise of the Lesser Notables in Misr Al Qadima', *Mediterranean Politics* 17(3) (2012): 322–39.
66. Mustafa Yousef Abdel-Salam (Yousef Abdel-Salam's son), *Interview*, Kerdasa, 23 April 2016.
67. Ibid.
68. Ibid.
69. For a variety of perspectives on the role of customary law in contemporary and historical contexts within the Arab World, see Baudouin Dupret et al., *Legal Pluralism in the Arab World* (The Hague: Kluwer Law International, 1999).
70. Hans Christian Korsholm Nielsen, 'State and Customary Law in Upper Egypt', *Islamic Law and Society* 13(1) (2006): 123–51.
71. Hans-Christian Korsholm Nielsen, 'Men of Authority – Documents of Authority: Notes on Customary Law in Upper Egypt', in Nicholas S. Hopkins and Kirsten Westergaard (eds), *Directions of Change in Rural Egypt* (Cairo: American University in Cairo Press, 1998), 353–68, 359.
72. Ibid., 359. See also Mohamed Abdo Mahgoub, *Customary Laws and Social*

Order in Arab Society: Socio-Anthropological Field Studies in Egypt (Newcastle: Cambridge Scholars Publishing, 2015), 26.

73. Jacques Berque, *Histoire sociale d'un village égyptien au XXème siècle*, vol. 3 (Paris: Mouton, 1957). Cited by Binder, *In a Moment of Enthusiasm*, 75.
74. The Omars believe that their clan are descendants of the tribe of A'amar in the Arab peninsula from the 1500s. They came to Kerdasa and established two mosques in Darb Omar (now al-Haswaya), one of them being the Qasim Mosque, which is currently in the centre of town. According to them, the Omars were Islamic scholars (*uluma*) who established a religious centre that later evolved to become Kerdasa (different interviews conducted in May 2016). The Omar clan consists of seven families: the Saleh, al-Ghizlani, al-Jamal, Abu-Ghrara, Abu-Zak, al-Asa'al and al-Sayfi.
75. I managed to interview a few elders from Kerdasa who confirmed that during their life they had witnessed many disputes between the Mikkawis and the Omars, but all of these disputes were small and did not evolve to become large-scale disputes between two families. Ismail Abu Hussain, *Interview*, Kerdasa, 12 April 2016; Aysha Ghizlani, *Interview*, Kerdasa, 29 April 2016; Ahmed Hulail, *Interview*, Kerdasa, 24 April 2016.
76. In his study on an Egyptian village in Aswan in the 1940s, Berque considered both the *duwwar* and *madyafa* as symbols of the patriarchal power of rural notability and their social statuses in their villages. Berque, *Histoire sociale d'un village égyptien*, 49–50. Cited in Binder, *In a Moment of Enthusiasm*, 66.
77. Mahjoub, *Interview*.
78. Ibid.
79. Ibid.
80. Ibid.
81. It was long ago established that patrilineal endogamy in the Middle East has rarely been more than an idiom for marrying close and has not been purely based on blood relations (i.e., marrying exclusively from the father's bloodline). In this case, the kinship pattern has always been prone to fissure, resulting in a situation in which everyone has multiple ways of reckoning kinship to everyone else in the group. See Robert F. Murphy and Leonard Kasdan, 'The Structure of Parallel Cousin Marriage', *American Anthropologist* 61(1) (1959): 17–29. The same conclusion can also be drawn with respect to the evolution of tribes and clans in rural and urban settings. Many scholars in the Middle East have stressed that tribes or clans are fluid and hence difficult to conceptualise structurally. They expand and shrink, include and exclude, as they are redefined constantly by social actors.
82. M. M., *Interview*.

83. Pascale Ghazaleh, 'Organizing Labour: Professional Classifications in late Eighteenth to early Nineteenth Century Cairo', in Suraiya Faroqhi and Randi Deguilhem (eds), *Crafts and Craftsmen of the Middle East: Fashioning the Individual in the Muslim Mediterranean* (London: I. B. Tauris, 2005), 235–60, 243.
84. Khaled Abbas, *Interview*, Kerdasa, 4 June 2016.
85. This is also applicable to nationalism and sectarianism. See Benedict Anderson, *Imagined Communities: Reflections on the Origin and Spread of Nationalism* (London: Verso, 1983). On sectarianism and sects, see Azmi Bishara, *aṭ-Ṭā'ifa, aṭ-Ṭā'ifiyya, aṭ-Ṭawā'if al-Mutakhayyala (Sect, Sectarianism, Imagined Sects)* (Doha and Beirut: ACRPS, 2018).
86. To this day, many Kerdasians still question the claimed history of the Sheikhs. Even some of the Sheikhs themselves tell the story with some hesitancy.
87. Different interviews.
88. Mahjoub, *Interview*.
89. Ibid.
90. Ibid.
91. Masoud, *Counting Islam*, ch. 7.

5

SYSTEM COLLAPSED: THE ADVENT OF REVOLUTIONARY LOCAL POLITICS

On 14 August 2013, there was a massacre at the police station in Kerdasa. A group of armed and masked assailants attacked the town's police station firing bullets and rocket-propelled grenades (RPGs). They killed eleven police officers in revenge for the break-up of the Rabia al-Adawiya sit-in, a huge protest camp that had been set up by the MB and its allies against the military coup led by Abdel Fatah al-Sisi and the removal of the elected president Mohammad Morsi. Over the following thirty-five days, the Egyptian press and satellite TV channels produced dozens of reports on the criminality of the people of Kerdasa, accusing them of dealing in arms, committing acts of terrorism and supporting armed groups. In response, many of the families and activists there tried to deny any connection between Kerdasa and the attackers, claiming that 'unknown people' from other towns had committed the massacre.

At dawn on Thursday, 19 September 2013, the operation to storm Kerdasa began. It was broadcast live on television by Egyptian channels in a carnivalesque atmosphere. Tanks and armoured cars surrounded Kerdasa. Over the course of a few hours, thousands of rounds of live ammunition and tear gas canisters were fired. Throughout the day and into the night dozens of homes were raided, their contents smashed and their inhabitants, be they men, women or juveniles, arrested in a humiliating manner. The following day, after Friday prayers, a large number of townspeople came out to condemn the raids. The police and army stationed in the town responded with gunfire and tear gas, leading to the asphyxiation of a number of children.

The media, purged of any semblance of independence, behaved as though the Egyptian army were going to war, rather than targeting a group of citizens for arrest, and inflaming public opinion with imaginary victories over 'enemies' who were most likely innocent. For a week, the homes of respectable local personalities, many of whom were Islamists, were attacked. Videos began circulating of burnt-out homes and the damage caused by the security forces. Anything that could be stolen was taken and the remaining possessions of these households trashed. Hundreds of townspeople of various political affiliations were arrested. According to many Kerdasians, the value of stolen cash and jewellery was estimated to be hundreds of thousands of Egyptian pounds.

Why did all this happen? Based on the theoretical framework proposed in the previous chapters, this chapter is an attempt to understand the underlying logic behind the post-military coup violence in Kerdasa. The August 2013 clashes in Kerdasa appeared to be part of a broader wave of political violence that pervaded many Egyptian cities after the overthrow of Mohammad Morsi in July 2013 and the August 2013 Rabeaa massacre. Thus, the violence has been interpreted as an expression of the struggle between the MB and the deep state. However, this chapter will show that these incidents were also locally driven. They were an expression of the collapse of the system of local governance which led to a power vacuum that was filled by revolutionary community-based organisations.

Nevertheless, an explanation for the August clashes may also require a return to the few years preceding the revolution, when the relationship between authoritarianism and its grassroots was distorted after the system of local governance went through a new process of upgrading which entailed abandoning a whole generation of NDP veterans. Hence, when the January 25 Revolution erupted, the regime found no local allies on the ground to offer assistance. Furthermore, this chapter will trace the emergence of a form of revolutionary local politics, which resulted from the withdrawal of the state's security agencies from the city after the limited clashes that took place on 28 January 2011 (the Friday of Rage). It will also explore the evolution of the relationship between Kerdasa's Popular Committee (PC) (*lajna sha'bya*) and the state's local institutions. While popular committees in many Egyptian cities had been formed spontaneously to protect neighbourhoods from crime and acts of *balṭaja* following the withdrawal of the police, popular committees evolved in the towns of Cairo's peri-urban fringe which saw themselves as representative entities that not only replaced the role played by the local NDP after the latter was politically delegitimised by the revolution, but also they introduced a revolutionary model of local politics that expanded the boundaries of the political field.

On the Eve of a Revolution

The previous chapters of this study proposed that a line could be drawn between two generations of the NDP. The first of these two generations began to decline from the late 1980s. It consisted of ASU veterans whose roles were mainly restricted to mediating between people in their localities and applying customary law. This generation was replaced by a new one that emerged as a result of an upgrading process in the system of local governance that led to changing the definition of local politics and assigned new roles to the local NDP leadership. We refer to this generation as the local NDP veterans. The previous chapters also concluded by stating that the local NDP veterans were later replaced by parachuted-in 'arrivals', who came with the rise of Gamal Mubarak and what has been known in Egypt as the 'money–power marriage'. By the late 2000s, it had become apparent among the NDP grassroots in towns of the Cairo peri-urban fringe that the regime had turned its back on them.

Nonetheless, it is important to shed some light on what was going on within the local NDP on the eve of that development. Local NDP veterans in Kerdasa have stated that in the early 2000s, a procedure was introduced that permitted the creation of new secretaries at the local level.[1] It became possible for any NDP member to apply to establish a new local secretary if he managed to collect 200 letters of attorney (*tawkīlāt*) from registered NDP members, while the NDP upper secretaries became more flexible in approving these applications.[2] As a consequence, it became not unusual to have more than one local secretary general in one town. In Ausim there were four, while in Kerdasa, Abdel-Wahhab Mahjoub managed to have his own secretary. Furthermore, the NDP veterans have stated that after the 2000 parliamentary election a new system was introduced to select the ruling party's candidates for parliamentary and local elections. Thus, the NDP members were to vote secretly in the local Electoral College (*majmaʿ intikhābī*) to choose the party's formal nominees.[3]

The previous chapters suggested that we can view these developments as adaptive mechanisms to manage the competition that ensued among the rising NDP men when they became too abundant in number and to enhance the mobilisation functions of the party's subnational structures. Local NDP veterans have stated that the system of the local Electoral College was fairly respected by the upper level of the ruling party at one time, prior to the 2005 election.[4] In the 2010 election, however, the local figureheads of the NDP enthusiastically mobilised their grassroots, mainly by kin-based means, but the results of the primaries were largely disregarded by the upper levels. The winners were surprised by a parachuting-in of formal candidates who had barely appeared in the primaries.[5] In the 2010 primaries, for instance, Ala'a Wali was chosen by the Electoral College, but the NDP nomination eventually went to Khaled Taiea' who had no chance in the primaries, according to Abdel-Wahhab Mahjoub.[6] Wali resisted by running as an independent, but the election's outcome was predetermined in favour of Taiea'.[7] It is no wonder, then, that the number of 'independent' candidates for the 2010 election was to rise dramatically.

The chaos at the NDP's lower level was explained as an expression of the struggle between the 'old' and the 'new' guard at the upper level, which was widely covered by both the Egyptian media and many academic analyses.[8] Nevertheless, it can also be assumed that in the context of this struggle, a new tendency within the upper level believed that the existing system of containment had been shown to have failed politically. As discussed in Chapter 3, the system's political outcomes were indeed contradictory. While the local NDP branches dominated local politics at the micro level (e.g., villages and towns), the party lacked a cultural framework that could translate political domination into political hegemony at the macro level (i.e., districts and governorates), where it was defeated by the politics of identity. Thus, it may be possible that there was a tendency in the thinking of the 'new' guard to consider it better to recruit supporters selectively in what was believed to be an efficient 'modern' way: through NGOs. For example, Moa'taz Mikkawi was an educated youth and a member of the NDP, who in 2007 was chosen by one of Gamal Mubarak's institutions (the Future Generation Foundation) to become a board member. Within a relatively short period of time, he had acquired further responsibilities in the national Secretariat of the NDP.[9]

Moa'taz stated that one of the local NDP veterans had reported to the SSIS that he was a member of the MB who was trying to infiltrate the NDP with malicious intentions. As a result, Moa'taz was interrogated for hours at the SSIS headquarters in Cairo before he was eventually released. Moa'taz could not understand why a local NDP veteran had made that accusation, especially since he shared no history with him and they belonged to different generations.[10] This story could not be verified, but if true, it might indicate how Gamal Mubarak's NGOs were conceived as dangerous by the local NDP veterans. By the late 2000s, the local NDP veterans found themselves the main victims of the struggle that took place in the upper level. They had to witness their 'unjust' replacement by amateurs with no history of public service. Many of them, as Mahjoub had done relatively early, were to quietly give up. Many others resisted, however, and were consequently subjugated and humiliated, mostly by the security apparatus. But how could the Egyptian authoritarian regime abandon its well-established grassroots in this way? Simply, through reliance on more authoritarian measures.

In the towns of the Cairo peri-urban fringe, the local NDP veterans from the mid-2000s realised that the old system had been substituted by a new informal system of local power in which the SSIS was in charge, and in which *balṭajiyya* frequently appeared to be on the side of the police.[11] *Balṭajiyya* had started to become noticeable in Kerdasa from the mid-1990s. Many Kerdasians saw groups of them hanging around the new mixed-gender business school. The school opened in 1994/5 and received students from the surrounding towns and villages. Thus, this semblance of *balṭajiyya* was associated with the way in which the town was increasingly taking the form of a city. At this time, the *balṭajiyya* were only small groups of street transgressors. But from the mid-2000s, Kerdasians started to notice some of them around the newly established police centre, where they chatted with police officers. They were also extensively used in the 2010 election to block access to voting stations. However, the *balṭajiyya* are too complex to be considered merely as figures exploited by security agents. They deserve a separate analysis.

On the eve of the January Revolution, it seemed to most local NDP veterans that the rules of the game had been changed forever. Local notables could no longer use the same strategies to defend or improve their position in the political field. Most positions had become fully controlled by the SSIS, which rented several apartments in Kerdasa as headquarters. Ironically, while the security intelligence, a few years before, had been oriented towards the NDP's opponents, mainly Islamists, now the local NDP was also targeted. Not only was this mirrored in the general elections, it was also reflected by smaller appointments, such as when both the local council (in 2008) and Kerdasa's sports club (in 2006) came to be headed by figures who had no history of public service and did not belong to large *'ā'ilāt*. This may be one of the reasons behind the dissolution of the local councils in March 2011 (one month after Mubarak's removal), which were considered, according to a judicial decision, 'the foundation of the NDP's power on the basis that they had corrupted the country's political life'.[12]

It is no surprise, then, that during the first days of the revolution, the police in Kerdasa found almost no sympathy among those who should theoretically have been their allies. The 2010 election was the last straw in the detachment of the authoritarian regime from its previously established grassroots. The Egyptian version of authoritarianism was consuming itself and its system of local governance was to collapse in the January 25 Revolution.

Filling the Gap: The Emergence of Revolutionary Local Politics

If there is one day that the Egyptian police will never forget, it must surely be 28 January 2011, later known as the Friday of Rage (*Jum'at al-Ghaḍab*), when for the first time in Egypt's contemporary history the Interior Ministry was literally defeated by hundreds of thousands of angry protesters. Following this event, the security forces 'disappeared' from all the major cities, including Cairo. For most observers then, it was a miracle. This was also how it seemed in Kerdasa when mass demonstrations took place for the first time in the town's history. Thousands of townspeople attacked the police station in the town centre after two protesters (Yousef Anwar Mikkawi and Husam Ahmed Jindi) had been killed by police. As a result, the townspeople stormed the police station, forced the police to evacuate and then destroyed it. The police did not return to the town for another eight months, following mediation by the PC.

As with many urban quarters and towns in Egypt, the police withdrawal from Kerdasa created a security vacuum. For this reason, local groups organised semi-armed popular committees (*lijān sha'biyya*) to protect their neighbourhoods. In Kerdasa, Sheikh Mohammad Mahdi Ghizlani (see Chapter 4) led the PC, which included more than a hundred young people from different families. The PC, which was driven by the revolutionary spirit, had little difficulty in administering the town during the eighteen days of the revolution until Mubarak stepped down. During the following eight months, which was known in the country as the transitional phase (*marḥala intiqāliyya*), the PC refused to allow the police to return without settling the cases of the two victims who had died during the 28 January clashes.

However, while most PCs in Egypt were dissolved spontaneously after the removal of Mubarak, Kerdasa's PC in fact expanded its role to take on the same functions and responsibilities as those previously held by the police and the local NDP in the town. What helped to facilitate this process was the previously mentioned judicial decision in March 2011 that forced the Egyptian government to dissolve local and popular councils. These were the places that usually accommodated the local branches of the NDP. It was believed at this time that the Supreme Council of the Armed Forces (SCAF) was trying to absorb popular anger by scapegoating the NDP and figures from the old regime. But as we saw in the previous section, this was also because these councils were subjected to reconfiguration by SSIS policies that aroused the indignation of the regime's grassroots. At the local level, this move established a power vacuum and allowed many groups in the towns of the Cairo peri-urban fringe and other areas to establish community organisations and govern themselves, especially after the subsequent step of dissolving the NDP itself. As this section will show, Kerdasa's PC during the transitional phase was a structural substitution for the local NDP branch, after the latter had been subjected to a process of marginalisation during the second half of the 2000s, and following the collapse of the subsequent informal system of power led by the SSIS due to the revolution.

As the previous chapters argued, the subnational level of the NDP could be viewed as an informal extension of the SLA. It was contended that both the local ruling party and the SLA were historically constructed to accommodate each other. This is because the Egyptian system of local governance evolved from interaction between the structure of the regime's networks of power and the expansion of state bureaucracy. The system, therefore, embraced two continua: one of centralisation of authority by deconcentrating the state apparatuses; and the other of decentralisation of patronage politics through decentralising the regime's networks. Both worked together to guarantee authoritarian control over constituencies.

However, as we saw in the previous section, while the early 2000's process of upgrading alienated the local NDP on the eve of January 2011, it was the revolution that completely paralysed it and excluded its players from the political field. From 2011, the local NDP was no longer able to assume its

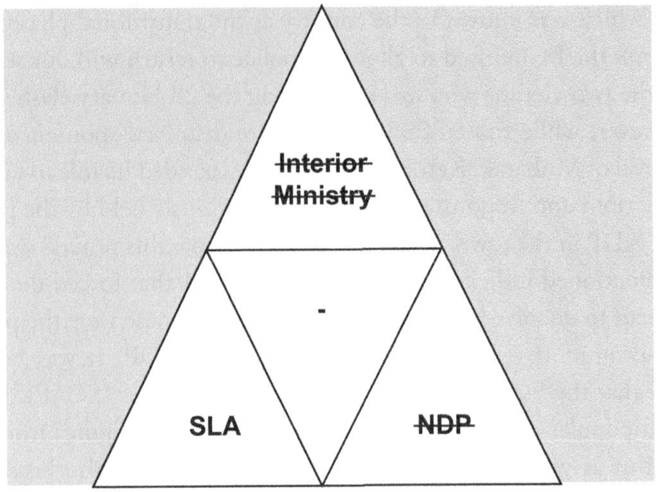

Figure 5.1 The system of local governance after the January 25 Revolution

functions not only due to the revolution, but also by law. Its agents suddenly found themselves with no social or political capital. The authoritarian restrictions on the political field were lifted (for a while) leading to a change in the structure of opportunity, and since many of the previous occupants were excluded, new occupants had to fulfil the vacant positions. Thus, a vacuum was created, which was immediately filled by new players who came to assume and revolutionise functions that had previously been performed by their predecessors. And so, the PC took charge.

The Popular Committee in Charge

From the Friday of Rage until Mohammad Morsi was elected as President of Egypt, Kerdasa was administered by the PC led by Sheikh Mahdi Ghizlani. In March 2011, Mohammad Nasr Ghizlani, a leading figure in the Jihad Organization who was active in the *da'wa* movement, was released from prison along with dozens of other jihadists.[13] The day after his release, Nasr Ghizlani became the vice chairman of the PC, before taking over Sheikh Mahdi's position after the latter's death in February 2013. He and Sheikh Mahdi Ghizlani launched many initiatives aimed at improving public-service delivery in the town. In eight months, from March to November 2011, the committee formed several subcommittees that were responsible for keeping an eye on different aspects of Kerdasa's socio-economic life, such as security, gas and wheat-flour supplies, cleaning, dispute settlements and even removing some illegal constructions.

In the first four months, until June 2011, most efforts were put into creating a kind of 'civilian police' to protect the town and put an end to the acts of *balṭajiyya* that flourished after the revolution. The PC succeeded in preventing many thefts, notably of automobiles. Apprehended criminals were handed over to a police station outside Kerdasa (on the Cairo–Alexandria desert road). Security subcommittees also brought an end to the phenomenon of teenage gangsters who were involved in purse-snatching and begging from townspeople in the streets. Most importantly, the PC led by Mahdi Ghizlani, using *da'wa* and Islamic preaching, invited many *balṭajiyya* to refrain from *balṭaja* acts and to repent to God. A few of them, such as Emad Sa'idi, would join the committee and bring their experience to bear in serving it.[14] On 15 May 2011, for example, a principal of a public school in Kerdasa asked the PC to send a 'force' to secure the examination from bullies.[15] On the eve of the presidential election in May–June 2012, the PC's security team had reached such a level that they were able to provide the police themselves with protection when they came to Kerdasa to take away a criminal arrested by the PC, according to members of the committee.[16]

The PC's services were not restricted to security matters. As mentioned above, another subcommittee was later formed to supervise the supplies of gas and wheat-flour. Dozens of young people volunteered in shifts to watch over government bakeries as well as stores of gas cylinders, the supply of which was notoriously subject to corruption. Members from the PC told the author that they succeeded within a short time in terminating most corruption and monopoly practices with the cooperation of the city council (*majlis al-madīna*).[17] In this period, according to an owner of a propane warehouse (*mustawdaʿ*), the stealing of gas nearly stopped altogether and the price of gas cylinders was strictly fixed at 5 LE, whereas its price had reached 50 LE on the black market.[18] According to Nasr Ghizlani, the PC at that time coordinated with Bassim Odah, who was responsible for the PCs in the al-Giza Governorate (later he would become a Minister of Supply and Interior Trade in the MB's government).[19] By November 2011, according to Ghizlani, the PC claimed that it had fundamentally solved the gas crisis in Kerdasa by prohibiting the selling and buying of gas cylinders on the black market and by coordinating with the Governorate to provide the city with more gas units.[20]

The PC also worked with the city council with regard to facilitating the process of issuing construction and building permits. This process is notorious for its complexity and corruption as well as its time-wasting due to bureaucratically slow procedures. In many cases, the PC succeeded in forcing violators to remove their construction sites from public properties or at least to settle their cases with the city council.[21] For instance, they negotiated with a few squatters who occupied small plots in the town's cemetery.[22] Eventually, they managed to persuade them to leave of their own volition by reminding them that this act is forbidden in *sharia* law (*haram*) and by paying them compensation.[23] Furthermore, the PC used its influence to force the city council itself to replace the building services engineer due to his involvement in receiving bribes from violators.[24]

A subcommittee was also formed to handle customary law issues, and to settle disputes and problems between families. Numerous documents, seen by the author, indicate that the PC was trusted by many townspeople to settle their cases.[25] Finally, it was said that the committee handled the issue of the town's hygiene successfully. Similar to many Egyptian cities and urban quarters following the removal of Mubarak, most of Kerdasa's streets, roads and public facilities were cleaned by groups of volunteers within weeks. Impressively, the PC also convinced the al-Giza Governorate to designate a plot of land in the town to become a garbage dump and recycling centre. It made arrangements with many *zabbālīn* (garbage collectors who make a living by collecting trash door-to-door from the residents and recycle most of it). They also recruited eighteen vans to collect the waste from every place in Kerdasa. Members of the committee told the author that the project was very successful. According to them, not only did it solve the problem of garbage in Kerdasa, it also contributed to the drawing of profits from the recycling process and created job opportunities for many young people.[26]

Independent sources (namely, many Kerdasians to whom I spoke) confirmed these claims and some of the PC's accomplishments were played-out in the Egyptian media.[27] The PC also created a YouTube channel and a Facebook page to show Kerdasians their activities and services. However, there is no way of knowing whether these 'accomplishments' were objectively stated by the leaders and members of the PC, or whether they were exaggerated. Furthermore, we do not know if this kind of civic work was carried out with the same level of enthusiasm that had characterised it immediately after the revolution. What we do know is that the PC considered itself to be the representative of Kerdasa and the guardian of its amenities, as well as its public institutions. In short, as Nasr Ghizlani put it, 'we were almost a self-government'.[28] Moreover, the state (represented by the city council, the Governorate of al-Giza and the Interior Ministry) acknowledged the PC and its claimed status. At least, this is what we can infer from the communications between the PC and the state's institutions.[29]

Given that the Egyptian state is extremely sensitive towards the issue of local governance, to the extent that it has never tolerated any semi-autonomous representative units at the local level, why was it willing to permit an independent entity like the PC in Kerdasa to gradually replace some of its functions locally? The fluidity of the political atmosphere following the revolution made the state's apparatus behave hesitantly towards any kind of popular movement on the peripheries, and their focus was then on inner cities, especially Cairo. However, Kerdasa's PC was aware of the capacity of local entities of the state to manifest hostility towards any kind of power outside the state. Consequently, they were keen to inform the state apparatus of all their activities and to coordinate with them at almost all times. For example, the PC had an IT expert who was responsible for issuing identification cards (with electronic barcodes) to all who volunteered for security subcommittees. All registered names, along with copies of their national identity cards, as the author was informed by the IT expert himself, were passed on to the city council as well as the Governorate of al-Giza.[30] (Ironically, this step would later provide the coup regime with a 'wanted list' – as a result, all members of the PC would later end up in prison or in exile.)

In fact, the Ministry of the Interior itself acknowledged the achievements of the PC. The Head of Security in the al-Giza Governorate, Abdin Yousef, honoured both Mahdi Ghizlani and Mohammad Nasr Ghizlani because the PC had succeeded in arresting a gang of thieves led by one of 'the most dangerous' of the *balṭajiyya* in al-Giza, Waleed Abu al-Dahab, after members of the PC in July 2011 laid a trap for his gang. The PC seized two machine guns, two rifles, a quantity of marijuana and 380,000 LE from them. Egyptian newspapers wrote about the incident, stressing that the police could not have arrested those criminals without the assistance of the PC.[31] Generally, the PC kept receipts and written acknowledgements from the police, Interior Ministry, the Governorate, and the city council, regarding everything (and everybody) they had handed to them.[32] The PC's activities were not restricted to working with the local institutions. It also tried to expand its coordination with the military. This took place when dozens of young people helped the army and police in protecting polling stations during the March 2011 constitutional referendum, the 2011–12 parliamentary election, and the 2012 constitutional referendum.

Even the local supervision of bakeries and gas cylinder stores in Kerdasa involved a degree of cooperation with the city council. The minutes of a meeting and a subsequent agreement (dated 21 May 2011), of which the author has received a copy, show that the PC took over bread and gas distribution points after having ensured that an official decision from the city council had been issued regarding this matter. The document stipulates that 'the dismissal of three public-sector workers [in Kerdasa] due to the dereliction of their duties and the appointment in their place of three members [recommended by] the Popular Committee'. The document also stipulated the right of the PC to supervise wheat-flour distribution points and to inform the authorities of any breach in protocol.[33] Nonetheless, the PC's work did not pass without some obstruction from corrupt employees in the city council. For instance, officials from the Supply Management (*'idārat at-tamwīn*) ruined some bakery machines in order to halt bread supplies and push local people to complain against the PC. The PC, in its turn, was aware of these attempts and informed the city council as well as the Governorate.

We have many accounts which indicate that the flourishing of PCs and their assumption of the roles of local governance was a general phenomenon, at least in Greater Cairo. It is observable that popular committees were devoted to 'community development and reform as well as neighbourhood watches'. In Basatin, an informal settlement southeast of central Cairo, the PCs 'extracted the provision of essential state services – gas lines, lighting and health clinics'.[34] This can also be observed in other Cairo neighbourhoods, such as Umraneya, Boulaq Abu Eila, Boulaq Dakrour, Maspero, Dokki, Dar al-Salam and Agouza, where the 'incredible political energy that accompanied the popular efforts . . . involved a huge array of community-oriented activities in which citizens took urgent issues into their own hands'. According to Harders and Wahba, the PCs proudly told stories of successful conflict with the local administration over water and electricity shortages, paving streets, acting in 'place of the dissolved local councils'.[35] The media also reported similar cases in many areas.

Scholarship, the international media and public opinion have all celebrated these initiatives, considering them to be the soul of the Egyptian revolution, a new chapter in the history of popular participation, and a demonstration of the incredible power of the real civil society that was unleashed after the break-up of authoritarian rule. No doubt these informal networks presented impressive examples of local energy and its will to reform. However, the following section will take a different position, and will argue that this form of popular participation in local governance was no novelty. Instead, it can be viewed as a continuity of the same form of local politics that had been monopolised by the local NDP prior to the revolution, rather than the advent of a something unprecedented. The novelty lay in replacing the old players with new ones, who had previously been excluded from the political field and were more capable of mobilising their local communities.

A Déjà Vu?

Who was in charge of the PC in Kerdasa? The head of committee was Sheikh Mahdi Ghizlani, a *Sheikh Arab* and real-estate entrepreneur. Those who ran the subcommittees were mainly respected figures who had been active in the *da'wa* movement from the 1970s to the early 1990s, such as Mohammad Sayed Ghizlani, Mohammad Nasr Ghizlani, Ali Qinawi, Khaled Sa'd and Sayid Zinnari, among others, who had previously been repressed as we saw in Chapter 3. However, the committee on the ground was not restricted to Islamists. It also encompassed dozens of youths from different social and ideological backgrounds, such as members of the April 6 Youth Movement, and even a few former members of the NDP, but the majority had not previously been politicised due to their age.[36] Nevertheless, there was an indication that the committee was also driven by kin-based mobilisation, since the leadership was dominated by figures from just one large family that was targeted by the SSIS from the late 1990s: the Omars. It also seems that many of the youths on the ground were either from the Omars or were linked to them by affinity and friendship. This latter aspect reminds us of the strategy that had previously been used by the NDP veterans to mobilise their grassroots: clannism.

This situation elicited some discreet criticism from a few youth members of the committee, such as Khaled Abbas. Abbas is a lawyer from Kerdasa who belonged to the initial group that founded the PC, but later left. He said that at its initial stage, the PC encompassed many Kerdasians with a vision of developing the town's facilities during the state's absence. Abbas has stressed, nevertheless, that 'a specific *'ā'ilā* and direction' [i.e., Islamists] seized the committee and, from May 2011, started to exclude all who disagreed with their agenda. Abbas, in a meeting with members of the PC in June 2011, accused Mohammad Nasr Ghizlani and his associates of having 'stolen the revolution from those who actually made it' (since Ghizlani himself was in prison prior to and during the eighteen days of the revolution). Nasr Ghizlani responded by arguing that 'it is not necessary for those who planted the tree to reap its fruits', according to Abbas.[37]

This early criticism, however, did not seem to prevent the PC from pursuing its work according to the same formula. In September 2011, the PC acted as a mediator to convene a reconciliation meeting between the families of the victims of the Friday of Rage and the police to enable the return of the police, after promises were given that those responsible would be held accountable. A conference was held on their return to confirm this precondition.[38] The Ministry of Interior gave official recognition to the PC's leadership after the latter contributed to the rebuilding of the police station. Official cards were printed for the PC leaders, which indicated acknowledgement of their organisational body. However, what made the situation complicated was that the PC did not dissolve itself after the return of the police, or after the presidential election in May–June 2012. Thus, what was supposed to be temporary turned out then to be permanent, or at least this is what members of the PC aspired to.

The PC was also aware that it needed a legal status to work under. Therefore, its leadership acted in the same way as many other PCs in Egypt during the transitional phase.[39] They founded an association under the name of 'Nahḍat Baladna' ('The Renaissance of our Town'), which they registered, and within which they carried out their activities. However, the PC insisted that they undertake roles that were beyond the limits of any association, such as monitoring the state's local institutions and maintaining security. Thus, the PC not only functioned as a local council, but also acted as civilian police. Over time, it was obvious that the PC would intimidate the local state, the police and the NDP veterans. The latter were threatened especially after the dissolution of their party by a court order in April 2011, and also because they had been stigmatised after the revolution, becoming known as *fulūl* (remnants of the old regime). Nevertheless, despite the fact that they were vulnerable and almost powerless, they still had one weapon that has proven to be effective in Egypt: the power of rumour.

Following the presidential election, and especially after Morsi's Constitutional Declaration in November 2012, rumours began to fly concerning the PC's activities. The PC was said to be forcing a 'brotherhoodisation'[40] of the town's institutions, to be involved in *balṭaja* acts, including the blackmail of workers in the informal market, and to have prevented police officers in July 2012 from prescribing penalties against members of the PC or their friends. The PC was also said to have harassed those who worked with the presidential candidates Hamdin Sabahi and Ahmed Shafik during the 2012 presidential election campaigns.[41] As usual with rumours, they came thick and fast, and could not be verified.

As can be seen, the 'brotherhoodisation of the state', as an accusation, was the perfect weapon used by local groups and national entities to defend their diminished status after the revolution. However, this accusation also had its foundations at the local level – not in terms of replacing the employees of the local state's institutions with Brotherhood members (who were a minority in Kerdasa's PC), but rather in terms of replacing the roles that had been undertaken by the local NDP. In this sense, it is not difficult to observe that most of the achievements (*'injāzāt*, sing. *'injāz*) of the PC in the transitional phase were no different to those of the NDP veterans when they were in charge.

As we discussed previously, the local NDP from the late 1980s to the early 2000s was an informal extension of the SLA, in which its figureheads manoeuvred among the state's institutions and pressured them to develop their localities. Abdel-Wahhab Mahjoub spoke, as we saw in Chapter 2, of his *'injāz* in convincing the state to allocate nine feddans for a school complex, a vehicle-licensing agency and a youth centre. He was proud – in a similar way to Ghizlani in this chapter – of the less than one feddan used for the recycling centre. This followed the same logic as Ghizlani, except that in the latter's time, the state's institutions were willing to concede anything to avert the people's anger during the months after the revolution, which made the PC's *'injāzāt* faster and easier to achieve.[42]

The members of Kerdasa's PC might be not aware that they were introducing the same model as that of the NDP in local politics. They believed that they were breaking new ground. But for the NDP veterans, it was a *déjà vu*. Therefore, when they came retrospectively to evaluate the PC's work, they did not criticise it for being Islamic, or for being dominated by the Omars. They castigated it for its lack of experience, or for behaving in a manner that they considered insane. Based on their experience, they were aware that the PC had misread the boundaries of local politics as a political field. They knew that you do not 'force' the state to do what you think it should do, but rather that you negotiate with it and convince it. Furthermore, they knew that there was no way that the state would accept the idea of a semi-armed informal network that would share responsibility for policing, not even in their dreams. The Egyptian state has no mercy towards those who challenge its 'ritual of presence'.[43]

Remarkably, both the local NDP in the Mubarak era and the PC after the revolution derived their legitimacy from the same source: servicing the local community. As elaborated in Chapters 2 and 3, it is more accurate to understand the NDP subnational branches as a sort of community organisation in Egypt, rather than as one unified national party. This was its weakness and its strength at the same time. Local NDP figures were often successful and well known in their localities, but they were barely known in neighbouring towns and villages. The PC also derived its legitimacy from its claims that it represented the local community. Its leadership and members perceived themselves to be the guardians of the town's amenities, institutions and public services. They introduced themselves as an entity that spoke for Kerdasa and represented the will of its residents. Nevertheless, the major difference between the local NDP and the PC was that the latter had a greater capacity of mobilising the local community, which made the new local leadership able to push the boundaries of the political field by assuming functions that historically had been cartelised by the government and the executive branch of the SLA. However, this situation did not last long. In July 2013, the country experienced a military coup. The PC organised demonstrations in the middle of town, near the police station, in solidarity with the elected president. But on the day of the break-up of the Rabia al-Adawiya and Nahda protest camps, violence would break out.

Social Capital vs Symbolic Capital

Kerdasa became known to the Egyptian media after the bloody clashes that occurred on 14 August 2014 after the break-up of the Rabia al-Adawiya and al-Nahda protest camps, when, as stated at the beginning of this chapter, hundreds of townspeople attacked the police station, firing bullets and RPGs. They killed eleven police officers. The Egyptian media circulated video clips showing the station totally burned. Blood covered the internal walls of the building and dead policemen were shown half-naked in their own blood, while voices around them could be heard celebrating and shouting '*allahu 'akbar'*.[44] Another video showed hundreds of townspeople protesting around the station and a few of them setting fire to it.[45]

One of the state-owned TV satellite channels interviewed a survivor of the tragedy, the deputy inspector Ashraf Abdel-Aziz, in his bed at the hospital immediately after the massacre.[46] In his testimony, Abdel-Aziz stated that when crowds had surrounded the police station, the police officers tried to protect themselves by shooting tear-gas and firing warning shots. However, when the situation span out of control, the policemen tried to flee, every man for himself. From his department there were no survivors except Abdel-Aziz himself, who managed to escape through al-Seyahi Street, where a smaller crowd surrounded him. They beat him up and yelled at him 'you *kāfir*' (infidel) until he passed out. Eventually he woke up in a mosque where a few Kerdasians took care of him.[47]

An eyewitness, who was later sentenced to death in the court case on the Kerdasa events, told the author that on the day of the Rabia al-Adawiya massacre, townspeople crowded around the police station from early morning, after news had come in from Cairo that two youths in the protest camps had been killed (Khaled Zandahi and Hisham al-A'waj). The police in turn tried to push them away by shooting tear-gas and birdshot (the usually non-lethal pellets being the favoured tool of the security forces for trying to disperse protests).[48] From midday, the clashes became seriously violent, especially when a group of armed and masked assailants attacked the police station, firing bullets and RPGs. After this, eleven police officers surrendered themselves to the townspeople, who beat them to death, while two young people among the protesters were killed by police who were defending the station.[49]

Another eyewitness, a former member of the PC, told the author that a subcommittee for managing the crisis was formed immediately after the military coup. The committee, according to him, was responsible for organising demonstrations in Kerdasa every Friday. On the day of the bloody dispersal of the protest camps, and after people had started to surround the police station, a delegation of local figures went to the police, asking them to leave the town with their arms to avoid hostilities. According to the eyewitness, who was actually one of those who surrounded the station, one of the officers sexually insulted the delegation. Less than an hour later, a group of assailants attacked the station. One of the assailants, according to him, was from the town and his wife had been harassed by an officer several days before. Eventually, he stated, 'When the policemen surrendered, we handed all the senior officers (*ḍubbāṭ*) over to the townspeople, while we released all the juniors.'[50]

How can we understand the violence that erupted in Kerdasa after the break-up of the Rabia al-Adawiya and al-Nahda protest camps? These clashes were conceived as part of a broader wave of political violence that pervaded the country for several months after the military coup, and which followed more than two years of extensive political polarisation. For example, *Wiki-Thawra*, a statistical database of the Egyptian Revolution, listed sixty-eight similar occurrences throughout Egypt in the month following the break-up of the two protest camps, in which people took revenge against state institutions.[51] Furthermore, in three days following the break-up, dozens of churches were set on fire, totally or partially.[52] Many governmental institutions were attacked or besieged, especially in towns around the cities. The logic behind these incidents was ambiguous, as the Egyptian regime preferred to accuse the MB of committing these attacks on state institutions, as well as Coptic churches, in order to retroactively justify the military coup against the elected president.[53]

My analysis agrees that what became known as the so-called 'massacre of Kerdasa' should be placed in the context of the political polarisation and struggle with the deep state that occurred after the revolution. However, I will also stress the importance of considering the local dynamics that facilitated violence in many areas. In the towns of the Cairo peri-urban fringe, political violence was also motivated by and resulted from what can be categorised under a community movement. In the clashes that took place in Kerdasa, and in the regime's subsequent 'revenge', an objectification of town was present not only among local groups, but also among state agencies, the media and the formal discourse. I will scrutinise the bloody clashes of August in Kerdasa, and the media campaign that accompanied it, from this perspective.

Community Activism?

Social movement research has usually neglected small-scale, localised movements. There are doubts that theories and concepts developed from studies of large-scale social movements are applicable at the local scale and territorialised level without significant modifications.[54] The reason behind this might be the lack of theoretical bridging between two very established academic fields: community studies and social movements research, albeit both having a long history of theoretical development. While the emphasis in the latter has historically been on the organisation and mobilisation of movements, the former emphasises local community mobilisation and neighbourhood associations.[55] Social movement literature has already promulgated the concept of 'social movement community', but the concept lacks a territorial proximity, as with the residents of a neighbourhood or a town, and instead, stresses social networks and collective identity.[56] On the other hand, community activism research has been poorly utilised in the MENA to the extent that it led Asef Bayat to concluding that the region is a 'blank space' on the 'global map of community action'[57] because this kind of activism 'seems to be largely a Latin American model rooted in socio-political conditions of that region'.[58]

However, community-based movements or localised social movements have been present in the MENA in tandem with the acceleration of neo-liberal policies in most Arab countries. In Egypt, for example, Lisa Blaydes observed an emerging major trend regarding the politics of infrastructure development beginning from 2007, whereby locals protested against the deteriorating public services in a number of areas. In many cases, according to her, demonstrators refused to yield to what they considered threats from the security forces to pressure them to break up their protests.[59] In southern Tunisia, in 2008, the Gafsa phosphate-mining region experienced a six-month-long local uprising triggered by corrupt hiring practices. The movement has been regarded as one of the precursors to the revolution of 2010–11.[60] In Syria, immediately after its revolution (March 2011), the country experienced the emergence of the Local Coordination Committees (*tansīqiyyat*), which were neighbourhood associations established by civilians after the first protests to organise media coverage and local demonstrations.[61] Last, but not least, the eight-month-long Rif Movement in northern Morocco that took place in El Hoceima city in 2016–17 serves as another important example. The movement was triggered by the death of a local fishmonger who was crushed to death after climbing into the back of a rubbish truck, following the confiscation of his allegedly illegal fish merchandise by municipal authorities.

All of these movements have been conceived as community-based and locally driven. In explaining the dynamics and the logic of these localised social movements, recent scholarship has stressed the role of local leadership,[62] the collective memory,[63] shared marginalisation,[64] local solidarity as well as spatial proximity.[65] From my field research, I would also stress the existence of a leadership that has capacities and resources beyond social and economic capitals. In the case of Kerdasa, symbolic capital was existent.

Chapter 3 has discussed the different historical and social dynamics that contributed to the deterioration of the subordinated political institutional spheres including the local branches of the NDP. These dynamics were also responsible for the emergence of more competitive and mobilisative alternative local politics, represented by the *da'wa* movement. The movement, however, was eventually neutralised by coercion. The previous section has shown how the revolution paralysed the subordinated political field and led to the emergence of a new revolutionary one that rehabilitated those local political agents who had been excluded from local politics in the Mubarak era. They became the new local leadership of the community in the revolutionary era. The rest of this chapter will show how this local leadership, equipped with symbolic capital, was able to mobilise the local community in Kerdasa to initiate what can be considered a community-based movement.

We will begin with the testimony of Mohammad Nasr al-Ghizlani, who became the chairman of Kerdasa's PC after Sheikh Mahdi al-Ghizlani died in March 2013. Al-Ghizlani told the author that he and other 'respected personalities' went to the police station days after the military coup in July 2013. Police officers were very clear: 'From now on, it will never be the same as before.' Al-Ghizlani added: 'We had a deal, but they reneged on the promises they had made when they returned to Kerdasa. We were worried about them stealing our efforts, *'injāzāt*, sacrifices and dreams. We realized then that this was a counter-revolution and that businessmen, the media and the old regime were all involved in it.'[66] Thus, until the 14 August, Kerdasa's PC organised non-violent demonstrations almost on a daily basis, condemning the military coup and demanding that the police leave the town.

The verdict of the Giza Criminal Court on the Kerdasa case elaborated in detail the official view of what happened to the police station on 14 August (against 183 defendants). The court questioned 104 witnesses, including police officers and townspeople. Sixteen videos and seventeen pictures were also analysed by the public prosecutor. Although the court was biased and politicised and the head of it was Mohammad Nagy Shehata (a controversial judge who had sentenced hundreds of defendants to death in previous court cases), the testimonies of witnesses offer interesting details of how townspeople reacted on that day, some of which intersect with the narratives that I have gathered.[67]

For example, nearly all the police officers testified that the chairman of the PC had come with other Kerdasians to demand that they evacuate the station, and that the head of the police station had refused point blank, saying 'over our dead bodies!' Police officers and many townspeople stated that the crowd was chanting Islamic slogans such as 'come to Jihad!' (*ḥaī 'alā al-jihād*). 'Islamic . . . Islamic, the Interior Ministry are *balṭajiyya* (*'islāmiyya 'islāmiyya . . . id-dakhliyya balṭagiyya*).' The verdict also intended to criminalise the PC by accusing it of planning to seek revenge on the police station, and by linking it to *balṭajiyya* who were accused of firing RPGs to force the police to surrender and to steal the station's contents. The verdict also stressed the tensions between *balṭajiyya* and the police and concluded that the PC exploited this kind of hostility to push *balṭajiyya* into attacking the station.[68]

Most important is what was said to the police officers when they had surrendered. According to the verdict, the attackers were chanting slogans that invoked the name of Kerdasa as they murdered the police officers. An attacker shouted: 'the government is no match for Kerdasa' (*il-ḥukūma ma ti'darsh 'alā Kerdasa*). Another police officer told the court that Kerdasian women came to the station at 6:00 am the same day, threatening the police and saying: 'if anyone from Kerdasa dies, you will be killed here!' Other testimonies also described townspeople attacking the station and throwing stones and Molotov cocktails while crying out the name of Kerdasa.[69] Finally, the court emphasised that what made the large crowds surround and attack the station was that the defendants were trusted by the townspeople (*kilmithum masmū'a*). According to the verdict, the defendants took advantage of their influence over the townspeople because some of them were *imams* at mosques or teachers in schools. Thus, they were able to convince more than two thousand people to participate in the crime. Ironically, the court concluded: 'due to the fact that the majority of Kerdasa inhabitants are from the MB, they [i.e., the people of Kerdasa] have in their hearts malice and hatred towards the police, which led them to organise and commit the crime'.[70] As a result, the criminal court sentenced 183 defendants to death.[71]

Obviously, the verdict in its essence, as well as the majority of the testimonies of the police officers, not only criminalised a group of defendants, it was also a collective condemnation and stigmatisation of the whole town of Kerdasa, or at least the majority of its inhabitants. It is also obvious that the court's decision was affected by the narrative produced by Egyptian media in the weeks following the incident. In the thirty-five days after the massacre, Egyptian satellite TV channels and newspapers painted a black picture of the town, turning its residents into criminals who deserved what was coming.

Dozens of news stories described Kerdasa as a hotbed of terrorism (*'irhāb*), a source of violent crime and a stronghold of *takfīrī* groups (predicated on declaring other Muslims to be apostates). The media behaved as though the Egyptian army were going to war, rather than going to arrest a citizen or group of citizens, inflaming public opinion with imaginary victories over victims who were most likely innocent.[72]

This was a typical discourse in such situations and it resembles – to a large extent – what was documented by Singerman in 'The Siege of Imbaba', when Egyptian newspapers constructed an image of the residents of Imbaba as an uncivilised, almost savage 'other'.[73] On the eve of the security operation, for example, the then president of the Free Egyptians Party, Ahmed Said, attributed the police station massacre in Kerdasa to informal settlements there. Terrorism according to him was 'entrenched in thousands of mosques and sanctuaries (*zawaya*) that are deployed in *aṣ-Ṣa'īd* [Upper Egypt] and the *al-'ashwā'iyyāt* [informal housing districts].'[74] The day after, the *al-Masry al-Youm* newspaper published a caricature celebrating 'the national day of liberating Kerdasa'.[75]

As can be observed from the testimonies regarding the attack on the police station, a significant motivation for the clashes between Kerdasa's townspeople and the state was a local solidarity that had emerged due to the presence of a sense of community. Nevertheless, discernible evidence indicates that the role of the local leadership, who were equipped with an Islamic ideological discourse, was also a determining factor. This is what enabled the new local leadership to mobilise the community in a way that the local NDP leaders never dreamed of doing. In brief, while the latter were armed with social capital, which allowed them to employ clan-based strategies in political mobilisation, the new players had – in addition – symbolic capital, which allowed its holders to mobilise social segments beyond the scope of kinship networks.

This might be one of the reasons that made the state, through its security apparatus, the military forces, the judicial institutions and the media, not restrict antagonism towards the leaders and members of the PC but expand it to include the whole town of Kerdasa and its people. The fact that the court's verdict described Kerdasa's inhabitants in terms of their collective status indicates not just the Egyptian state's tendency to construct and categorise its citizens on spatial criteria; Egyptian state agencies also criminalised the local community itself by assuming that it had been a hotbed of 'brotherhoodisation' and terrorism. This was a pejorative discourse that can be placed within the elite discourse, which has viewed and constructed the residents of informal settlements, peri-urban towns and villages as savages and uncivilised.

Many young people of the town attempted, mainly on social media, to defend Kerdasa's reputation; first, by claiming that the massacre's perpetrators were outsiders (that is to say, from other towns, or Bedouins), and, secondly by blaming the Ministry of Interior itself for liquidating its staff and leaving the police station poorly guarded. However, all local narratives and justifications were futile in the face of dozens of media reports accusing the townspeople of dealing in arms, committing acts of terrorism and embracing armed groups. Over eight weeks, the people of the town spent every night waiting for retribution and persecution.

The State is Back

At dawn on 19 September 2013, the security operation to storm Kerdasa began. As detailed in this chapter's introduction, the operation was broadcast live on television by Egyptian channels. Dozens of homes were raided, their contents smashed and their inhabitants randomly arrested. The following day, after Friday prayers, many of the townspeople of Kerdasa and Nahia came out to condemn the raids. The police and army stationed in these two towns responded with gunfire and tear gas, leading to the asphyxiation of a number of children.[76]

Subsequently, images began circulating of burnt-out homes and the damage caused by the security forces to the houses of many local personalities. Anything that could be stolen was taken and the remaining contents trashed.[77] Over the course of one week, the homes of the leaders and members of the PC were raided. Many of them managed to flee, but many also were arrested along with members of their families. The string of arrests was not restricted to the PC; it included hundreds of the townspeople of various political affiliations. Security forces also raided the home of Abdel Salam Bashendi, the Freedom and Justice Party (FJP) member of the dissolved People's Assembly, and the home of Ahmad Muqallad, the town's registrar of marriages. The value of stolen cash and jewellery was estimated to be hundreds of thousands of Egyptian pounds.[78]

Videos published in the Egyptian media showed groups of security forces searching almost every corner of the town. The security forces suspected anybody walking in streets and they entered many houses searching for weapons, drugs and items stolen from the police station. A video posted on YouTube showed several members of the Special Forces (*quwwāt khāṣa*) interrogating a middle-age man and accusing him of stealing the door of the police station while the man tried his best to convince them that he had bought it a long time prior to the incident.[79] It was not difficult to see that this propaganda was intended to construct an image of the townspeople as thieves and savages, who were hostile and irrational, as if the state as well as its allies among the elites had only just discovered Kerdasa (which is only 8 km from the capital).

Another video published by *Al-Youm Al-Sabi'* newspaper on its website purported to present the sound of gunfire and a firefight between members of the military forces and unknown opponents. No camera was able to capture footage of any terrorist or gunman. Opponents of the regime, including Islamists, therefore suspected that these videos had been forged in order to suggest that there was a real battlefield in Kerdasa.[80] The Ministry of Interior claimed that a police major general was killed during the operation, but according to the forensic report, his death was caused by a 9mm bullet fired at close range that entered his right side and lodged in the lung wall. This makes it likely that he was killed by friendly fire.[81]

Over the course of a week, the Egyptian media celebrated what it called 'the liberation of Kerdasa'. The headlines inflamed public opinion with fabricated victories. In actuality, the Egyptian security forces did not confront any resistance, simply because there were no gunmen in the city on the day of the operation. In all likelihood, the Egyptian regime simply used Kerdasa to give the public a 'quick' example of its 'war on terrorism', especially after the then Minister of Defence and the leader of the military coup, Abdel Fattah al-Sisi, had called for mass demonstrations to grant the Egyptian military and police a 'mandate' to combat 'terrorism' (a call understood by the public as granting popular support for using violence against Islamist civilians in Rab'a and Nahda squares).

Nevertheless, the operation also had other goals. The case of Kerdasa shows precisely the way in which the Egyptian state dealt with its peripheries. As mentioned earlier, the Kerdasa incident was only one among a series of assaults against the state's institutions after the break-up of Cairo's sit-ins. In Egypt's peripheries – both urban and rural – the state usually avoids applying the framework of the law and prefers to deal with whole communities collectively. In Sinai, or in some regions in Upper Egypt, for instance, journalists have documented various examples of collective punishment applied by the Interior Ministry and the military forces in response to terrorist attacks or outlaw activities.

Thus, when the Egyptian state decides to engage in a security operation against a village, the predominant approach is one of collective punishment because in the state's view the town's basic legal unit is not the citizen, as it should be, but the collective as a whole. An entire village might be punished, or an extended family, which may comprise dozens of families and hundreds of individuals. For this reason, frequently during the course of security campaigns, homes are set on fire and a number of relatives of the person sought are arrested and abused. A curfew is imposed, most likely involving 'informally' the theft from shops and houses.

In such cases, the Egyptian army operates alongside another army made up of broadcasters and journalists, who paint a black picture of the targeted village, turning its residents into criminals who deserve what is coming. Most importantly, the state, using naked power, intends to humiliate and punish many local figures and respected personalities who might have some sympathy towards any group that challenges the state. In Kerdasa, the security forces were not content simply to raid the homes of all those known to belong to the MB. In fact, the homes of many local community figures were raided, trashed and robbed, while members of their families were arrested. These actions can only be understood as intended to humiliate the town's elite that had administered affairs following the January 25 Revolution.

In her study of Bulaq al-Dakrur, Ismail has stressed that a space of tolerance is offered by the authorities on condition that local networks have a kind of connection with the regime's networks or at least its implicit approval. The case of the crushing of Islamic movements by the heavy hand of the state in the 1990s showed that not respecting this implicit power structure led to the demise of local figures. For Ismail, the key to understanding how informal-local government works is the politics of conviviality, which 'binds ruler and ruled'.[82] *Sha'bi* quarters' residents accumulate an intimate knowledge of the everyday state. They cultivate an 'intimacy with power in the sense of knowing it closely' in order to create 'the context for complicity among the ruled'. The state, in return, publicly keeps for itself the 'ritual of presence' which must not be challenged at all.[83] This explains why the state would not tolerate any communal structure that might question its upper hand on society.

In Kerdasa, it was obvious from the performative way in which the police and military forces behaved that they were practising what Ismail has termed a 'ritual of presence', whereby the state was asserting its existence by raiding selective targets that represented the local community. The way in which the Egyptian security forces arrested people shows that this was not based on information or even intuition, but on pre-formed attitudes and a tendency to inflict punishment and revenge. For instance, the security forces went to raid the home of Sheikh Mahdi al-Ghizlani (the former chairman of the PC) and arrest him, only to be informed by his neighbours that he had died seven months previously. In this pattern, arrests were random and those sought came from a range of backgrounds (Islamists, local figures, etc.).[84] In short, the pattern of attacking and humiliating local figures and representatives of Kerdasa demonstrates that the state was intent on flexing its hegemonic muscles.

No individual can elaborate on the way the state apparatus dealt with the case of Kerdasa in the way that a state institution can. In February 2016, Egypt's Court of Cassation, the country's highest appeals court, overturned the death sentences of 149 defendants issued by the Giza Criminal Court and ordered a retrial. The court accepted the appeals of defendants for several reasons. One reason is that the Giza Criminal Court's verdict entailed 'combining both collective solidarity and personal responsibility . . . which led to a contradiction in the decision'.[85] In other words, the Court of Cassation overturned the verdict because it equalised the perpetrators of the police station massacre and the thousands of townspeople who crowded around the station who were viewed as potential accessories to the crime by inciting it. Another reason for overturning the verdict was that the Giza Criminal Court, according to the Court of Cassation, had relied on the heavily biased police investigations as its main evidence for finding the defendants guilty of the crime.[86]

Thus, even one of the most prestigious judicial institutions of the state admitted that there had been serious problems in the handling of the Kerdasa incident by the state. The state's tendency to view the townspeople collectively suggests that the logic of citizenship, which treats every adult individually, is simply not applicable except to certain segments of society. In the peripheries, the *state of exception*, to use Giorgio Agamben's concept,[87] has actually been the rule during the post-military coup era. In this regard, people on the outskirts of cities are usually associated with their towns, villages and suburbs and categorised as dangerous or hostile according to the space in which they live.

From 19 to 24 September 2013, a curfew was imposed. The security forces not only raided dozens of Kerdasa houses, they also set five of them on fire (the homes of Jamal M. Imbabi, Ashraf A. al-Zindahi, Sa'd Abu A'mira-Omar and two other houses owned by Mohammad N. Ghizlani). They also burned down a clinic owned by Mahmoud Sayed Ghizlani, and raided the hospital of his father (Mohammad Sayed Ghizlani), which they smashed up and robbed. During this operation, a special force was responsible for preventing local people from putting out fires and even arresting anyone who tried to film the burnt and wrecked houses. Police also stormed sixteen other homes, again trashing them and looting the contents.

During this period, the security forces' tanks roamed Kerdasa and through loudspeakers insulted the town, its men, the MB and the recently ousted President Mohammad Morsi. The town then lived through a horrifying period in which most of its people were afraid of being brutalised. Immediately after the operation, Egyptian satellite TV channels conducted studio interviews with commanders and colonels from the Interior Ministry, who had been in charge in the operation. The main aim of this propaganda was to emphasise to the viewers the legendary status of the operation in Kerdasa. For instance, a colonel and a major general from the Special Forces appeared on the MBC Misr satellite channel in order to explain how complex the operation had been and how it had needed much planning. Colonel Mahmoud Nazih said that Kerdasa after the police station massacre had been a 'ghost town'. The town, he said, is a 'group of very narrow roads and haphazard neighbourhoods (*'ashwā'iyyāt*), which made the operation very complex and dangerous'.[88]

Neither of these claims was true. Leaving aside the fact that a city of more than 1000,000 people cannot be considered, in any case, a ghost town, Kerdasa, like many cities, towns and suburbs at that time, was highly mobilised due to the political polarisation after the military coup. The whole country in the months after the coup, and after the bloody dispersal of the Rabia al-Adawiya and Nahda protest camps, witnessed demonstrations of tens of thousands of citizens, most of which were suppressed by naked power. Secondly, it may be true that parts of Kerdasa can be considered as informal areas (which is the case for 40 per cent of Greater Cairo), but the area targeted by the security forces cannot be deemed *'ashwā'ī*. Finally, the same town after the January 25 Revolution, as we have seen earlier, had been presented and praised by the Egyptian media and the Interior Ministry as a model that should be considered by all other local governments in Egypt.[89]

Facts were beside the point. The aim of the media coverage was to celebrate and praise the police as the protectors of the nation after more than two years of sabotaging it with its brutality and disregard of its human rights record, which actually led to the 2011 revolution. Praise for the Interior Ministry, as well as the Egyptian army, was not based on genuine achievements. Instead, the regime found it easier to fabricate a victorious story to broadcast to public opinion. This was, indeed, at the expense of the status of tens of thousands of people on the outskirts of Cairo, whom the capital's elites simply dismissed or disparaged.

Conclusion

The January 25 Revolution marked a turning point in Egypt's contemporary history. It also represented the beginning of a new chapter in the history of the system of local governance. The NDP, which for three decades had been one of the main pillars of the power structure at the local level, was dissolved and politically de-legitimised, leaving a vacuum that was filled immediately by an organised sort of community activism, whose version of local politics was indeed revolutionary. However, as this chapter has shown, the revolutionary aspect in this model did not lie in the quality of public work, which was more or less a substitution for the role that had been undertaken by the local branches of the NDP through the local councils.

Instead, the PC's model of local politics was revolutionary in two interrelated respects. First, in terms of the independence of the new occupants of the political field who were not subordinated to the state and its agencies compared with their predecessors in the local branches of the NDP. This was clear since most local agents who were in charge of the PC had previously been suppressed, imprisoned and excluded from any sort of public work during the Mubarak era. Secondly, in terms of their capacity to mobilise their communities, because the new occupants had previously been active in the *da'wa* movement, therefore, were able to articulate their public work discourse within a cultural framework. In other words, while the local NDP leadership's influence was based, at best, on social capital (most prominently kinship-based social resources), that of their counterparts in the PCs on the Cairo peri-urban fringe was based on symbolic capital.

This is what emboldened the leadership of the PC in Kerdasa to expand the boundaries of local politics to include roles that historically had been held exclusively by the government (especially security issues) and the executive branch of the SLA. Furthermore, this is what made this leadership able to initiate a community movement following the military coup that would later lead to the unfortunate incidents of October 2013. However, the state response was prompt and decisive: a point-blank refusal of any compromise that could undermine its authoritarian domination over local politics. Thus, by late 2013, the authoritarian regime regained full control over local governance after exercising a large wave of naked power all over the country. Ever since, no grassroots have been needed, just the rule of fear.

Notes

1. Mahjoub, *Interview*; Hasanin Mikkawi, *Interview*; Abu Ismail, *Interview*; Gabiri, *Interview*.
2. Ibid.
3. Ibid.
4. Ibid.
5. Ibid.
6. Mahjoub, *Interview*.
7. The following report reflects on the indignation among the NDP rivals in Kerdasa's district on the day of elections: Al-Masri al-Yowm, 10 November 2010, available at: http://today.almasryalyoum.com/article2.aspx?ArticleID=276709.
8. See, for example, Jason Brownlee, 'The Decline of Pluralism in Mubarak's Egypt', *Journal of Democracy* 13(4) (2002): 6–14.
9. Mo'ataz Mikkawi, *Interview*.
10. Ibid.
11. Cilja Harders has discussed this phenomenon, which she calls 'the authoritarian social contract of informality'. Cilja Harders, 'A Revolution of Logics of Action? Renegotiating the Authoritarian Social Contract in Egypt', in Jakob Horst et al. (eds), *Euro-Mediterranean Relations after the Arab Spring: Persistence in Times of Change* (Farnham: Ashgate, 2013), 103–22. However, she places all the different social agents involved, such as Islamists, *balṭajiyyas*, the NDP men, businessmen and security forces, in one and the same basket.
12. Bruce K. Rutherford, *Egypt after Mubarak: Liberalism, Islam, and Democracy in the Arab World*, 6th edn (Princeton, NJ: Princeton University Press, 2013), xxii.
13. See the report on the release of Mohammad Nasr Ghizlani at *Al-Ahram Online*, 5 March 2011, available at: http://gate.ahram.org.eg/News/46277.aspx. In

my interview with Nasr Ghizlani, he suggested that the SCAF might have released jihadists in March 2011 in order to manipulate them against the MB. (Mohammad N. Ghizlani, *Interview*, Istanbul, 21 March 2016). Later, however, many jihadists would be on the side of the MB against the deep state and others became embroiled in terrorism in Sinai.

14. Later on 9 March 2016, the Egyptian Security Forces assassinated Emad Sa'idi in Pyramids Gardens west of al-Giza Governorate. See *Al-Shorouk*, 9 March 2016, available at: https://goo.gl/ZaASCs.
15. See Appendix IV.
16. Mohammad Ghizlani, *Interview*; Hussain Omar, *Interview*; Shadi Beik, *Interview*.
17. Ibid.
18. Mohammad A. Khattab, *Interview*, Kerdasa, 23 December 2016. According to Khattab, this situation was sustained until May 2013, nearly a month before the military coup.
19. Mohammad Ghizlani, *Interview*.
20. Ibid.
21. Ibid.
22. Hussain Omar, *Interview*.
23. Ghizlani, *Interview*; Omar, *Interview*.
24. Ibid.
25. See Appendix VI and Appendix VII.
26. The following link contains fifteen videos that document Kerdasa's recycling centre: *Ikhwan*, October, March 2013, https://www.youtube.com/watch?v=YvTPCtL6lxI. See specifically the following videos, which contain interviews with many employees there, including *zabbalin*: Ikhwan, October, 18 March 2013, part 1: https://www.youtube.com/watch?v=w-q-sOEdq78; part 2: https://www.youtube.com/watch?v=THd0BQSoXlk. Finally, the following videos contain an interview with two of the founders of the recycling centre. They explain how the project developed and how the PC was able to convince Kerdasa's families and townspeople to embrace it: Ikhwan, October, 17 March 2017, part 1: https://www.youtube.com/watch?v=YvTPCtL6lxI, part 2: https://www.youtube.com/watch?v=JBbJPBneZts, part 3: https://www.youtube.com/watch?v=JBbJPBneZts.
27. See, for example, ON TV (Report), *YouTube*, 16 July 2011, https://www.youtube.com/watch?v=KFZKRCe59a4. In December 2013, the Egyptian Central Bank confiscated funds of the project, along with those of 1,054 other institutions across the whole country that were considered affiliated with the MB. See Akher Alanba', 26 December 2013, https://goo.gl/Hkg3z8.

28. Ghizlani, *Interview.*
29. See Appendix V(A) and (B); Appendix VIII.
30. Shadi al-Baik, *Interview*, Istanbul, 1 April 2016.
31. See, for example, *Al-Youm Al-Sabi'*, 17 July 2011, available at: http://www.youm7.com/story/0000/0/0/-/456093.
32. See Appendix V(A) and (B).
33. See Appendix I.
34. Asya El-Meehy, 'Egypt's Popular Committees from Moments of Madness to NGO Dilemmas', *Middle East Review – Egypt*, 42 (2012): 246, available at: http://www.merip.org/mer/mer265/egypts-popular-committees#_7_.
35. Cilja Harders, '"State Analysis from Below" and Political Dynamics in Egypt after 2011', *International Journal of Middle East Studies* 47(1) (2015): 148–51; Cilja Harders and Dina Wahba, 'New Neighborhood Power: Informal Popular Committees and Changing Local Governance in Egypt', in T. Cambanis and M.W. Hanna (eds), *Arab Politics Beyond the Uprisings: Experiments in an Era of Resurgent Authoritarianism* (New York: Century Foundation Press, 2017), 400–19.
36. M. A. M., *Interview*, Kerdasa, 22 December 2016; H. U., *Interview*, Kerdasa, 21 December 2016.
37. Khaled Abbas, *Interview*, Kerdasa, 4 June 2016.
38. ON TV, *YouTube*, 21 September 2016, https://www.youtube.com/watch?v=LAl-hU0bS5k. See also Appendix II and Appendix IX.
39. El-Meehy, 'Egypt's Popular Committees'.
40. 'Brotherhoodisation of the state' (*'akhwanat ad-dawla*) was a discourse that the MB's opponents used to accuse the MB and its supporters of taking over the state's apparatus by replacing the bureaucracy's senior officials with its members. Later, these accusations would be used by non-Islamists and the Egyptian deep state to topple the elected president. Some accounts considered Brotherhoodisation was real. According to Alexander Kazamias, Brotherhoodisation was the process that President Mohammad Morsi used to confront the military by 'concentrating semi-dictatorial power around himself in order to create a party state'. The aim of this process, Kazamias says, was to establish a semi-dictatorship of the MB in which 'the army would share power as the junior partner in the arrangement'. Alexander Kazamias, 'From Popular Revolution to Semi-Democracy: Egypt's Transition to Praetorian Parliamentarism', in Reem Abou-El-Fadl (ed.), *Revolutionary Egypt: Connecting Domestic and International Struggles* (London: Routledge, 2015), 112–33, 127. Patrick Haenni, on the other hand, contends that Brotherhoodisation was an overused expression, but 'it does aptly describe the organization's relationship to weak state institutions' such as the state-

owned media and the Ministry of Religious Endowments. Patrick Haenni, 'The Reasons for the Muslim Brotherhood's Failure in Power,' in Bernard Rougier and Stéphane Lacroix (eds), *Egypt's Revolutions: Politics, Religion, and Social Movements* (Basingstoke: Palgrave Macmillan, 2016), 19–40, 29. However, both accounts neglect the fact that the MB members were informally prohibited from working in public institutions prior to the January 25 Revolution. Hence, it should be no surprise that the public sector's door was opened to the MB members as citizens. At any rate, the July 2013 military coup showed that the claimed 'penetration' of the state by the MB was very limited since the army did not have much difficulty in toppling the elected president and the FJP.

41. Abdel-Wahhab Mahjoub himself told the author that he was subjected to *balṭaja* acts by members of the PC who accused him of receiving 2 million LE from Hamdeen Sabahi (a prominent left-wing politician and a presidential candidate in 2012 and 2014 elections) in order to guarantee his family's votes. According to Mahjoub, Sheikh Mahdi Ghizlani intervened to prevent three youths from making trouble for him (Mahjoub, *Interview*).
42. From February to September 2011, Egypt's foreign currency reserves fell from $29.8 billion to $19.4 billion according to figures published by the Central Bank of Egypt. *The Financial Times*, 'Turmoil Hits Egypt's Foreign Currency Reserves', 5 October 2011, https://www.ft.com/content/c9edcc1a-ef71-11e0-941e-00144feab49a.
43. Ismail, *Political Life in Cairo's New Quarters*, 134.
44. *YouTube*, 21 August 2013, https://www.youtube.com/watch?v=9cd0dyZljig.
45. *YouTube*, 14 August 2013, https://www.youtube.com/watch?v=LpO9unifghE.
46. *YouTube*, 20 August 2013, https://www.youtube.com/watch?v=suBOdblZta4.
47. Ibid.
48. *YouTube*, 5 July 2013, https://www.youtube.com/watch?v=4tM9tRrjlic.
49. Hussain, Omar, *Interview*.
50. S. K., *Interview*, Istanbul, 12 April 2016.
51. The documentation is available at: *Wiki-Thawra* (blog), http://wikithawra.wordpress.com
52. EIPR, June 2014, available at: https://eipr.org/sites/default/files/reports/pdf/weeks_of_killing-en.pdf.
53. Ishaq Ibrahim, 'Who Bears Responsibility for What Happened to the Copts?' *Egyptian Initiative for Personal Rights*, 10 September 2014, available at: https://goo.gl/3Vp279.
54. Randy Stoecker, 'About the Localized Social Movement', in Ram A. Cnaan and Carl Milofsky (eds), *Handbook of Community Movements and Local Organizations in the 21st Century* (Cham: Springer, 2018), 211–27.

55. Albert Hunter, 'Conceptualizing Community', in Ram A. Cnaan and Carl Milofsky (eds), *Handbook of Community Movements and Local Organizations in the 21st Century* (Cham: Springer, 2018), 3–23, 17.
56. Suzanne Staggenborg, 'Social Movement Communities and Cycles of Protest: The Emergence and Maintenance of a Local Women's Movement', *Social Problems* 45(2) (1998): 180–204, 182.
57. Bayat, *Life as Politics*, 76.
58. Ibid., 78.
59. Blaydes, *Elections and Distributive Politics*, 76.
60. J.-P. Vatthauer and I. Weipert-Fenner, 'The Quest for Social Justice in Tunisia: Socioeconomic Protest and Political Democratization post-2011', *PRIF Reports*, 143 (Frankfurt am Main: Hessische Stiftung Friedens- und Konfliktforschung, 2017), available at: https://nbn-resolving.org/urn:nbn:de:0168-ssoar-51866-3.
61. José Ciro Martínez and Brent Eng, 'Stifling Stateness: The Assad Regime's Campaign against Rebel Governance', *Security Dialogue* 49(4) (2018): 235–53.
62. Al-Mouldi al-Ahmar, 'Inhiyār Muʿaddalāt al-Tabādul fī Sūq Siyāsiyya Maḥaliyya Muzayyafa' ('The Collapse of Social Resources Exchange in a Pseudo Political Market'), in al-Mouldi al-Ahmar (ed.), *Ath-Thawra at-Tūnisiyya: al-Qādiḥ al-Maḥalī Taḥt Mijhar al-ʿUlūm al-ʾInsāniyya* (*The Tunisian Revolution: Examining the Local Triggers through the Prism of Humanities*) (Doha and Beirut: ACRPS, 2014).
63. Muhammad Saadi, *Ḥirāk ar-Rīf: Daynāmiyyāt al-Huwiyya al-Iḥtijājiyya* (*The Rif Movement: Dynamics of Protest Identity*) (Rabat: Slaiki Frères – Akhawayne, 2020).
64. Gilbert Achcar, *The People Want: A Radical Exploration of the Arab Uprising* (Berkeley: University of California Press, 2013).
65. Mounira M. Charrad and Nicholas E. Reith, 'Local Solidarities: How the Arab Spring Protests Started', *Sociological Forum* 34 (2019): 1174–96.
66. Mohammad al-Ghizlani, *Interview*.
67. The verdict was published in several Egyptian newspapers. See *Al-Shorouk*, 16 February 2015, available at: http://www.shorouknews.com/news/view.aspx?cdate=16022015&id=3a295b07-9b22-439d-b75e-cb973f336daf.
68. Ibid.
69. Ibid.
70. Ibid.
71. Ibid.
72. The following are examples of such coverage: *Al-Wafd*, 19 September 2013, http://goo.gl/j6WKFq; ONA News Agency, 19 September 2013, http://onaeg

.com/?p=1172674; *Al-Watan* (Egypt), 20 September 2013, http://www.elwatannews.com/news/details/326462; *Al Masry Al Youm*, 20 September 2013, http://www.almasryalyoum.com/node/2134951.

73. Diane Singerman, 'The Siege of Imbaba: Egypt's Internal "Other", and the Criminalization of Politics', in Diane Singerman (ed.), *Cairo Contested: Governance, Urban Space, and Global Modernity* (Cairo: American University in Cairo, 2009), 111–43.
74. *Rose al-Yūsuf*, 19 September 2013, http://goo.gl/PGkOpU.
75. See Appendix III.
76. See, for example, Kerdasa Tube, *YouTube*, 20 October 2013, https://www.youtube.com/watch?v=F89s8YMfQ3w.
77. I. M., *Interview*, Kerdasa, 10 October 2013; S. M., *Interview*, 15 October 2013; al-Ghizlani, *Interview*.
78. Ibid.
79. *YouTube*, 6 October 2013, https://www.youtube.com/watch?v=eVXurxoiDss.
80. *Al-Akhbar* (Lebanon), 25 September 2013, http://www.al-akhbar.com/node/191975.
81. Ibid.
82. Ismail, *Political Life in Cairo's New Quarters*, 130.
83. Ibid., 134.
84. Ismail al-Iskandrani (journalist), *Interview*, 4 October 2013.
85. To view the verdict's details, see *al-Shorouk*, 16 March 2016, available at: http://goo.gl/EYCMZq.
86. Ibid.
87. Giorgio Agamben, *State of Exception*, trans. Kevin Attell (Chicago: University of Chicago Press, 2005).
88. MBC MASR, *YouTube*, 22 September 2013, https://www.youtube.com/watch?v=hcM0RHBah3Y.
89. Examples of which can be found at ON TV, *YouTube*, 16 July 2011, https://www.youtube.com/watch?v=KFZKRCe59a4.

EPILOGUE
A REGIME TRUSTS NO GRASSROOTS: LOCAL GOVERNANCE UNDER SISI: SECURITISATION, UNTRUST AND UNCERTAINTY

Ten years on from the Egyptian Revolution of 2011 and around seven years since the July 2013 military coup led by Abdel Fattah Al-Sisi, what are the elements of continuity and change in the politics of local governance in Egypt?

Since the very first days following the July 2013 *coup d'état*, Egyptian politics has undergone major changes in different aspects of institutional configuration that have affected most Egyptians. State violence has erupted and become arbitrary, ubiquitous and deadly. Political dissidents have either gone to prison or been exiled. Independent Egyptian-based media channels and newspapers have been shut down. Journalists, human rights activists and researchers have been persecuted. In just two years (2017–19), al-Sisi extended the nationwide state of emergency seven consecutive times. Emergency measures have become a principal paradigm of governance and *the state of exception* has become the dominant form of political life.[1]

Under al-Sisi, furthermore, the state's fiscal health has continued to deteriorate. Unemployment rates have increased and foreign investors have not yet shown signs of interest in investing. The country's economic stability has become dependent on regional powers and is under the thumb of the International Monetary Fund (IMF). The Egyptian pound was devalued in November 2016, as part of an economic reform programme tied to a three-year, $12 billion loan from the IMF, causing a steep hike in core inflation of 32 per cent, and resulting in the cost of basic foodstuffs and fuel rising by 60 per cent.[2] The Egyptian economy is unlikely to return even to the level of growth achieved under Mubarak. According to Springborg, Egypt is en route to becoming a 'basket case similar to Yemen or Sudan'.[3]

Egypt's economy under the al-Sisi administration has become dominated by a business empire led by the army. While the generals had taken a backseat in ruling the country since Sadat, the military now has expanded its penetration to various sectors of the economy, including agribusinesses, manufacturing, private and public construction, trade, the hydrocarbon industry, telecommunication and media production.[4] As Zeinab Abul-Magd puts it: 'In today's Egypt you cannot miss it: the omnipotent presence of the military institution everywhere across the country. The Egyptian military intensively occupies the economic realms and social spaces of citizens from all social classes in every urban locality.'[5] The result of the military control of the state, as Heba Khalil and Brian Dill have concluded, is a conflicting model of statist neo-liberalism, which partially 'seeks neo-liberal reforms, while reinforcing the state's centralized control over the economy'.[6]

Yet the authoritarian shift from pre- to post-revolutionary Egypt still lacks conceptualisation. Joshua Stacher argues that the ejection of long-time leader Mubarak as a result of a popular revolution in 2011 was not a case of state collapse, neither was it an instance of regime continuity.[7] An incumbent ejection, Stacher says, means that the predictable interactions between the state and society may no longer hold. Incumbent ejection marks an end of a regime but not its immediate replacement.[8] Instead, a political vacuum emerges leading to reframing of the time horizon, giving new state elites the chance to build a regime from the ashes of the old order that has already been discredited.[9] Similarly, Walter Armbrust considers that the outcome of Egypt's January 25 Revolution is *Liminal Crisis*. Liminality is understood as the intermediate stage in a transition that allows us to view the rise of al-Sisi not as a 'straightforward restoration of the old regime', but as 'both a revolutionary outcome and as an instantiation of a New Authoritarianism' that has been structured by 'permanentized precarity'. This situation, according to Armbrust, creates a crisis that demands both rebellion and an efficient incubator of authoritarian politics.[10]

On the other hand, Bruce K. Rutherford argues that the transition from Mubarak to al-Sisi is 'an attempt to shift from a provision pact, grounded in a robust and extensive patronage network, to a protection pact, in which elites back the regime because it provides protection against internal and external threats'.[11] The first pact entails an authoritarian regime gaining the support of elites through patronage politics, whereas a robust ruling party is essential to develop a durable relationship with elites. The second pact is a type of governing that is founded on a single consideration: a shared sense of threat posed by political Islam.[12]

At the subnational level, nevertheless, our knowledge of the continuity and change in local politics in post-revolutionary Egypt is still underdeveloped; perhaps due to the extreme difficulty at the moment in conducting safe fieldwork in Egypt. The outcome, unsurprisingly, is that local politics has been relatively disregarded in the literature produced after 2011.[13] However, there are rare exceptions. Mohammed Menza's recent assessment in Misr al-Qadima shows that the regime still rests on lesser notables, who proved to be durable intermediaries between the grassroots level and bureaucracy.[14] Yet it is hard to argue otherwise since creating new grassroots and networks of power is not an automatic decision, it is a process (that is to say, it needs time).

In contrast, Mohammad Yaghi has noted that Sisi's neo-liberal reforms transformed the nature of patron–client relations, from volitional into forceful. The regime's grassroots, therefore, are subjected to a set of forceful relationships of dependency.[15] I agree. In fact, based on the theoretical approach introduced in this book, I will show that the relationship between the Sisi regime and the pre-2011 grassroots is characterised by mistrust and uncertainty. However, it is neither a change nor a continuity. The authoritarian system of local governance is still in the process of upgrading, sorting out new methods of managing its power networks. A comparative analysis of the results of two rounds of general elections (2015 and 2020), with a focus on Kerdasa, will show that the new regime does not trust or even respect its grassroots. Yet, because of the lack of alternatives, the regime is forced to work with them.

The logic behind this unhealthy relationship might be that the current regime accused Mubarak's corrupted networks, especially in the NDP, of being the reason for the January 25 Revolution (in fact, it was the only institutional frame that the regime scapegoated after the fall of Mubarak). Therefore, these networks have now become subjected to police surveillance, brutality and exploitation. However, although it is an unhealthy relationship, it is not novel. As this study showed, the Mubarak regime, since the mid-2000s at least, started to view its grassroots as a burden. Under a fiscal crisis and electoral disasters, the regime turned its back on a whole generation of local leaderships, and increased the role of the SSIS in local governance. Therefore, securitising local governance under al-Sisi could be regarded as a continuity not as a change. It is the acme of a molecular process of securitising local governance that was already building up in the late 2000s.

In my opinion, the change is reflected in the process of centralising–decentralising the regime's networks of power at the subnational level. As will be shown in this Epilogue, analysing the changes in election laws and legislation between the 2015 and 2020 parliamentary elections suggests that the regime manoeuvres between strategies of informal centralisation and decentralisation in a way that serves building and consolidating new loyal networks of power at the subnational level. However, the lack of trust between the Sisi regime and its networks makes the former in continuous need of coercion.

Securitising Local Governance: Police Instead of the Ruling Party?

As discussed in Chapter 5, on the eve of the January 25 Revolution the Mubarak regime implemented informal institutional reconfigurations that expanded the influence of the SSIS in local governance. In the towns of the Cairo peri-urban fringe, this practically marginalised a generation of NDP local leaders and notables who used to mobilise their kin-based socio-political resources in their competition over the political field. In Kerdasa, the SSIS rented several apartments as centres for its operations. It took charge of deciding even the lowest appointments such as membership of popular and local councils and the sports club, leaving no room for quasi-competitive local politics. On the eve of the 2010 primaries, local NDP leaders mobilised their networks, but they were stunned by winners who had been parachuted in and lacked rootedness in their localities and had barely appeared in the primaries. Those NDP local notables who objected to the controlled results were repressed by coercion.

The previous chapters viewed these developments as a result of a realisation that the old system of local governance in which the NDP's local branches had been expected to mobilise local communities failed to yield the desirable political outcomes. Backed by the government, the local NDP branches indeed dominated local politics at the micro level (for example, villages and towns). However, they lacked the means to translate political domination into political hegemony at the macro level (namely, districts and governorates), where they were defeated by the politics of identity. This crisis, as this book has argued, reflected the authoritarian dilemma of bridging micro–macro relations. Evidence from the fieldwork suggests that the Mubarak regime in its last few years abandoned the idea of overcoming this dilemma. Instead, it reconfigured authority–power relations in the system of local governance in a way that turned the system into an exploitative machine consistent with the accelerating neo-liberal policies that marked the governmental economic agendas.

The process of alienating the second generation of local NDP leaders, who were relatively rooted in their local communities, and favouring a newly brought-in generation of local businessmen reflected the authoritarian confidence of ruling constituencies with no need of established grassroots. The January 25 Revolution, however, proved that wrong. In the very first days after the revolution, the system collapsed. Later, in April 2011, the NDP was dissolved and, in March 2011, the SSIS was renamed the National Security Agency *al-ʿamn al-watany* (NSA). It shrank in size after the then Interior Minister Mansour al-Issawi restructured it.[16] This resulted in leaving the SLA to stand alone in the face of local communities. A power vacuum was created, and thus, the popular committees partially filled it.

As also discussed in Chapter 5, the popular committees, at least in the towns of the Cairo peri-urban fringe, represented organic community organisations that did not only substitute the roles that had been assigned to the local branches of the NDP from the early 1990s to the mid-2000s, but also introduced a revolutionary model that had a greater capacity to mobilise local communities. However, the July 2013 military coup put an end to this model of local politics. From then and until early 2014, the towns of the Cairo peri-urban fringe witnessed demonstrations and unrest on a weekly basis. A group of Kerdasian youths established a local organisation under the name of 'Ultras Masr al-Siyasi', which later extended its activism against the military coup to reach the surrounding towns.[17] Nevertheless, they were ignored by the Egyptian authorities as most of the security focus was on public squares in the cities.[18]

From the middle of 2014, the Egyptian regime turned its attention to the peripheries. However, due to the fluidity of the Egyptian political landscape and the absence of a robust ruling party, the NSA was not able alone to counter political domestic security issues. Therefore, other security agencies, most notably the Criminal Intelligence Services (CIS), *al-mabahith al-gina'iya*, also gave assistance. This created problems since the CIS lacked training and therefore had no experience in implementing politically-related security missions.

One Kerdasian told the author that he was detained in February 2017 for 24 hours by CIS officers who suspected him of being a member of the MB. After hours of interrogation, however, the police officer came to realise that not only had the detainee nothing to do with the MB, but also that he had been an active member of the dissolved NDP before the revolution. Before he was released, one of the police officers complained that the police are assigned missions that they are not trained to do, the interviewee claimed.[19]

Since the end of the military campaign against Kerdasa in September 2013 and until the present day, thousands of citizens from the towns of the Cairo peri-urban fringe have been detained and arrested. Hundreds of youths were tried before exceptional courts. Dozens received sentences ranging from three years to the death penalty. In court case No. 1273 of 2016 in the name of 'The Center of Kerdasa's felonies', the court sentenced six Kerdasian youths to death, forty-one to life imprisonment, seven to 15 years' imprisonment, and a thirteen-year-old child to 3 years. The NSA also arrested Ahmad Khattab, the defendants' lawyer, and accused him of joining a terrorist group. Khattab spent 11 months in prison, and then in 2018 went into exile.[20]

The latest security campaign was in September–October 2020 after hundreds of Egyptians in many towns such as Kerdasa, Nahia, Abu Rawash, Kiddaya and Ayat and Kafr Qandil took to the streets in response to al-Sisi's televised threats to deploy the army in villages to demolish illegal houses.[21] The government claimed that informal constructions did not comply with engineering safety standards.[22] Nevertheless, the government ratified a law allowing settlement with the state over building violations by paying compensation, setting a six-month deadline to reach such settlement. This suggests that the regime's intentions were exploitative rather than reformative or developmental. Given the fact that informal settlements constitute more than 40 per cent of Greater Cairo and house more than 60 per cent of its residents,[23] the regime's move may be explained as an obsessive quest to extract funds from Egypt's poorest. Media reported that the government asked residents of villages to pay around $1,000 to regularise their houses, while they struggle to earn $100 monthly.[24]

As was discussed in Chapters 1 and 2, the strategies of decentralising the regime's networks of power from the late 1980s entailed local NDP leadership being assigned the role of mobilising their communities. The NDP's local secretaries until 2005 helped to organise the collection of various kinds of donations from the community to develop local amenities, facilities and infrastructure, therefore, helping to reduce governmental expenditure on urban development. From the mid-2000s, however, the regime bypassed its established local leaders who were replaced by corrupt local businessmen who paid the donations directly to the government. Under al-Sisi, there are indicators that the police themselves, perhaps temporarily, are carrying out this task instead of a robust ruling party. The situation requires more securitising of local governance. However, it is unlikely that this would be a durable situation since it fuels further grievances against the state as the case of the villages' protests in September–October 2020 suggests. Other recent indicators, nevertheless, point to the securitisation of local governance being an interim stage until the new regime establishes and consolidates its own reliable networks of power at the subnational level. The next section discusses the limitations of this strategy.

From the NDP to the NFP: Insecure Grassroots?

For decades, the NDP represented the major institutionalised patronage machine through which the authoritarian regime not only intended to dominate local politics, but also contributed constantly to redefining it. At the subnational level, the relationship between the state and the ruling party was subjected to major shifts based on the regime's strategies of horizontal centralisation–decentralisation. Motivated by the politics of succession, the first decade of the Mubarak era was marked by strategies of centralisation on structures of both authority and power. As we saw in Chapter 2, Mubarak re-engineered electoral laws and legislation in a way that retained the NDP's centralist control. He reduced the number of electoral constituencies and banned independents from running in the elections. The change had devastating consequences on the local NDP leadership. It practically led to the degradation of the semi-autonomous character of the political field and created a gap between the authoritarian regime and its local networks of power, leaving room for an alternative local politics to emerge: the politics of identity.

Starting from the second decade of Mubarak's presidency and accompanied by a shift in the country's political economy, the regime again used elections to retain strategies of decentralisation by gradually liberating both local and general elections. This move brought local networks of power closer to the structure of authority. Consequently, as we have seen in this book, the conception of local politics was changed. While local leaders had been expected to be social mediators among the locals, their roles after the process of upgrading evolved into service deputies, helping to provide services to their localities and in return mobilising local communities to reduce the cost of public expenditure. From the mid-2000s, this formula was informally changed. A new generation of SSIS-backed NDP men, who had no roots in their local communities but had money to finance their networks, emerged. However, they lacked sufficient time to enjoy their clientelistic positions. In January 2011, a popular revolution erupted leading to the collapse of the system of local governance, but by late 2013 authoritarian control had been reinstated.

How can we understand the authoritarian strategies of managing the networks of power at the subnational level in post-revolutionary Egypt? Although it might be too early to answer this question, an assessment of the most recent developments in the politics of local governance suggests that the regime is manoeuvring between the strategies of informal centralisation and decentralisation through manipulating election laws and procedures.

Under al-Sisi, Egypt has experienced a series of plebiscites and elections: two constitutional referendums in March 2014 and April 2019; two presidential elections in May 2014 and March 2018; two parliamentary elections in October and December 2015 and October–November 2020; senate elections in August 2020, but no local council elections at all. The 2015 parliamentary election filled 596 seats, of which 448 were individual candidates in 205 constituencies; 28 seats were appointed by the president; 120 seats were elected through winner-take-all party lists competing in just four huge constituencies. The 120 list seats were filled by 56 women, 24 Copts, 16 workers and farmers, 16 youths, 8 Egyptians abroad, and 8 Egyptians with disabilities. The post-military coup parliament was the largest in the country's history, more than 100 members larger than the parliament it was to replace.[25]

Scholars of the politics of Egypt consider al-Sisi's parliament 'a rubber stamp that provided them little if any representation'.[26] Contrary to the parliamentary elections during Mubarak's presidency, which served as a strategy of authoritarian upgrading through updating and outsourcing the regime's grassroots, elections under al-Sisi's presidency appear far more circumscribed, fabricated, controlled and 'less effective for extending state power into society'.[27] As Stacher has stressed, 'elections in Egypt today transmit a message that citizens will vote as they are told and nothing else',[28] and, according to Sahar Aziz, the 2015 parliamentary election facilitated the return of powerful local figures who had been the backbone of the NDP: 'Instead of Mubarak as their patron, it was now Sisi.'[29]

Although in the 2015 election, the military-backed 'For the Love of Egypt' bloc won all 120 party-list seats, the number of electoral constituencies for individual candidates was relatively high. A total of 5,420 candidates were approved to compete for the 448 independent seats, which allowed for the local notables from the marginalised second generation of the NDP to assume their roles in local politics as service deputies. In Kerdasa, Ala'a Wali, whom the NDP had turned down in the 2010 election though he had been chosen by the local Electoral College in the primaries, won the seat designated for individuals in 2015. Wali worked very hard in his five-year term as an MP, in the same way and using the same logic as any NDP parliamentarian from the early 1990s to the mid-2000s. As a service deputy, he lobbied the state institutions and mobilised local communities to improve public services, such as opening a medical centre in Kerdasa, solving the problem of sanitation in west Nahia, establishing a unit for dialysis in Birak al-Khiyam and a post office in al-Moatamadeyah, as well as expanding a school in Kafr Hakeem. However, in the most recent election, Wali withdrew his candidacy. Why?

In the 2020 parliamentary election, electoral legislation was fundamentally changed. First, the number of electoral constituencies was significantly reduced from 205 to 143, therefore, the number of seats designated for individual candidates dropped from 448 to 284. Secondly, the party-list's share was increased from 120 in the 2015 parliament to 284 seats. The result was that over 4,000 candidates ran as individuals competing for 50 per cent of the seats. The other 50 per cent were reserved for over 1,100 candidates running on four party lists, while the president could appoint some members, but no more than 5 per cent of the total.[30]

In Kerdasa, this meant that individual candidates were to compete over only one seat, since the other one was transferred to the party list. Those local figures who wanted to join the pre-selected list had literally to purchase a guaranteed seat from a newly-backed regime party, Mostaqbal Watan or the Nation's Future Party (NFP). Alternatively, they had the choice of purchasing the official party nomination for the individual seat, which was cheaper but not guaranteed. According to press reports, the price of a seat ranged from LE 10 to LE 25 million ($600,000–$1,500,000) for a party-list seat and started from LE 2 million for an individual one.[31] The NFP's pre-selected lists, consequently, won all 284 seats allocated to the 596-seat chamber through a winner-takes-all system. Its candidates also secured a majority in seats contested by individual candidates.

The NFP was founded in November 2014 by members of the Egyptian Military Intelligence and Reconnaissance Administration. In the 2015 parliamentary election, it was one of the largest parties in the pro-Sisi coalition of 'For the Love of Egypt', holding fifty-seven seats in the parliament. The Egyptian constitution stipulates that the president cannot assume the leadership of any political party and the NFP officially denied on many occasions that it was the party of the state. However, many indicators, most notably the results of the 2020 election, suggest that not only is the NFP a revival of the dissolved NDP, but it is also a return to Gamal Mubarak's version just before the January 25 Revolution; albeit this time with no Gamal. It is the party of the men of the security business.

After he had officially submitted his candidacy, Wali realised that he had no chance of winning this election. On his Facebook page, he released a statement announcing the withdrawal of his candidacy in the 2020 election. He justified his decision by his refusal to buy politics with money, which he considered disrespectful to the voters of Kerdasa whose 'votes are priceless'.[32] Obviously, however, Wali was expressing his resentment at what he saw as his unjust replacement by Khaled Tamer Taiea', a local tycoon from Abu Rawash of whom it is said that he is one of the prominent monopolists of the antiquities trade on the Cairo peri-urban fringe. Taiea' was nominated on behalf of the NFP to compete for the individual seat although he lacked popularity in his locality, to the extent that a YouTube video has shown him threatening to jail the people of the village of Kombra because they refused to back his electoral campaign.[33]

As we saw in Chapter 5, ironically, both Wali and Taiea' contested Kerdasa's parliament seat in the 2010 election. Wali represented the second generation of the local NDP leadership (the NDP veterans), while Taiea' emerged as an expression of the emergence of a third generation who came with the rise of Gamal Mubarak. In 2010, Wali resisted his unfair deprivation of an official NDP nomination by running as an independent, but the election's outcome was predetermined in favour of Taiea'. This time, however, he learned that resistance was pointless. If he had had any hope of challenging the circles of power in the last few years of Mubarak's presidency, under al-Sisi it had become extremely dangerous, foolish and reckless; a point that was realised not only by Wali but also by others in Shubra, Bulaq and other electoral constituencies.[34]

The regime's politics of local governance, as can be concluded from the 2020 election, manoeuvres between strategies of informal centralisation and decentralisation in order to recreate its own networks of power. On the one hand, increasing the share of party lists to 50 per cent of the parliament means that the regime is insisting on supervising the selection of at least half of its power centres at the subnational level. This strategy reminds us of Mubarak's move in the first decade of his rule when he reduced the number of electoral constituencies and banned individuals from running for elections. As discussed in Chapter 2, Mubarak was motivated by politics of secession. He had a negative attitude towards the Sadatian version of the ruling party and wanted to create a new party loyal to him. Therefore, he used local and parliamentary elections as a strategy of horizontal centralisation, which empowered the NDP centralist control and gave its senior leadership a formidable power even in deciding the lowest appointments, which subsequently undermined the role of the local leadership, leading to degradation of the semi-autonomous character of the political field at the subnational level.

The logic of the 2020 election tells us that al-Sisi may also have been motivated by the politics of succession, which made him preoccupied with implementing strategies of centralisation on the structure of power in order to create new loyal networks at the subnational level, even if this was at the expense of other pro-regime parties and political groups. For example, a report revealed that the Republican People's Party (RPP) – the main partner of the NFP on the electoral list – which is made up of a group of former government ministers, proposed a preliminary list featuring its suggested forty-six candidates for election. However, the RPP leadership was shocked to find that only eight names on the list were active members of their party. All the other names on the list came from the NFP. The result was mass resignation from the RPP, one of whose leaders describing what had happened as the 'nationalisation of his party'.[35] However, this incident also tells us that the current authoritarian regime has no trust in its grassroots, nor any respect.

On the other hand, the regime's eagerness to maintain half of the parliamentary seats to be contested by individual candidates suggests that it still deems the strategies of decentralising networks of power to be of importance. As we have discussed in this book, the Egyptian regime since the late 1970s has had a great deal of experience in how to utilise elections as a strategy of political decentralisation in favour of more authoritarian resilience. In his last years, Sadat tended to conduct elections on an individual basis, allowing a relatively large number of independent candidates as a way of mobilising rural support and also to weaken the central control of the ruling party to prevent the emergence of a strong party leadership. Mubarak also used the individual system from the early 1990s to regularise intra-elite competition, outsource the cost of political mobilisation, as well as mobilise local communities to fill the financial void that was left as a result of the state's withdrawal from the mission of urban development due to the acceleration of neo-liberal policies (see Chapter 2).

It is unlikely that al-Sisi's regime will give up the political benefits brought by the individual electoral system as a mechanism of informal political decentralisation. In fact, both the 2015 and 2020 parliamentary elections show the regime's commitment to it. It is also expected that once the regime consolidates its networks at the subnational level, it would again retain the full capacity of the individual system. This is because the alternative of abandoning the strategies of informal decentralisation would lead to more securitisation of local governance or the inevitability of decentralising the structure of authority of the state. Both options, however, are not economically and politically affordable to Egyptian authoritarianism.

From my own perspective, I do not think that Egyptian authoritarianism can afford to rule subnational levels by coercion. Not only because of the lack of recourse, but also because people are not just ruled by force, but by ideology, too, which the regime lacks (except if we consider the current trickster politics, and the discourse of developmentalism, a substitution for ideology, which I doubt). Eventually, the regime would face the same dilemma the previous regime failed to confront. The fact that the *untrusted* regime's multi-level informal networks share nothing except their *uncertain* closeness to the state will make them never able to cooperate voluntarily, or gain popular support or even prevent the emergence of new challengers on the ground. It will merely make them insecure. Only time and further research will tell us if Egyptian authoritarianism would resolve this dilemma.

Notes

1. Lucia Ardovini and Simon Mabon, 'Egypt's Unbreakable Curse: Tracing the State of Exception from Mubarak to al Sisi', *Mediterranean Politics* 25(4) (2020): 456–75.

2. Joshua Stacher, *Watermelon Democracy: Egypt's Turbulent Transition* (New York: Syracuse University Press, 2020), 158.
3. Robert Springborg, 'Egypt's Economic Transition: Challenges and Prospects', in Giacomo Luciani (ed.), *Combining Economic and Political Development: The Experience of MENA* (Leiden: Brill, 2017), 184–210.
4. Robert Springborg, 'The Rewards of Failure: Persisting Military Rule in Egypt', *British Journal of Middle Eastern Studies* 44(4) (2017): 478–96; Zeinab Abul-Magd, İsmet Akça and Shana Marshall, 'Two Paths to Dominance: Military Businesses in Turkey and Egypt', Carnegie Endowment for International Peace, 2020, available at: https://carnegieendowment.org/files/Magd_Akca_Marshall_-_PathsDominance.pdf .
5. Abul-Magd, *Militarizing the Nation*, 228.
6. Heba Khalil and Brian Dill, 'Negotiating Statist Neoliberalism: The Political Economy of Post-Revolution Egypt', *Review of African Political Economy* 45(158) (2018): 574–91.
7. Stacher, *Watermelon Democracy*, 19.
8. Ibid., 26.
9. Ibid.
10. Walter Armbrust, 'Trickster Defeats the Revolution: Egypt as the Vanguard of the New Authoritarianism', *Middle East Critique* 26(3) (2017): 221–39.
11. Bruce K. Rutherford, 'Egypt's New Authoritarianism under Sisi', *Middle East Journal* 72(2) (2018): 185–208, 185.
12. Ibid.
13. de Elvira et al., *Networks of Dependency*, 2.
14. Mohamed Fahmy Menza, 'Cairo's New Old Faces: Redrawing the Map of Patron–Client Networks against the Background of the January 25 Revolution and the 2015 Elections', in Ruiz de Elvira et al., *Clientelism and Patronage in the Middle East and North Africa: Networks of Dependency* (London: Routledge, 2018).
15. Mohammad Yaghi, 'Neoliberal Reforms, Protests, and Enforced Patron–Client Relations in Tunisia and Egypt', in Ruiz de Elvira et al., *Clientelism and Patronage in the Middle East and North Africa: Networks of Dependency* (London: Routledge, 2018).
16. Al-Masry Al-Youm, 27 April 2011, available at: https://www.almasryalyoum.com/news/details/128155.
17. Othman Mousa, *Interview*, November 2020.
18. Hani Awad, 'Egypt after Rabia Al-Adawiya: Ongoing Protests and Open-Ended Transitions', ACRPS Policy Analysis, February 2014, available at: https://www

.dohainstitute.org/en/PoliticalStudies/Pages/Egypt_after_Rabia_Al-Adawiya _Ongoing_Protests_and_Open-Ended_Transitions.aspx.

19. K. S., *Interview*, November 2020.
20. Ahmad Khattab, *Interview*, 3 December 2020.
21. *Middle East Eye*, 'Egypt: Villages Witness Limited anti-Sisi Protests amid Fears of Crackdown', 21 September 2020, available at: https://www.middleeasteye.net /news/egypt-villages-witness-limited-anti-sisi-protests-despite-fear-crackdown; *Middle East Monitor*, '"Sisi is the Enemy of God", Chants on Egypt's Fourth Day of Protest against His Rule', 24 September 2020, available at: https://www .middleeastmonitor.com/20200924-sisi-is-the-enemy-of-god-chants-on-egyp ts-fourth-day-of-protests-against-his-rule; Amnesty International, 'Egypt: Rare Protests Met with Unlawful Force and Mass Arrests', 2 October 2020, available at: https://www.amnesty.org/en/latest/news/2020/10/egypt-rare-protests-met -with-unlawful-force-and-mass-arrests.
22. Ahram online, 'Egypt Will no Longer Allow Building Violations in Villages and Cities, says PM', 9 September 2020, available at: http://english.ahram.org.eg /NewsContent/1/64/379657/Egypt/Politics-/Egypt-will-no-longer-allow-buil ding-violations-in-.aspx.
23. Sims, *Understanding Cairo*, 92.
24. *The Guardian*, 'Threat of Home Demolitions Sparks Protests among Egypt's Poorest', 6 October 2020, available at: https://www.theguardian.com/world/20 20/oct/06/egypt-security-forces-target-rare-anti-government-protests; Reuters, 'Crackdown on Illegal Housing Leaves some Egyptians Struggling to Pay Fees', 5 October 2020, available at: https://www.reuters.com/article/us-egypt-politi cs-demolitions/crackdown-on-illegal-housing-leaves-some-egyptians-struggling -to-pay-fees-idUSKBN26Q0ZP?il=0.
25. Robert Springborg, *Egypt* (Cambridge: Polity, 2008), 104.
26. Ibid., 105.
27. Stacher, *Watermelon Democracy*, 59.
28. Ibid., 57.
29. Sahar F. Aziz, 'Military Electoral Authoritarianism in Egypt', *Election Law Journal: Rules, Politics, and Policy* 16(2) (2017): 280–95, 293.
30. Mada Masr, 'Giza House Race Sheds Light on Egypt's Shifting Political Machinery', 26 October 2020, available at: https://www.madamasr.com/en/20 20/10/26/feature/politics/giza-house-race-sheds-light-on-egypts-shifting-politi cal-machinery.
31. *The Economist*, 'Another Sham Election Highlights Egypt's Problems the Country's Rulers are Making a Mess of Politics and Business', 22 October 2020, available at: https://www.economist.com/middle-east-and-africa/2020/10/22

/another-sham-election-highlights-egypts-problems; *Middle East Monitor*, 'Egypt Parliament Seat Costs $3.2m, Reveals MP', 9 October 2020, available at: https://www.middleeastmonitor.com/20201009-egypt-parliament-seat-costs-3-2m-reveals-mp.

32. Ala'a Wali, '*Bayan Ham*' ('Important Statement'), Facebook, 7 October 2020, available at: https://www.facebook.com/Alaa.walyyy/posts/2857100844567940.
33. *Al-Watan*, 29 September 2020, available online at: https://www.elwatannews.com/news/details/4990995; *Bawabit al-Barlaman* (*The Parliament Gate*), 11 October 2020, available at: https://www.parlgate.com/59070.
34. *Bawabit al-Barlaman* (*The Parliament Gate*) 10 October 2020, available at: https://www.parlgate.com/59015.
35. Mada Masr, 'The Cost of Playing Monopoly: How the Nation's Future Party has Caused Rifts among Parties in House Elections', 1 October 2020, available at: https://madamasr.com/en/2020/10/01/feature/politics/the-cost-of-playing-monopoly-how-the-nations-future-party-has-caused-rifts-among-parties-in-house-elections.

APPENDICES

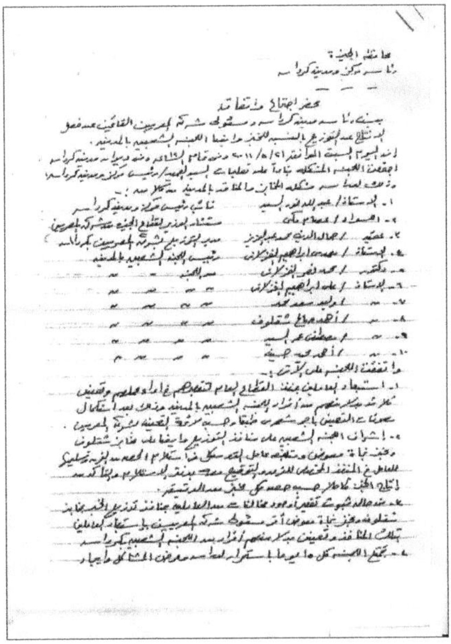

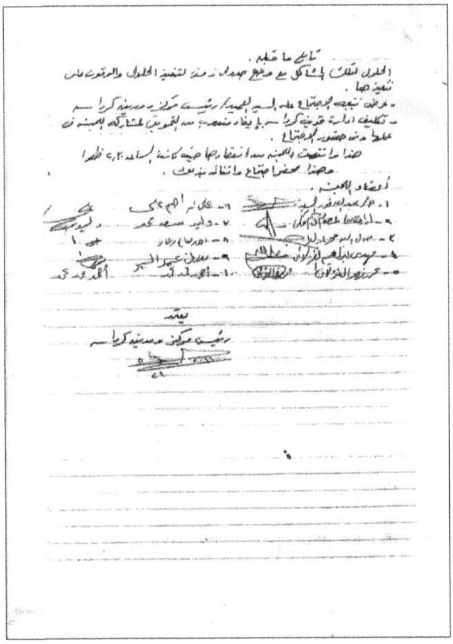

Appendix I Minutes of a meeting and agreement between the Popular Committee and the City Council of Kerdasa regarding the organisation of bread distribution points in the town

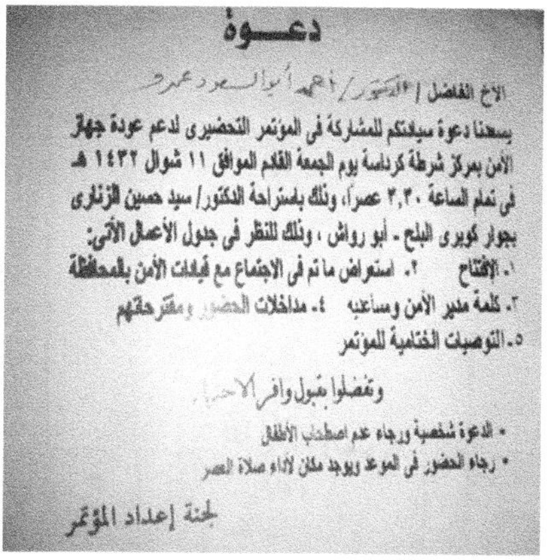

دعـــوة

الأخ الفاضل / الدكتور/ أحمد أبو السعود

يسعدنا دعوة سيادتكم للمشاركة فى المؤتمر التحضيرى لدعم عودة جهاز الأمن بمركز شرطة كرداسة يوم الجمعة القادم الموافق ١١ شوال ١٤٣٢ هـ فى تمام الساعة ٢,٣٠ عصراً، وذلك باستراحة الدكتور/ سيد حسين الزناري بجوار كوبرى البلح - أبو رواش ، وذلك للنظر فى جدول الأعمال الآتى:

١. الافتتاح ٢. استعراض ما تم فى الاجتماع مع قيادات الأمن بالمحافظة

٣. كلمة مدير الأمن ومساعديه ٤. مداخلات الحضور ومقترحاتهم

٥. التوصيات الختامية للمؤتمر

وتفضلوا بقبول وافر الاحترام

- الدعوة شخصية ورجاء عدم اصطحاب الأطفال
- رجاء الحضور فى الموعد ويوجد مكان لأداء صلاة العصر

لجنة إعداد المؤتمر

Appendix II Kerdasa public meeting invitation

Translation: We have the pleasure to invite you to attend the preparatory conference in support of the return of the police to Kerdasa's police station next Friday, Shawwal 11, 1432 AH at 2:30 pm. This will take place at the rest house of Dr Sayyid Hussein al-Zanari next to the Balah Bridge, Abu Ruwwash. The agenda is as follows: 1. Opening. 2. Review of the meeting with governorate security chiefs. 3. Address by the Director of Security and his assistants. 4. Questions and proposals from those present. 5. Concluding recommendations.

Please note the following:

The invitation is personal, please do not bring children.

Please arrive on time. Space is available for the afternoon prayer.

The Conference Committee

Appendix III 'The national day of liberating Kerdasa'

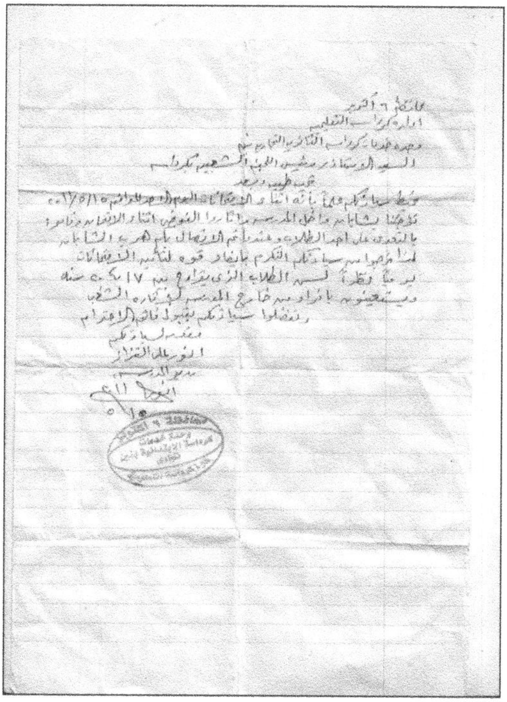

محافظة ٦ أكتوبر
إدارة كرداسة التعليمية
مدرسة [illegible] كرداسة الثانوية التجارية بنين
السيد الأستاذ / رئيس اللجنة الشعبية بكرداسة
تحية طيبة وبعد
نحيط سيادتكم علماً بأنه أثناء الامتحانات اليوم الأحد الموافق ١٥/٥/٢٠١١
فوجئنا بشباب من داخل المدرسة [illegible] أثاروا الفوضى أثناء الامتحانات وقاموا
بالتعدي على أحد الطلاب وعندما تم الاتصال [illegible] الشباب
لذا نرجو من سيادتكم التكرم بإيفاد قوة لتأمين الامتحانات
[illegible] نظراً لسن الطلاب الذي يتراوح من ١٧ [illegible] سنة
ويستعينوا بأفراد من خارج المدرسة [illegible]
وتفضلوا سيادتكم بقبول فائق الاحترام
مقدمه لسيادتكم
[illegible]
مدير المدرسة
[illegible]

Appendix IV A letter (dated 15 May 2011) from a principal of a public school in Kerdasa asking the Popular Committee to send a 'force' to secure the examination from bullies

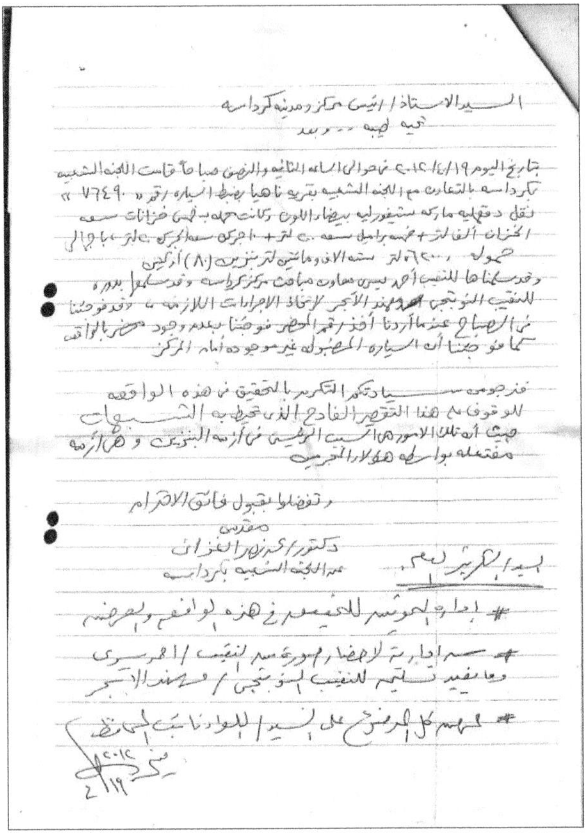

السيد الأستاذ / رئيس مركز ومدينة كرداسة
تحية طيبة ... وبعد

بتاريخ اليوم ١٩/٤/٢٠١٢ في حوالي الساعة الثانية والنصف صباحاً قامت اللجنة الشعبية
بكرداسة بالتعاون مع اللجنة الشعبية بقرية ناهيا بضبط السيارة رقم « ٧٦٤٩٠ »
نقل دقهلية ماركة شيفروليه بيضاء اللون وكانت محملة بخمس خزانات سعة
الخزان ألف لتر + خمسة براميل سعة ٢٠٠ لتر + ١٠ جركن سعة الجركن ٢٠ لتر بإجمالي
حمولة ٦٢٠٠ لتر ستة آلاف ومائتين لتر بنزين (٨٠) أوكتين
وقد سلمناها للنقيب أحمد يسري معاون مباحث مركز كرداسة وقد سلمها بدوره
للنقيب [illegible] لاتخاذ الإجراءات اللازمة .. وقد فوجئنا
في الصباح عندما أردنا أخذ رقم المحضر فوجئنا بعدم وجود محضر بالواقعة
كما فوجئنا أن السيارة المضبوطة غير موجودة أمام المركز

فنرجو من سيادتكم التكرم بالتحقيق في هذه الواقعة
للوقوف على هذا التقصير الفادح الذي تحيط به الشبهات
حيث أن تلك الأمور هي السبب الرئيسي في أزمة البنزين وهي أزمة
مفتعلة بواسطة هؤلاء المجرمين

وتفضلوا بقبول فائق الاحترام
مقدمه
دكتور / [illegible] الغزالي
عضو اللجنة الشعبية بكرداسة

[illegible]

Appendix V(A) A letter (dated 19 April 2012) from the Popular Committee to the President of the City Council in Kerdasa demanding an investigation into the disappearance of a van that contained 6,200 litres of smuggled petrol after it had been handed in to the police

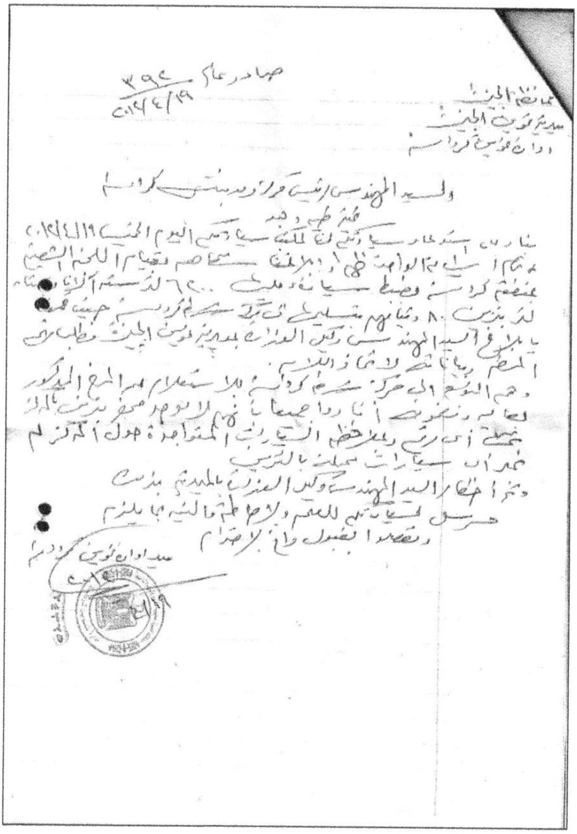

Appendix V(B) A letter (dated 19 April 2012) from the head of the Supply Management in Kerdasa responding to the disappearance of the van

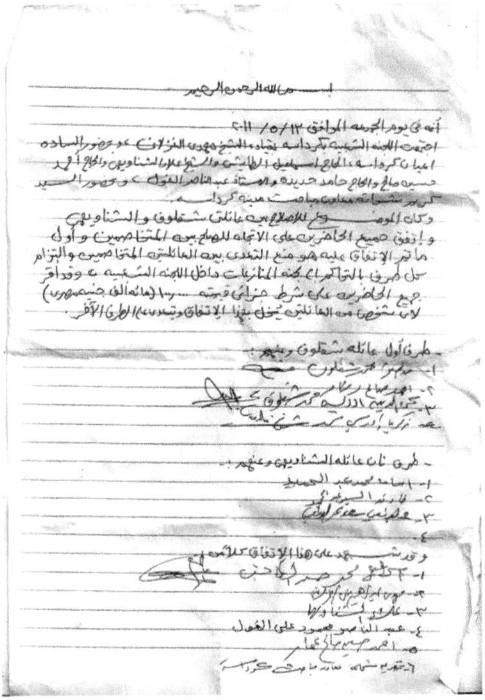

بسم الله الرحمن الرحيم

أنه في يوم الجمعه الموافق ١٣/٥/٢٠١١
اجتمعت اللجنه الشعبيه بكرداسه بقياده الشيخ مهدي الغزلاني وحضور السادة
اعيان كرداسه الحاج اسماعيل الطايش والشيخ علاء الشناويهي والحاج أحمد
حسين صالح والحاج حامد حديده والاستاذ عبد الناصر الغول وحضور السيد
[illegible] مباحث مدينه كرداسه.
وكان الموضوع للاصلاح بين عائلتي شقلوف والشناويهي
واتفق جميع الحاضرين على الاتجاه للصلح بين المتخاصمين وأول
ما تم الاتفاق عليه هو منع التعدي بين العائلتين المتخاصمين والتزام
كل طرف بالتحاكم الى لجنه المنازعات داخل اللجنه الشعبيه ووافق
جميع الحاضرين على شرط جزائي قيمته ١٠٠٠٠٠ (مائه الف جنيه مصري)
لأي شخص من العائلتين يخل بهذا الاتفاق ويسدد للطرف الآخر.

- طرف أول عائلة شقلوف ومنهم:
١- [illegible] شقلوف
٢- [illegible]
٣- [illegible] شقلوف
٤- [illegible]

- طرف ثاني عائلة الشناويهي ومنهم:
١- اسامه محمد عبد الحميد
٢- [illegible]
٣- [illegible]
٤-

وقد شهد على هذا الاتفاق كل من:
١- [illegible]
٢- [illegible]
٣- [illegible]
٤- عبد الناصر محمود علي الغول
٥- [illegible]
٦- [illegible] كرداسه

Appendix VI A dispute settlement (dated 13 May 2011) between two families in Kerdasa settled by the Popular Committee

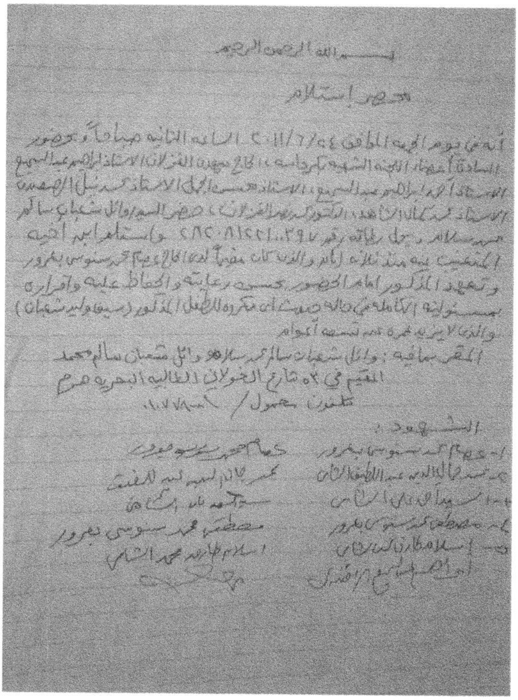

بسم الله الرحمن الرحيم

محضر إستلام

أنه في يوم الجمعة الموافق ٢٤/٦/٢٠١١ الساعة الثانية صباحاً ، وبحضور السادة أعضاء اللجنة الشعبية [illegible]
[illegible]
[illegible]
[illegible] وإستلم ابن أخيه [illegible]
وتعهد المذكور امام الحضور بحسن رعايته والحفاظ عليه وإقراره بمسئوليته الكاملة في حالة حدوث اي مكروه للطفل المذكور [illegible]
والذي لا يزيد عمره عن تسعة أعوام
المقر بما فيه : وائل شعبان سالم [illegible]
المقيم في [illegible] شارع [illegible]
تلفون محمول / [illegible]

الشهود :
[illegible]

Appendix VII A letter (dated 24 June 2011) that a person received from the Popular Committee about his nine-year-old nephew after the boy had been missed for three days

بسم الله الرحمن الرحيم

السيد العميد / رئيس مركز ومدينة كرداسه

تحيه طيبه .. وبعد

- نحيط سيادتكم بأن المنطقه الواقعه بين كوبرى صفط اللبن وكوبرى الأورمان
كانت بمثابه مقلب للقمامه ومخلفات المبانى وقد حول أصحاب سيارات
النقل أصحاب النفوس الخربه تلك المنطقه الى تلال وجبال من المخلفات
التى شكلت مناخاً خصباً للمجرمين لتعاطى وبيع المخدرات فى هذه المنطقه
وقد قامت اللجنه الشعبيه بكرداسه بضبط العديد من المجرمين من هذه المنطقه
وتسليمهم الى مركز كرداسه فى القريه الذكيه وقد بذلت اللجنه الشعبيه
جهداً كبير فى الحفاظ على تلك المنطقه بعد تنظيفها من قبل المسئولين
فى مدينه كرداسه والذى استغرق جهداً ووقتاً ومالاً لا يستهان به
- ولذلك نحيطكم علماً بأن اللجان الشعبيه بكرداسه ستقوم بتشجير
تلك المنطقه وتحويلها الى متنزهات خضراء تمهيداً لتحويلها إلى حديقه
عامه يستفيد منها كل أهالى كرداسه والمناطق المحيطه بها

وتفضلوا بقبول وافر الاحترام

عن اللجنه الشعبيه بكرداسه

١- محمد ابراهيم الغزلانى
٢- عاطف شحات الجندى
٣- احمد سامح يحى
٤- محمد فاروق عمار
٥- محمد احمد على الصيفى
٦- محمد نصر مزروع
٧- ابراهيم عبد السميع الجندى
٨- محمد حسنى الشاهد

Appendix VIII A letter from the Popular Committee (dated June 2011) informing the City Council that they will reforest a plot of land in Kerdasa and develop it into a public park; the City Council (in red) responded positively.

Appendix IX The former chairman of the Popular Committee Sheikh Mahdi Ghizlani with the then head of Kerdasa's police station, and to the right, the chief of police in al-Giza Governorate (*Hikimdar*); the picture was taken during one of the reconciliation councils (*majalis al-sulh*) to settle the cases of the two victims who died during the 28 January clashes

Appendix X Central interviews used in the study

Name	Occupation/career/ political affiliation	Location	Date(s) of interview	Notes
Abdel Salam Zaki Bashandi	MB	Khartoum	26 January 2017	Through research assistant
Ismail Abu Hussain	Merchant (old man)	Kerdasa	23 April 2016	Through research assistant
Ahmed Abdel-Wahhab Mahjoub	NDP	Kerdasa	(a) 16 April 2016 (b) 25 December 2016	(a) On Skype (b) Through research assistant
Ahmed Hulail	The mosque movement	Germany	18 April 2016; 22 April 2016	VoIP
Ahmed Nizili	Son of Sayed Nzeili	Cairo	18 September 2013	VoIP
Ashraf Rajab	MB	Istanbul	22 March 2016	Personally
Aysha Ghizlani	Yousef Abdel-Salam Saleh's sister	Istanbul	29 April 2016	Through research assistant
Hussain Saleh Omar	PC	Istanbul	Several interviews	Personally
Ismail al-Iskandrani	Journalist	USA	4 October 2013	VoIP
K. S. M.	Jihadist	Istanbul	Withheld	Withheld
Khaled Sa'd	The mosque movement	Istanbul	Several interviews	Personally
Khaled Abbas	PC	Kerdasa	Several interviews	VoIP
M. A. M.	NDP	Kerdasa	Withheld	Withheld
M. H.	NDP	Kerdasa	Withheld	Withheld
M. I.	PC	Kerdasa	Withheld	Withheld
M. S.	PC	Kerdasa	Withheld	Withheld
M. M.	MB	Saudi Arabia	Withheld	Withheld
Moa'z Tareq Mikkawi	Tareq Mikkawi's son	Kerdasa	30 April 2016	VoIP

Mo'ataz Mikkawi	NDP	Kerdasa	Several interviews	VoIP
H. U.	NDP	Kerdasa	Withheld	Withheld
Mohammad Abu Mousa	NDP	Kerdasa	25 December 2016	Through research assistant
Mohammad Ghizlani	The mosque movement, al-Jihad Organisation, the head of the PC	Istanbul	21 March 2016; 23 March 2016	Personally
Mohammad A. Khattab	SLA (gas warehouse)	Kerdasa	21 Mar 2016	Through research assistant
Mohammad Azayzeh	Textile workshop owner	Kerdasa	28 May 2016	Through research assistant
Mohammad Hasanin Mikkawi	NDP	Kerdasa	24 February 2017	Through research assistant
Mohammad Khamis Abu Issa	Textile workshop owner	Kerdasa	12 April 2016	VoIP
Mustafa Yousef Abdel-Salam	Yousef Abdel-Salam's son	Kerdasa	23 April 2016	VoIP
Sayed Hussain Zinnari	The mosque movement	Kerdasa	4 February 2016	Personally
Shadi al-Baik	PC	Istanbul	1 April 2016	Personally
Othman Mousa	Activist	Istanbul	28 November 2020	VoIP
Ahmad Khattab	Lawyer and activist	Istanbul	3 December 2020	VoIP

BIBLIOGRAPHY

Abdel-Fadil, Mahmoud, *Development, Income, Distribution and Social Change in Rural Egypt (1952–1970): A Study in the Political Economy of Agrarian Transition* (Cambridge: Cambridge University Press, 1975).

Abou-El-Fadl, Reem. *Revolutionary Egypt: Connecting Domestic and International Struggles* (London: Routledge, 2015).

Abu Ismail, Salah, *ash-Shahāda: Shahādat ash-Shaykh Ṣalāh 'Abu 'Ismā'īl fī Qaḍiyyat Tanẓīm al-Jihād* (*The Testimony: The Testimony of Sheikh Salah Abu Ismail on the Case of the Jihad Organization*) (Cairo: Dar al-I'tiṣām, 1984).

Abul-Magd, Zeinab, *Militarizing the Nation: The Army, Business, and Revolution in Egypt* (New York: Columbia University Press, 2017).

Abul-Magd, Zeinab, İsmet Akça and Shana Marshall, 'Two Paths to Dominance: Military Businesses in Turkey and Egypt', Carnegie Endowment for International Peace, 2020.

Achcar, Gilbert, *The People Want: A Radical Exploration of the Arab Uprising* (Berkeley: California University Press, 2013).

Agamben, Giorgio, *State of Exception*, trans. Kevin Attell (Chicago: University of Chicago Press, 2005).

Aidi, Hisham, *Redeploying the State: Corporatism, Neoliberalism, and Coalition Politics* (London: Springer, 2008).

Al-Anani, Khalil, *Inside the Muslim Brotherhood: Religion, Identity, and Politics* (Oxford: Oxford University Press, 2016).

al-Awadi, Hesham, 'A Struggle for Legitimacy: The Muslim Brotherhood and Mubarak, 1982–2009', *Contemporary Arab Affairs* 2(2) (2009): 214–28.

Al-Jabarti, A. al-Rahman, *Aja'ib al-athar fi al-tarajim wal-akhbar* (Cairo: Ktab Inc, 2013).

al-Mouldi al-Ahmar (ed.), *Ath-Thawra at-Tūnisiyya: al-Qādiḥ al-Maḥalī Taḥt Mijhar al-ʿUlūm al-ʾInsāniyya* (*The Tunisian Revolution: Examining the Local Triggers through the Prism of Humanities*) (Doha and Beirut: ACRPS, 2014).

Ambrosio, Thomas, 'Constructing a Framework of Authoritarian Diffusion: Concepts, Dynamics, and Future Research', *International Studies Perspectives* 11(4) (2010): 375–92.

Amin, Galal, *Whatever Happened to the Egyptians? Changes in Egyptian Society from 1950 to the Present* (Cairo: American University in Cairo Press, 2000).

Ammar, Hamed, *Growing up in an Egyptian Village: Silwa, Province of Aswan* (London: Routledge, [1954] 2013).

Anderson, Benedict, *Imagined Communities: Reflections on the Origin and Spread of Nationalism* (London: Verso, 1983).

Ansell, Chris, 'Network Institutionalism', in R. A. W. Rhodes, S. A. Binder and B. A. Rockman (eds), *The Oxford Handbook of Political Institutions* (Oxford: Oxford University Press, 2006), 75–89.

Antoun, Richard and Iliya Harik (eds), *Rural Politics and Social Change in the Middle East* (Bloomington: Indiana University Press, 1972).

Ardovini, Lucia and Simon Mabon, 'Egypt's Unbreakable Curse: Tracing the State of Exception from Mubarak to al Sisi', *Mediterranean Politics* 25(4) (2020): 456–75.

Armbrust, Walter, 'Trickster Defeats the Revolution: Egypt as the Vanguard of the New Authoritarianism', *Middle East Critique* 26(3) (2017): 221–39.

Arnold, Thomas Walker et al., *The Encyclopaedia of Islam: A Dictionary of the Geography, Ethnography and Biography of the Muhammadan Peoples*, vol. VI (Leiden: E. J. Brill, 1908).

Atia, Mona, *Building a House in Heaven: Pious Neoliberalism and Islamic Charity in Egypt* (Minneapolis: Minnesota University Press, 2013).

Ayubi, Nazih, *Bureaucracy and Politics in Contemporary Egypt* (Oxford: Middle East Centre, 1980).

Ayubi, Nazih, *The State and Public Policies in Egypt since Sadat*, Political Studies of the Middle East Series, No. 29 (Reading: Ithaca Press, 1991).

Ayubi, Nazih, *Over-Stating the Arab State: Politics and Society in the Middle East* (London: I. B. Tauris, 1995).

Ayubi, Nazih, *Political Islam: Religion and Politics in the Arab World* (London: Routledge, 2003).

Aziz, Sahar F., 'Military Electoral Authoritarianism in Egypt', *Election Law Journal: Rules, Politics, and Policy* 16(2) (2017): 280–95.

Baedeker, K., *Egypt: Handbook for Travelers*, 2nd edn (London: Karl Baedeker Publisher, 1885).

Baer, Gabriel, *Studies in the Social History of Modern Egypt* (Chicago: University of Chicago Press, 1969).

Baker, Raymond William, *Sadat and After: Struggles for Egypt's Political Soul* (Cambridge, MA: Harvard University Press, 1990).

Barakat, Halim, *The Arab World: Society, Culture, and State* (Berkeley: California University Press, 1993).

Barber, Bernard, *The Logic and Limits of Trust* (New Brunswick, NJ: Rutgers University Press, 1983).

Batatu, Hanna, *Syria's Peasantry, the Descendants of its Lesser Rural Notables, and Their Politics* (Princeton, NJ: Princeton University Press, 1999).

Bates, Thomas R., 'Gramsci and the Theory of Hegemony', *Journal of the History of Ideas* (1975): 351–66.

Bayat, Asef, *Life as Politics: How Ordinary People Change the Middle East?* (Amsterdam: Amsterdam University Press, 2010).

Beach, Derek, 'Process-tracing Methods in Social Science', in *Oxford Research Encyclopaedia of Politics* (Oxford: Oxford University Press, 2017).

Benton, Allyson Lucinda, 'How "Participatory Governance" Strengthens Authoritarian Regimes: Evidence from Electoral Authoritarian Oaxaca, Mexico', *Journal of Politics in Latin America* 8(2) (2016): 37–70.

Berque, Jacques, *Histoire sociale d'un village égyptien au XXème siècle*, vol. 3 (Paris: Mouton, 1957).

Bevir, Mark (ed.), *Encyclopedia of Governance* (Thousand Oaks, CA: Sage, 2007).

Binder, Leonard, *In a Moment of Enthusiasm: Political Power and the Second Stratum in Egypt* (Chicago: University of Chicago Press, 1978).

Bishāra, Azmi, *al-Mojtama' al-Madany: Dirāsa Naqdiyya* (*Civil Society: A Critical Study*) (Beirut: Center for Arab Unity Studies, 1998).

Bishāra, Azmi, *Fy-l-Mas'ala al-'Arabiyya: Muqaddima li-Bayān Dīmuqrāty 'Araby* (*The Arab Question: Introduction to an Arab Democratic Statement*) (Beirut: Center for Arab Unity Studies, 2007).

Bishāra, Azmi, *aṭ-Ṭā'ifa, aṭ-Ṭā'ifiyya, aṭ-Ṭawā'if al-Mutakhayyala* (*Sect, Sectarianism, Imagined Sects*) (Doha and Beirut: ACRPS, 2018).

Blaydes, Lisa, *Elections and Distributive Politics in Mubarak's Egypt* (Cambridge: Cambridge University Press, 2010).

Boex, Jamie. 'Democratization in Egypt: The Potential Role of Decentralization', Center for International Development and Governance, Urban Institute, Washington, DC, February 2011, 3.

Bono, Irene and Béatrice Hibou (eds), *Development as a Battlefield*, International Development Policy Series No. 8 (Geneva: Graduate Institute Publications, Brill-Nijhoff, 2017).

Booth, David, 'Towards a Theory of Local Governance and Public Goods Provision', *IDS Bulletin* 42(2) (2011): 11–21.

Bourdieu, Pierre and Loi'c Wacquant, *An Invitation to Reflexive Sociology* (Cambridge: Polity, 1992).

Brown, Nathan, *The Rule of Law in the Arab World: Courts in Egypt and the Gulf* (Cambridge: Cambridge University Press, 1997).

Brownlee, Jason, 'The Decline of Pluralism in Mubarak's Egypt', *Journal of Democracy* 13(4) (2002): 6–14.

Calhoun, C., E. LiPuma and M. Postone (eds), *Bourdieu: Critical Perspectives* (Chicago: University of Chicago Press, 1993).

Cambanis T. and M. W. Hanna (eds), *Arab Politics Beyond the Uprisings: Experiments in an Era of Resurgent Authoritarianism* (New York: Century Foundation Press, 2017).

Canales, Oliver D. Meza, 'From Local Government to Local Governance', *Journal of Public Governance and Policy: Latin American Review* 1(1) (2015): 5–22.

Charrad, Mounira M. and Nicholas E. Reith, 'Local Solidarities: How the Arab Spring Protests Started', *Sociological Forum* 34 (2019): 1174–96.

Choueiri, Youssef (ed.), *A Companion to the History of the Middle East* (Oxford: Blackwell, 2005).

Clark, Janine A., *Islam, Charity, and Activism: Middle-Class Networks and Social Welfare in Egypt, Jordan, and Yemen* (Bloomington: Indiana University Press, 2004).

Clark, Janine A., *Local Politics in Jordan and Morocco: Strategies of Centralization and Decentralization* (New York: Columbia University Press, 2018).

Cnaan, Ram A. and Carl Milofsky (eds), *Handbook of Community Movements and Local Organizations in the 21st Century* (Cham: Springer, 2018).

Craig, David Alan and Doug Porter, *Development beyond Neoliberalism? Governance, Poverty Reduction and Political Economy* (New York: Routledge, 2006).

Cromer, 1st Earl of, *Modern Egypt* (London: Macmillan, 1908).

Daly, Martin W. and Carl F. Petry (eds), *The Cambridge History of Egypt*, vol. 2 (Cambridge: Cambridge University Press, 1998).

De Elvira, Laura Ruiz, Christoph H. Schwarz and Irene Weipert-Fenner (eds), *Clientelism and Patronage in the Middle East and North Africa: Networks of Dependency* (London: Routledge, 2018).

Deeb, Marius, *Party Politics in Egypt: The Wafd and its Rivals, 1919–1939* (London: Ithaca Press, 1979).

Demmelhuber, Thomas, Roland Sturm and Erik Vollmann, 'Decentralization in the Arab World: Conceptualizing the Role of Neopatrimonial Networks', *Mediterranean Politics* (2018): 1–23.

Doornbos, Martin, *Global Forces and State Restructuring* (London: Palgrave Macmillan, 2006).

Dorman, W. J., 'The Politics of Neglect: The Egyptian State in Cairo, 1974–98', PhD dissertation, SOAS, University of London, 2007.

Dorman, W. J., 'Exclusion and Informality: The Praetorian Politics of Land Management in Cairo, Egypt', *International Journal of Urban and Regional Research* 37(5) (2013): 1584–610.

Dupret, Baudouin, Maurits Berger and Laila Al-Zwaini (eds), *Legal Pluralism in the Arab World*, vol. 18 (The Hague: Kluwer Law International, 1999).

Eickelman, Dale and James Piscatori, *Muslim Politics* (Princeton, NJ: Princeton University Press, 2004).

Eisenstadt S. N. and Luis Roniger, *Patrons, Clients, and Friends: Interpersonal Relations and the Structure of Trust in Society* (Cambridge: Cambridge University Press, 1984).

El-Meehy, Asya, 'Egypt's Popular Committees from Moments of Madness to NGO Dilemmas', *Middle East Review – Egypt*, 42 (2012): 246.

Emmenegger, Rony, 'Decentralization and the Local Developmental State: Peasant Mobilization in Oromiya, Ethiopia', *Africa: The Journal of the International African Institute* 86(2) (2016): 263–87.

Evans-Pritchard, E., *The Sanusi of Cyrenaica* (Oxford: Clarendon Press, 1954).

Fahmy, N. S., *The Politics of Egypt: State–Society Relationship* (London: Routledge, 2012).

Farah, Nadia Ramsis, *Egypt's Political Economy: Power Relations in Development* (Cairo: American University in Cairo Press, 2009).

Faroqhi, Suraiya and Randi Deguilhem, *Crafts and Craftsmen of the Middle East: Fashioning the Individual in the Muslim Mediterranean* (London: I. B. Tauris, 2005).

Ferlie, Ewan, Laurence E. Lynn Jr. and Christopher Pollitt (eds), *The Oxford Handbook of Public Management* (New York: Oxford University Press, 2005).

Fox, Vincente (ed.), *Reinventing Government for the Twenty-first Century: State Capacity in a Globalizing Society* (West Hartford, CT: Kumarian Press, 2003).

Fukuyama, Francis, 'Social Capital, Civil Society and Development', *Third World Quarterly* 22(1) (2001): 7–20.

Gauvain, Richard, *Salafi Ritual Purity: In the Presence of God* (London: Routledge, 2013).

Gellner, Ernest and John Waterbury, *Patrons and Clients in Mediterranean Societies* (London: Duckworth, 1977).

Ghazaleh, Pascale, 'Trading in Power: Merchants and the State in 19th-Century Egypt', *International Journal of Middle East Studies* 45 (2013): 71–91.

Gill, Graeme and James Young (eds), *Routledge Handbook of Russian Politics and Society* (London: Routledge, 2013).

Godelier, Maurice, *The Metamorphoses of Kinship*, trans. Nora Scott (London: Verso, 2011).

Goffman, Erving, *Frame Analysis: An Essay on the Organization of Experience* (Cambridge, MA: Harvard University Press, 1974).

Gramsci, Antonio, *The Gramsci Reader: Selected Writings, 1916–1935* (New York: New York University Press, 2000).

Habashi, Mohammad Moustafa, 'Social Values and its Impacts on Rural Development: A Field Study in the Village of Kerdasa in al-Giza Governorate', PhD dissertation, University of Asyut, 1982.

Halliday, Fred and Hamza Alavi (eds), *State and Ideology in the Middle East and Pakistan* (London: Macmillan Education, 1988).

Ḥamdān, Jamāl, *Shakhsiyyat Miṣr: Dirāsa fy ʿAbqariyyat al-Makān* (*The Personality of Egypt: Reflections on the Genius Loci*), 4 vols (Cairo: Dār al-Hilāl, 1967).

Hamied, Ansari, *Egypt: The Stalled Society* (New York: SUNY Press, 1986).

Harders, Cilja, '"State Analysis from Below" and Political Dynamics in Egypt after 2011', *International Journal of Middle East Studies* 47(1) (2015): 148–51.

Harik, Iliya, 'The Single Party as a Subordinate Movement: The Case of Egypt', *World Politics* 26(1) (1973): 80–105.

Harik, Iliya and Denis J. Sullivan (eds), *Privatization and Liberalization in the Middle East* (Bloomington: Indiana University Press, 1992).

Harrison, Lawrence E. and Peter L. Berger, *Developing Cultures: Case Studies* (London: Routledge, 2006).

Hefny, Kadry, 'Content Analysis for Counselling Meetings Committee in the Local Unit of Kerdasa, Giza-Egypt', *Population Studies* 10(66) (1983): 41–58.

Heydemann, Steven, 'Upgrading Authoritarianism in the Arab World', *Analysis Paper*, Saban Center for Middle East Policy at the Brookings Institution, October 2017.

Heydemann, Steven and Reinoud Leenders, 'Authoritarian Learning and Authoritarian Resilience: Regime Responses to the "Arab Awakening"', *Globalizations* 8(5) (2011): 647–53.

Hinnebusch, Raymond, 'The Reemergence of the Wafd Party: Glimpses of the Liberal Opposition in Egypt', *International Journal of Middle East Studies* 16(1) (1984): 99–121.

Hinnebusch, Raymond, *Egyptian Politics under Sadat: The Post-Populist Development of an Authoritarian-Modernizing State* (Cambridge: Cambridge University Press, 1985).

Hinnebusch, Raymond, 'Syria: From "Authoritarian Upgrading" to Revolution?' *International Affairs* 88(1) (2012): 95–113.

Hinnebusch, Raymond, *The International Politics of the Middle East* (Manchester: Manchester University Press, 2013).

Hopkins, Nicholas S. and Kirsten Westergaard (eds), *Directions of Change in Rural Egypt* (Cairo: American University in Cairo Press, 1998).

Hornemann, Friedrich Conrad, *The Journal of Frederick Horneman's Travels, from Cairo to Mourzouk, the Capital of the Kingdom of Fezzan, in Africa, in the Years 1797–8* (London: G. & W. Nicol, 1802).

Horst, Jakob, Annette Jünemann and Delf Rothe (eds), *Euro-Mediterranean Relations after the Arab Spring: Persistence in Times of Change* (London: Routledge, [2013] 2016).

Houtsma, Martijn Theodoor, *The Encyclopaedia of Islam: A Dictionary of the Geography, Ethnography and Biography of the Muhammadan Peoples*, vol. 1 (Leiden: E. J. Brill, 1913).

Howell, Jude, 'Governance Matters: Key Challenges and Emerging Tendencies', in Jude Howell (ed.), *Governance in China* (Lanham, MD: Rowman & Littlefield, 2004), 1–18.

Hunter, Robert F., *Egypt under the Khedives, 1805–1879: From Household Government to Modern Bureaucracy* (Cairo: American University in Cairo Press, 1984).

Hutchcroft, Paul D., 'Centralization and Decentralization in Administration and Politics: Assessing Territorial Dimensions of Authority and Power', *Governance* 14(1) (2001): 23–53.

Hydén, Göran, Julius Court and Kenneth Mease, *Making Sense of Governance: Empirical Evidence from Sixteen Developing Countries* (Boulder, CO: Lynne Rienner, 2004).

Immergut, Ellen M., 'The Theoretical Core of the New Institutionalism', *Politics & Society* 26(1) (1998): 5–34.

Ismail, Salwa, *Political Life in Cairo's New Quarters: Encountering the Everyday State* (Minneapolis: Minnesota University Press, 2006).

Ismail, Salwa, 'Authoritarian Government, Neoliberalism and Everyday Civilities in Egypt', *Third World Quarterly* 32(5) (2011): 845–62.

Ivanyna, Maksym and Anwar Shah, 'How Close is Your Government to its People? Worldwide Indicators on Localization and Decentralization', *Economics: The Open-Access, Open-Assessment E-Journal* 8 (2014): 1–61.

Iwan, James L., 'From Social Welfare to Local Government: The United Arab Republic (Egypt)', *Middle East Journal* 22(3) (1968): 265–77.

Jong, F., *Turuq and Turuq-linked Institutions in Nineteenth-Century Egypt: A Historical Study in the Organization Dimensions of Islamic Mysticism* (Leiden: E. J. Brill, 1978).

Kamrava, Mehran, *Inside the Arab State* (Oxford: Oxford University Press, 2018).

Kandil, Hazem, *Soldiers, Spies, and Statesmen: Egypt's Road to Revolt* (London: Verso, 2014).

Khalil, Heba and Brian Dill, 'Negotiating Statist Neoliberalism: The Political Economy of Post-Revolution Egypt', *Review of African Political Economy* 45(158) (2018): 574–91.

Kienle, Eberhard, *A Grand Delusion: Democracy and Economic Reform in Egypt* (London: Bloomsbury, 2001).

Kim, Harris Hyun-Soo, 'Generalised Trust, Institutional Trust and Political Participation: A Cross-National Study of Fourteen Southeast and Central Asian Countries', *Asian Journal of Social Science* 42(6) (2014): 695–721.

King, Stephen Juan, *The New Authoritarianism in the Middle East and North Africa* (Bloomington: Indiana University Press, 2009).

Lamaison, Pierre, 'From Rules to Strategies: An Interview with Pierre Bourdieu', *Cultural Anthropology* 1(1) (1986): 110–20.

Landry, Pierre Francois, *Decentralized Authoritarianism in China: The Communist Party's Control of Local Elites in the post-Mao Era* (New York: Cambridge University Press, 2008).

Lapidus I. (ed.), *Middle Eastern Cities* (Berkeley: California University Press, 1986).

Lawson, F. H., 'Rural Revolt and Provincial Society in Egypt, 1820–1824', *International Journal of Middle East Studies* 13 (1981): 131–53.

Levi, Margaret and Laura Stoker, 'Political Trust and Trustworthiness', *Annual Review of Political Science* 3(1) (2000): 475–507.

Luciani, Giacomo (ed.) *Combining Economic and Political Development: The Experience of MENA* (Leiden: Brill, 2017).

Mahgoub, Mohamed Abdo, *Customary Laws and Social Order in Arab Society: Socio-Anthropological Field Studies in Egypt* (Newcastle: Cambridge Scholars Publishing, 2015).

Mahmood, Saba, *Politics of Piety: The Islamic Revival and the Feminist Subject* (Princeton, NJ: Princeton University Press, 2005).

Mann, Michael, *The Sources of Social Power, vol. 1: A History of Power from the Beginning to AD 1760* (Cambridge: Cambridge University Press, 1986).

Martinez-Vazquez, Jorge and François Vaillancourt, *Decentralization in Developing Countries: Global Perspectives on the Obstacles to Fiscal Devolution* (Cheltenham: Edward Elgar, 2011).

Martínez, José Ciro and Brent Eng, 'Stifling Stateness: The Assad Regime's Campaign against Rebel Governance', *Security Dialogue* 49(4) (2018): 235–53.

Mason, S. C., *Saidy Date of Egypt: A Variety of the First Rank Adapted to Commercial Culture in the United States* (Washington, DC: US Department of Agriculture, 1924).

Masoud, Tarek, *Counting Islam: Religion, Class, and Elections in Egypt* (Cambridge: Cambridge University Press, 2014).

Mayfield, James B., *Local Government in Egypt: Structure, Process, and the Challenges of Reform* (Cairo: American University in Cairo Press, 1996).

Menza, Mohamed Fahmy, 'Neoliberal Reform and Socio-Structural Reconfiguration in Cairo's Popular Quarters: The Rise of the Lesser Notables in Misr Al Qadima', *Mediterranean Politics* 17(3) (2012): 322–39.

Menza, Mohamed Fahmy, *Patronage Politics in Egypt: The National Democratic Party and Muslim Brotherhood in Cairo* (London: Routledge, 2012).

Metz, Helen Chapin (ed.), *Egypt: A Country Study*, 5th edn (Washington, DC: GPO for the Library of Congress, 1991).

Mills, Albert J., Gabrielle Durepos and Elden Wiebe (eds), *Encyclopedia of Case Study Research* (Thousand Oaks, CA: Sage, 2009).

Mills, C. Wright (ed.), *From Max Weber: Essays in Sociology*, vol. 4 (London: Routledge, 2007).

Milofsky, Carl (ed.), *Community Organizations: Studies in Resource mobilization and Exchange* (Oxford: Oxford University Press, 1988).

Milton-Edwards, Beverley, *Islamic Fundamentalism since 1945* (London: Routledge, 2014).

Mitra, Subrata K., 'Making Local Government Work: Local Elites, Panchayati Raj and Governance in India', *The Success of India's Democracy* 6 (2001): 103–26.

Mkandawire, Thandike, '"Good Governance": The Itinerary of an Idea', *Development in Practice* 17(4/5) (2007): 679–81.

Moharram, Sobhi, 'The Process of Controlled Decentralization in Egyptian Local Finance', *Developing Economies* 30(4) (1992): 450–81.

Moustafa, Tamir, 'The Dilemmas of Decentralization and Community Development in Authoritarian Contexts', *Journal of Public and International Affairs* 13 (2002): 123–44.

Mubārak, 'Alī Pasha, *Khiṭāṭ at-Tawfiqīyah al-Jadīdah. al-Matba'a al-Kubra al-Amiriyya* (Bulaq Masr [Cairo], 1886).

Murphy, Robert F. and Leonard Kasdan, 'The Structure of Parallel Cousin Marriage', *American Anthropologist* 61(1) (1959): 17–29.

Murray, G. W., *Sons of Ishmael: A Study of the Egyptian Bedouin* (London: George Routledge, 1935).

Nagi, Mostafa H., 'Internal Migration and Structural Changes in Egypt', *Middle East Journal* 28(3) (1974): 261–82.

Nanda, Ved P., 'The "Good Governance" Concept Revisited', *Annals of the American Academy of Political and Social Science* 603(1) (2006): 269–83.

Needham, Rodney, *Remarks and Inventions: Skeptical Essays about Kinship* (Abingdon: Routledge, 2004).

Nellis, John R., 'Tutorial Decentralisation in Morocco', *Journal of Modern African Studies* 21(3) (1983): 483–508.

Nielsen, Hans Christian Korsholm, 'State and Customary Law in Upper Egypt', *Islamic Law and Society* 13(1) (2006): 123–51.

O'Donnell, Guillermo, *Modernization and Bureaucratic Authoritarianism: Studies in South American Politics* (Berkeley: University of California Press, 1973).

Owen, Roger, 'The Middle East in the Eighteenth Century: An "Islamic" Society in Decline? A Critique of Gibb and Bowen's Islamic Society and the West', *Bulletin (British Society for Middle Eastern Studies)* 3(2) (1976): 110–17.

Pappé, Ilan, *The Modern Middle East*, 2 edn (London: Routledge, 2010).

Pargeter, Alison, *The Muslim Brotherhood: From Opposition to Power* (London: Saqi, 2013).

Perlmutter, Amos, *Egypt: The Praetorian State* (New Brunswick, NJ: Transaction Publishers, 1974).

Perthes, Volker (ed.), *Arab Elites: Negotiating the Politics of Change* (Boulder, CO: Lynne Rienner, 2004).

Pierre, Jon, 'Models of Urban Governance: The Institutional Dimension of Urban Politics', *Urban Affairs Review* 34(3) (1999): 372–96.

Portes, Alejandro, Manuel Castells and Lauren A. Benton (eds), *The Informal Economy: Studies in Advanced and Less Developed Countries* (Baltimore, MD: Johns Hopkins University Press, 1989).

Rabīʿ, ʿAmru Hāshim et al. (eds), *Intikhābāt Majlis al-Shaʿb 2005* (*The 2005 Elections of the People's Assembly*) (Cairo: Al-ʾAhram Center for Political and Strategic Studies, 2006).

Ranko, Annette, *The Muslim Brotherhood and Its Quest for Hegemony in Egypt: State-discourse and Islamist Counter-discourse* (Hamburg: Springer, 2012).

Ritzer, George (ed.), *Sociological Theory*, 8th edn (New York: McGraw-Hill, 2010).

Rothstein, Bo and Dietlind Stolle, 'The State and Social Capital: An Institutional Theory of Generalized Trust', *Comparative Politics* 40(4) (2008): 441–59.

Rougier, Bernard and Stéphane Lacroix, *Egypt's Revolutions: Politics, Religion, and Social Movements* (Basingstoke: Palgrave Macmillan, 2016).

Rudolph, Lloyd I. and Susanne Hoeber Rudolph, 'Authority and Power in Bureaucratic and Patrimonial Administration: A Revisionist Interpretation of Weber on Bureaucracy', *World Politics* 31(2) (1979): 195–227.

Rutherford, Bruce K., *Egypt after Mubarak: Liberalism, Islam, and Democracy in the Arab World*, 6th edn (Princeton, NJ: Princeton University Press, 2013).

Rutherford, Bruce K., 'Egypt's New Authoritarianism under Sisi', *Middle East Journal* 72(2) (2018): 185–208.

Ryzova, Lucie, *Age of the Efendiyya: Passages to Modernity in National–Colonial Egypt* (Oxford: Oxford University Press, 2014).

Saadi, Muhammad, *Ḥirāk ar-Rīf: Daynāmiyyāt al-Huwiyya al-Iḥtijājiyya* (*The Rif Movement: Dynamics of Protest Identity*) (Rabat: Slaiki Frères – Akhawayne, 2020).

Sadanandan, Anoop, 'Patronage and Decentralization: The Politics of Poverty in India', *Comparative Politics* 44(2) (2012): 211–28.

Sadat, Anwar, *al-Baḥth 'an al-dhāt: Qiṣat Hayātī* (*In Search of Identity: An Autobiography*) (Cairo: Egyptian Office for Publishing & Distribution, 1979).

Sadiki, Larbi (ed.), *Routledge Handbook of the Arab Spring: Rethinking Democratization* (London: Routledge, 2014).

Sahlins, Marshall, 'What Kinship Is (Part One)', *Journal of the Royal Anthropological Institute* 17(1) (2011): 2–19.

Saouli, Adham, *The Arab State: Dilemmas of Late Formation* (London: Routledge, 2012).

Sauer, Christof, 'Reaching the Unreached Sudan Belt: Guinness, Kumm and the Sudan-Pionier-Mission', PhD dissertation, University of South Africa, 2001.

Shah, Anwar and Sana Shah, 'The New Vision of Local Governance and the Evolving Roles of Local Governments', *Journal of Public Administration* 3(1) (2009): 2–15.

Sharma, Aradhana and Akhil Gupta (eds), *The Anthropology of the State: A Reader* (Chichester: John Wiley & Sons, 2009).

Shefter, Martin, *Political Parties and the State: The American Historical Experience* (Princeton, NJ: Princeton University Press, 1993).

Shehata, Dina, *Islamists and Secularists in Egypt: Opposition, Conflict, and Cooperation* (London: Routledge, 2013).

Siisiainen, Martti, 'Two Concepts of Social Capital: Bourdieu vs. Putnam', *International Journal of Contemporary Sociology* 40(2) (2003): 183–204.

Sims, David, *Understanding Cairo: The Logic of a City Out of Control* (Cairo: American University in Cairo Press, 2011).

Sims, David, *Egypt's Desert Dreams: Development or Disaster?* (Cairo: American University in Cairo Press, 2014).

Singerman, Diane, *Avenues of Participation: Family, Politics, and Networks in Urban Quarters of Cairo* (Princeton, NJ: Princeton University Press, 1995).

Singerman, Diane, 'Restoring the Family to Civil Society: Lessons from Egypt', *Journal of Middle East Women's Studies* 2(1) (2006): 1–32.

Singerman, Diane (ed.), *Cairo Contested: Governance, Urban Space, and Global Modernity* (Cairo: American University in Cairo Press, 2009).

Springborg, Robert, 'Patrimonialism and Policy Making in Egypt: Nasser and Sadat and the Tenure Policy for Reclaimed Lands', *Middle Eastern Studies* 15(1) (1979): 49–69.

Springborg, Robert, *Mubarak's Egypt: Fragmentation of the Political Order* (Boulder, CO: Westview Press, 1989).

Springborg, Robert, *Egypt* (Cambridge: Polity, 2008).

Springborg, Robert, 'The Rewards of Failure: Persisting Military Rule in Egypt', *British Journal of Middle Eastern Studies* 44(4) (2017): 478–96.

Stacher, Joshua, *Adaptable Autocrats: Regime Power in Egypt and Syria* (Stanford, CA: Stanford University Press, 2012).

Stacher, Joshua, *Watermelon Democracy: Egypt's Turbulent Transition* (New York: Syracuse University Press, 2020).

Staggenborg, Suzanne, 'Social Movement Communities and Cycles of Protest: The Emergence and Maintenance of a Local Women's Movement', *Social Problems* 45(2) (1998): 180–204.

Stanley, C. V. B., 'The Oasis of Siwa', *Journal of the Royal African Society* 11(43) (1912): 290–324.

Starrett, Gregory, *Putting Islam to Work: Education, Politics, and Religious Transformation in Egypt* (Berkeley: California University Press, 1998).

Stoker, Gerry, 'Was Local Governance Such a Good Idea? A Global Comparative Perspective', *Public Administration* 89(1) (2011): 15–31.

Sulayman, Samir, *The Autumn of Dictatorship: Fiscal Crisis and Political Change in Egypt under Mubarak* (Stanford: Stanford University Press, 2011).

Sullivan, Denis J., *Private Voluntary Organizations in Egypt: Islamic Development, Private Initiative, and State Control* (Gainesville: University Press of Florida, 1994).

Swartz, David, *Culture and Power: The Sociology of Pierre Bourdieu* (Chicago: University of Chicago Press, 2012).

Tammam, Husam, *'Abd-l-Mun'im Abu-l-Futūḥ: Shāhid 'alā Tārīkh al-Ḥaraka al-'Islamiyya fi Maṣr 1970–1984* (*Abdel-Moneim Aboul-Fotouh: A Witness of the History of the Islamic Movement in Egypt 1970–1984*) (Cairo: Dar El Shorouk, 2012).

Third World Quarterly, 'Mosque and State in Egypt', 7(4) (1985): 11–16.

Tilly, Charles, 'Trust and Rule', *Theory and Society* 33(1) (2004): 1–30.

Tonkiss, Fran, 'Trust, Confidence and Economic Crisis', *Intereconomics* 44(4) (2009): 196–202.

Tosun, Mehmet Serkan and Serdar Yilmaz, *Centralization, Decentralization, and*

Conflict in the Middle East and North Africa (Washington, DC: The World Bank, 2008).

Uslaner, Eric M., *The Moral Foundations of Trust* (Cambridge: Cambridge University Press, 2002).

Uslaner, Eric M. (ed.), *The Oxford Handbook of Social and Political Trust* (Oxford: Oxford University Press, 2018).

Vollmann, Erik, Miriam Bohn, Roland Sturm and Thomas Demmelhuber, 'Decentralisation as Authoritarian Upgrading? Evidence from Jordan and Morocco', *Journal of North African Studies* (2020): 1–32.

Walker, Andrew, 'The Rural Constitution and the Everyday Politics of Elections in Northern Thailand', *Journal of Contemporary Asia* 38(1) (2008): 84–105.

Walz, Terence, 'Libya, the Trans-Saharan Trade of Egypt, and 'Abdallah Al-Kahhal, 1880–1914', *Islamic Africa* 1(1) (2010): 85–107.

Waterbury, John, *The Egypt of Nasser and Sadat: The Political Economy of Two Regimes* (Princeton, NJ: Princeton University Press, 1983).

Whidden, James, *Monarchy and Modernity in Egypt: Politics, Islam and Neo-Colonialism between the Wars* (London: I. B. Tauris, 2013).

Whiteley, Paul F., 'Economic Growth and Social Capital', *Political Studies* 48(3) (2000): 443–66.

Wickham, Carrie Rosefsky, *Mobilizing Islam: Religion, Activism, and Political Change in Egypt* (New York: Columbia University Press, 2002).

Wittfogel, Karl S., *Oriental Despotism: A Comparative Study of Total Power* (New Haven, CT: Yale University Press, 1957).

INDEX

Note: *italic* indicates figures; n indicates notes